EAGLES OVER
BRITANNIA

THE ROMAN ARMY IN BRITAIN

EAGLES OVER
BRITANNIA

THE ROMAN ARMY IN BRITAIN

GUY DE LA BÉDOYÈRE

TEMPUS

First published 2001
First paperback edition 2003

PUBLISHED IN THE UNITED KINGDOM BY:
Tempus Publishing Ltd
The Mill, Brimscombe Port
Stroud, Gloucestershire GL5 2QG

PUBLISHED IN THE UNITED STATES OF AMERICA BY:
Tempus Publishing Inc.
2 Cumberland Street
Charleston, SC 29401

British Library Cataloguing in Publication Data.
A catalogue record for this book is available from the British Library.

ISBN 0 7524 2923 X

Typesetting and origination by Tempus Publishing.
Printed in Great Britain by Midway Colour Print, Wiltshire.

CONTENTS

MAPS

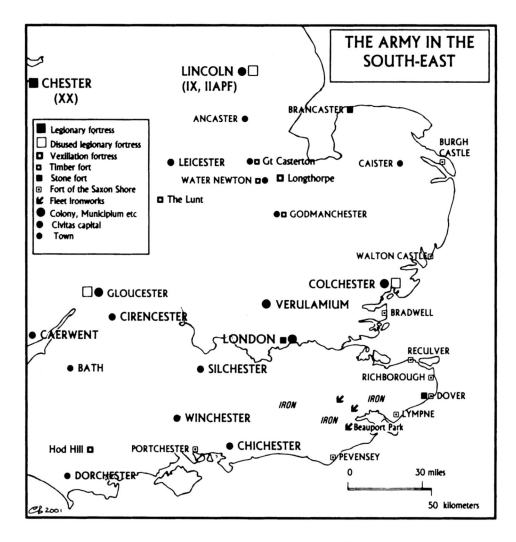

THE ARMY IN THE SOUTH-EAST

■ CHESTER (XX)

LINCOLN ●□ (IX, IIAPF)

BRANCASTER ■

ANCASTER ●

BURGH CASTLE

Legend:
■ Legionary fortress
□ Disused legionary fortress
◧ Vexillation fortress
□ Timber fort
■ Stone fort
◉ Fort of the Saxon Shore
⚒ Fleet Ironworks
● Colony, Municipium etc
● Civitas capital
● Town

● LEICESTER   ●◧ Gt Casterton   CAISTER ●

WATER NEWTON ◧●   □ Longthorpe

□ The Lunt

●◧ GODMANCHESTER

WALTON CASTLE◉

□● GLOUCESTER

COLCHESTER ●□

● VERULAMIUM

◉ BRADWELL

● CIRENCESTER

● CAERWENT

LONDON ■●

RECULVER ◉

● BATH

● SILCHESTER

RICHBOROUGH ◉

IRON   ⚒   IRON   ■◉ DOVER

● WINCHESTER

IRON   ◉ LYMPNE

⚒ Beauport Park

Hod Hill □   PORTCHESTER ◉   ● CHICHESTER

◉ PEVENSEY

● DORCHESTER

0   30 miles

50 kilometers

CB 2001

Map 1 *South-east Britain, showing the principal military and civilian sites of all periods, together with those mentioned or illustrated in the text*

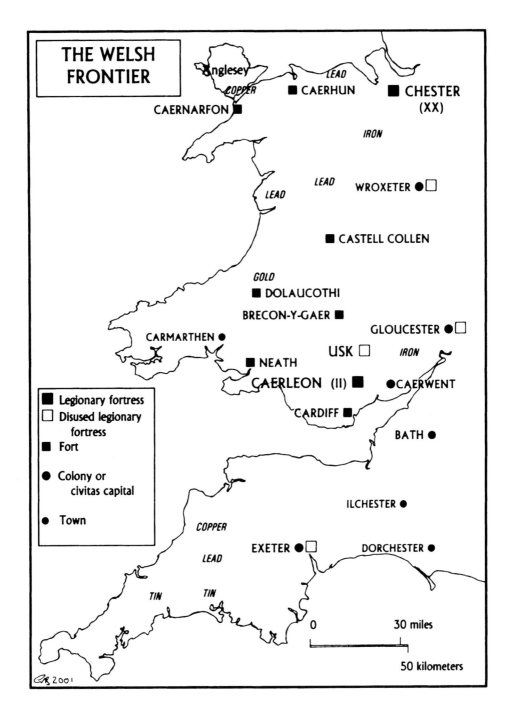

Map 2 *Wales and the south-west, showing the principal military and civilian sites, together with mineral sources, known to have been exploited in the Roman period*

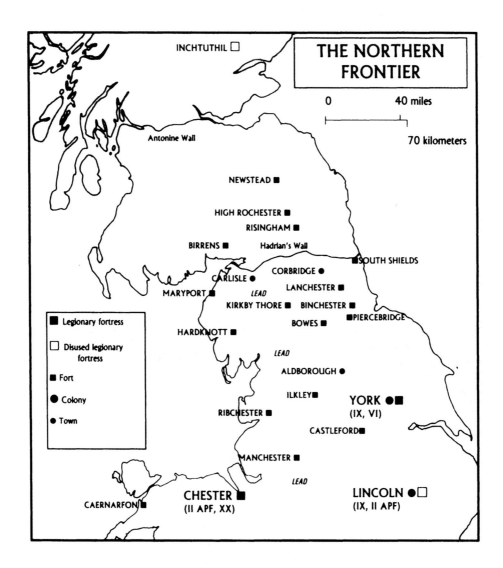

Map 3 *Northern Britain, showing the principal military and civilian sites, together with mineral sources, known to have been exploited in the Roman period. See* **Map 4** *for details of forts on Hadrian's Wall and its vicinity*

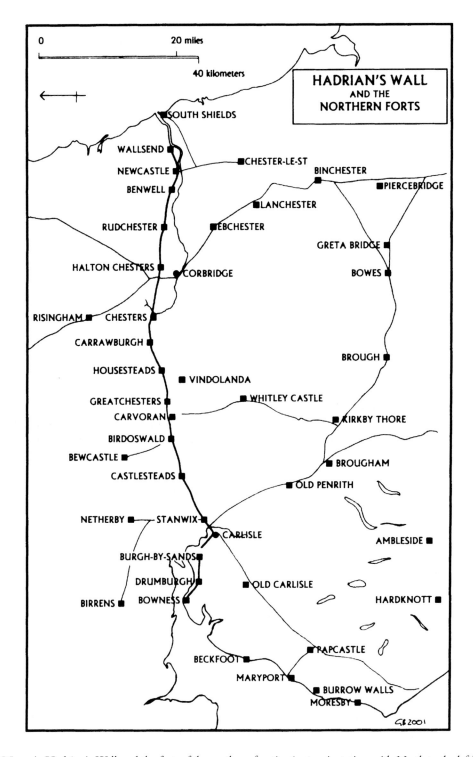

Map 4 *Hadrian's Wall and the forts of the northern frontier (note orientation with North to the left)*

FOREWORD

Virgil described the inhabitants of Britain, some 60 years before the invasion, as *penitus toto divisos orbe Britannos*, 'the Britons, entirely segregated from the whole world' (*Eclogues* i.66). Although Roman Britain is well known for her villas, mosaics, and towns, the Roman army came to define this remote part of the greatest empire of the ancient world. The Britons themselves continued to be regarded by the rest of the Roman world as a curiosity, and the possession of their island home a vanity, partly because of their comparatively limited take-up of Roman culture. Consequently, a surprisingly large amount of what we regard as Britain's Roman identity can be attributed directly or indirectly to the army. Subtract the military from the total and most of our historical, epigraphic, and even much of our artefactual, evidence for the impact of Roman culture disappears. Did the Britons then, remain largely 'segregated from the whole world'?

Of marginal interest to much of the Roman Empire, Britannia made occasional appearances on mainstream Roman coinage, invariably personified as a martial female, seated with shield and spear, or as a name in association with a traditional Roman Victory figure (**colour plate 15**). Unlike so much of the Roman Empire, Britain's Roman form was created out of what the Roman army brought into the island. It was the army which brought the classical world through what Shakespeare called 'the pristine wars of the Romans'. The army created the infrastructure and communications, and forced its way into the wildest parts of the north. Here Roman Mars met British Cocidius and these warrior gods were merged into a new hybrid form.

This is not to say that the Roman army was some sort of prefabricated example of pure Romanization. It was a vibrant mix of individuals from across the Empire who had been absorbed into the Roman world, just as the modern United States is the conflated consequence of a thousand cultures from across the world but still essentially American. Every member of every legion and auxiliary unit brought his own brand of Romanized living, whether that was a Thracian cavalryman (or even a Frisian posing as one) who was buried beneath a tombstone with a characteristically triumphant figure on horseback crushing his foe (**2**), or the poet Juvenal who took his experiences as the commander of an auxiliary unit in Britain back to Italy and into his poetry. It was this capacity for adaptation which made Roman culture so relentlessly successful. It was an oppressive and rapacious culture that did nothing to discourage people from accepting its comforts and security. It meant that classical Venus could be depicted in an entirely unselfconscious piece of provincial art at the fort of High Rochester while not far to the south Roman officers set up dedications to Persian Mithras and the British water nymph Coventina, and relaxed with imported wine while their troops sank British beer with beakers from the Rhineland.

Underlying all this was the institution of the Roman army — an organization belonging at once with the ruthless physical barbarity of antiquity and the anaesthetized mechanical brutality of our own world. Capable of moving men and horses from one end of the known world to the other, it could also sustain an international homogeneity of existence now only matched by the US forces. The dynamic of this extraordinary force is almost impossible to appreciate now, but for all their faults the epic motion pictures have done something to reproduce a sense of the sheer breadth of power. Perhaps the finest of all these is the motion picture *Gladiator*, followed shortly behind by *Spartacus*. Set around the decadent reign of Commodus and with reckless indifference to historical accuracy, the film opens with what must surely be the most brilliant, devastating and grimmest of all re-enacted battles. The army of the Rhine engages German tribesmen with an orgy of artillery, burning arrows, spears and cavalry. Horrific in its sheer force and unmitigated cruelty, the most memorable feature is the dirt-engrained pores and stolid expressions of the career Roman soldiers. Pursuing that most successful of all Roman military scenarios, the set-piece battle, the troops do little more than press the buttons of their equivalent of high-tech artillery before setting into hand-to-hand combat. Pedantic objections about the accuracy of equipment depicted are irrelevant to the effect of the whole.

Thanks to Roman historians, inscriptions and documents, we know more about the individuals, experiences, and institutions of the Roman garrison in Britain than any other aspect of Romano-British society. The army monopolizes the historical and epigraphic record. The forts of Hadrian's Wall have presented us with the names of hundreds of people and gods, while Verulamium — one of the province's largest and most prosperous cities — has left us almost nothing at all when it comes to the urban population. Even when cities do yield inscriptions, more often than not they record soldiers passing through, on detachment, or based in the garrison when the city lay in the future and this was still a fort. The army influenced the goods brought in, and new goods manufactured, while army pay fuelled the liquid economy, and the need to pay the army fuelled the need to conquer.

The attractions of the Roman army to the historian and archaeologist are obvious, though it is not very popular these days to say so. Archaeologists face a fundamental, and irrevocable, problem: motive. The motive behind making, using, losing, removing, depositing or destroying an artefact or feature is never apparent unless there is documentary or epigraphic evidence to support it. Motive can be inferred from the circumstances of a deposit and indeed often is. But that is not the same as knowing the motive. The appearance of African-style wares in early third-century York has been attributed to the appearance of legionary reinforcements brought from Africa after the civil war of 193-7. This is an intelligent and plausible explanation, but so is the idea that they represent a new local fashion brought by no more than a handful of soldiers or even an imaginative potter. Neither is provable because there is no literary or epigraphic evidence for these or any other explanations. Without motive though, we lose sight of the past as a human experience. It is literally unrecognisable in pottery models, or coin date charts. Inventing motive is a poor substitute. But the army, more than any other part of Roman Britain, comes with enough evidence to start seeing it as an historical, and therefore ultimately a human, experience.

The traditional picture of the Roman army is the image peddled by Josephus, turncoat, philo-Roman and opportunist. His description of the Flavian army on campaign in Judaea is one of unadulterated order, discipline, effortless control and, above all, homogeneity. This has motivated and excited generals, dictators, and archaeologists ever since. The Confederate general, Joseph E. Johnston, said of William Tecumseh Sherman's relentless and triumphant march with the Union forces through the swamps of South Carolina in 1865 that 'there had been no such army in existence since the days of Julius Caesar'. John Collingwood Bruce confidently celebrated the Romans for 'Englishmen' as 'our great predecessors'. Military archaeologists in particular have spent lifetimes trying to find this order in the scattered and disparate evidence they dug from their excavations on the forts of Britain's northern and western frontiers. The image has taken a knocking ever since documents started to emerge from waterlogged deposits, and a more critical assessment made of inscriptions, excavations and the physical evidence.

As a result, the Roman army emerges as a far more complex organization, perpetually in a state of flux. In this it mirrors the state it represented. The idea of the Empire operating a long-term strategy of conquest and exploitation is difficult to sustain in this respect, and so is the idea that Romanization was a deliberated policy operated by generations of imperial social strategists. To some extent the progression to power was as much a question of momentum and opportunism. There is no doubt that the army was a magnificently effective tool for imperial aggrandisement, but it is also true that the political stability of some periods, mainly the reign of Augustus, the Flavian period and the second century, made that success possible. In the third century, the army became as much the Empire's tool of its own destruction as it had once been the mechanism to conquest.

No unit of the Roman army ever permanently functioned *en masse*, with troops more or less continuously dispersed on different duties within, and without, the military zone, and in the sick bay. The old one-fort, one-unit, concept has given way to the recognition that splitting up units was the norm, not an exception, and that details are essentially unrecoverable from the archaeological record. Equally, building programmes were begun, half-finished, abandoned, restarted, and plans changed. The question of whether Hadrian's Wall was a 'failure' is a perennially futile pursuit. It is impossible to say, as circumstances changed from week to week and year to year. If it was a barrier at one point, then alterations later might change that. The gate at the Knag Burn was installed in the fourth century and diverted trans-Wall traffic away from the nearby fort at Housesteads (**colour plate 12**). Changing features on the Wall were as likely to represent new circumstances as recognition that an earlier scheme might have needed revision. The Spitfire went through more than 20 versions in the space of six years during the Second World War, but no one would seriously suggest that the Spitfire Mark I, mainstay with the Hurricane during the Battle of Britain but shortly afterwards supplanted by the Mark II, V and then IX, was therefore a 'failure', anymore than that the pillboxes, built to house defenders in the event of an invasion in 1940, were failures because they were never used for that. Likewise, the dogma that Roman soldiers could not marry, complicating the interpretation of the status of their dependants and whether they even had any, falters when a letter from Pliny the Younger shows a citizen centurion appealing directly to the emperor to have his daughter's status elevated to his own. Rigidity and regularity give way to a world of *ad hoc* arrangements made on the fly, at a whim or personal policy, defying archaeology.

This state of flux, sinking the idea that incomplete projects necessarily equate with failure of a grand strategy, or that different equipment means different units, or different dates, is changing the way we look at the Roman past. The idea that the legions, for example, were installed in the fortresses beloved of reconstruction drawings, invariably replete with a full suite of facilities, is fading fast. Likewise, the individual soldiers have ceased to be members of neat ranks of identically uniformed troopers. Equipped with helmets, shields and armaments manufactured at different times, stored, passed on, damaged and repaired, the image of homogeneity which Josephus luxuriated in was only superficial. The idea that one could date the presence of a soldier from the typological detail of a cuirass hinge is as simplistic as it is an anachronism. Even the ethnic homogeneity of auxiliary units has crumbled as a much more colourful mix of backgrounds has been recognized — indeed some of it was even manufactured, while at the same time the long-term Roman fort has emerged as a kind of frontier town, filled with women, children, vagabonds and dealers, as well as soldiers.

This does nothing to diminish the dynamic force the army had in Romanizing the provinces. If anything, it increases it. Far from being a separate world, the army was within every part of Roman provincial society. But even if the army monopolizes the record, that record is tantalisingly incomplete. Epigraphy in Britain is dominated by the army, but whole periods and places are not represented in the record. That means relying on the evidence from other provinces to help supplement or confirm the information we have in Britain. Richard Alston has shown that there are very good reasons for treating what has survived from Roman Egypt as a vital, and relevant, part of the record. An exceptional quantity of documentation has survived which shows how Roman soldiers from all parts of the Empire passed through Egypt at some point in their careers, living and working amongst civilian communities. Not only did they work as administrators, police and legal officials, but also consorted with, socialised, and merged with those civilian communities. Some, as veterans, remained to serve as relatively affluent and influential members of the villages and towns in which they settled.

But Egypt is also a place from which a great deal of similar material has survived from those very civilian communities. Britain is different because a disproportionate amount of what has survived, in its relatively minimal record, can be directly associated with the military world. As we will see, towns such as Lincoln with even a brief military period generally yield a body of inscribed tombstones dominated by the soldiers from that phase. Towns with no known military phase, such as Verulamium, tend to produce few or none at all. Throughout its history, and this is the essential thesis of this book, the Roman army remained constantly the most conspicuous form of Romanization in almost all its forms.

The Roman army remained fundamental to the character of Roman Britain. Indeed, in the later years it spread further across the province, returning once more to the south to guard its shores. A procession of military usurpers chanced their luck on the greater imperial stage, utilising the garrison along the way in different forms. In the end, though the withdrawal of military pay presaged the collapse of almost everything, illustrating the vivid consequences of terminating the army in Britain as a centralised and meaningful institution. As the military engine of Romanization was switched off, so the provinces of Britannia died a death as Roman institutions. Elsewhere in the Empire, Roman culture seems to have been more deeply imbued. It proved more durable, while in Britain even basic skills, once fostered by the army, seem to have been forgotten within a generation, despite the efforts of an opaque élite culture of villa-owners who indulged in a clumsy version of the classical world they sought to emulate.

Referring to the Roman army at all though is at the heart of the issue. As a concept it is one of the most apparently clearly defined aspects of antiquity. The pages of Tacitus are replete with references to its exploits, members, problems and, above all, its central role in Rome's self-perception. The challenge for the archaeologists and historians of Roman Britain is how to identify the manifestation of this concept in the ground. The buildings of forts may seem an obvious place to start, but at many places and times the material culture excavated from the ground is almost impossible to distinguish from the excavated artefacts from civilian settlements, while military artefacts also turn up in 'civilian' contexts. With relatively few inscriptions in Britain, and such a piecemeal historical record, the excavated remnants are all we have to go on, but it is becoming increasingly clear that life is not as simple as clear divisions into 'civilian' and 'military' would have us believe. Can, for example, the finds of early military equipment at a town like Verulamium be taken to mean that there must be an undiscovered fort? Or, are they just representative of military individuals functioning within the more general community? Likewise, how far did the 'civilian' world invade the 'military'? It may be that what we would call civilians actually lived within the forts as well as outside them.

Even today, anyone with an interest in the Roman history of Britain cannot fail to be overwhelmed by the impact of the army. Not only do the inscriptions and sculptures produced by or for soldiers clutter museums, but also the wreckage of their buildings dominates the physical record as it survives. These include the vast ruins of the forts of the Saxon Shore and Hadrian's Wall, but there are also the colossal overnight marching camps, traced from the air, or even the derelict military bathhouses at Chesters, Ravenglass and Beauport Park: the best-preserved Roman buildings in the whole island. This book traces the impact of the army and argues that in every branch of what went to make Britain Roman it was the military world which was ultimately responsible, and that when what remained was removed to take part in distant wars, the Roman world also began a slow journey back across the Channel.

Dealing with references and footnotes in a work like this is always difficult. It would be impossible to provide references for every statement made. However, I have taken the view that it is reasonable to provide references for historical and epigraphic sources and also to point the reader in the direction of books and articles, which have provided the stimulus for some of the more significant points referred to, or challenged, in the text. I hope that readers for whom this is unnecessary detail will forgive the inclusion. The history and archaeology of the Roman period in Britain are in permanent flux, but it is as well always to look back at the source material, or have the chance to do so. It is also worth emphasising that this is *not* a book about the details of military equipment across time, place, units and individuals. That specialist field is already covered by many different works, creating a thriving and fertile source of debate for those with a particular interest in this aspect of the Roman army.

As the ancient sites of Verulamium (St Albans) and Vindolanda (Chesterholm) are known and marketed today by their Roman names, I have continued to use them throughout in non-italicised form. Other ancient names for cities, towns and forts are italicised, as are Latin terms for offices, goods and money. Provinces present a different problem because some Latin names trip more easily off the tongue than others. I have therefore used the most comfortable form and italicised none. So, the reader will find Gallia Aquitania and Britannia Superior, but Lower Moesia and Upper Germany. Unit names, such as *ala Sebosiana*, are italicised as a matter of routine. Italicised numerals, such as *XX*, refer to the legion of that number.

I would like to thank Peter Kemmis Betty and Anne Phipps for their efforts in seeing this book through to the press. For various comments and thoughts on different parts of the text I am grateful to Pat Southern and Richard Reece, and Bill Griffiths at Segedunum Roman Fort (Wallsend) for his help with illustrations. As a mark of how book production is now changing, the entire text, and all illustrations, including scanned and enhanced drawings, black and white photographs and colour plates, were submitted to Tempus in electronic format on CD-ROM.

Guy de la Bédoyère
Welby, by Ermine Street, Lincolnshire 2001

1
THE CLAUDIAN INVASION

Throughout Roman history, Britain remained one of the most garrisoned of all provinces. With around 16,000 legionaries, and the same number or more of auxiliaries, together with innumerable dependants and support services, Britain epitomised the Roman military zone. Forever a frontier, Britain was a source of mystery and wonder to the Romans who simultaneously shrugged her off as a place of obscurity and inconsequence. A trophy won, and held, for the sake of it, Britain's Roman-ness was defined by her experience of the Roman army (1).

This is reflected in the Roman perspective. Roman historians tended only to record military events in Britain. Politically and aesthetically, Britain was irrelevant to them. This was a stage on which great men might act out that military part of their great careers. So, we know a reasonable amount about the conquest period and then largely only because Tacitus, that most remarkable of all Roman historians, happened to have a father-in-law who was governor of Britain. Had Gnaeus Julius Agricola been governor of somewhere else then students of Roman Britain could kiss much of what is known goodbye. As it is, the moment Agricola's career moved away from Britain Tacitus ceased even to mention the place in which his father-in-law had made his name.

This bias in the literary record was also immensely attractive to the kind of archaeologists to whom military affairs appealed. The backdrop afforded by the imperial wars of the nineteenth century, and the world wars of the twentieth, encouraged this interest. Britain was a particularly appropriate subject. Not only are Roman military remains substantially more conspicuous than the remains of towns and villas, but Britain's own role in world affairs up to 1960 meant that many professional archaeologists had seen military service in what had been one of the most powerful armed services of the modern era. The consequence was something of a desire, or even a need, to construe organized patterns of behaviour in the Roman military record and to accentuate the army's role and impact. Much has changed in recent years, not least the gradual realization that the Roman army's impact was not only a good deal more haphazard than was thought, but that it was an aspect of the Roman world which was experienced at a very complex series of levels.

Nevertheless, whatever archaeologists might like to pretend, history provides a spine — a backbone for their chronologies and typologies of artefacts. Without our Roman historians we would have little detailed idea of Roman perceptions and achievements in Britain. A fundamental problem also exists for the archaeologist of the first century AD. For the period 43-84 we have, by ancient world standards, an exceptionally detailed account of the military conquest of Britain. By our standards it is tantalizingly and frustratingly fragmented. We also have a colossally rich archaeological record of sites and artefacts associated with this phase in Britain's history. Likewise, the sources describe a

1 *Bronze* as *issued by Hadrian c.119 from the mint of Rome. The figure depicted is Britannia in military garb, and in what appears to be a submissive posture. It exemplifies how the island province was seen by the rest of the Empire*

number of events and places which simply cannot now be located. What we cannot do is associate most of the known sites with individual governorships or individual campaigns. By their very nature armies on the move tend to leave little trace behind them, and after 1900 years it is hardly surprising that only by chance might we hope to locate what they did leave. The battered skeletal remains bearing Roman artillery bolts found at Maiden Castle in Dorset are powerful and evocative evidence for the Roman army in battle against an Iron Age community, but an army engaged in that sort of activity was not much involved in manufacturing pottery, commissioning goods from local suppliers, or spending money at opportunistically-established settlements. Once settled in a garrison fort, a unit of auxiliary infantry or cavalry might indeed engage in these but it means that the archaeologist may well find him or herself with a gap between the excavated material and the date at which the army was supposed to have begun its activity in the area.

This issue of a discrepancy becomes far less significant later on in being obscured by our ignorance of a chronology. Once Tacitus finished the *Agricola*, he left us bereft of the history we crave. Nevertheless, the archaeology provides a fabulous complement for it has yielded more evidence for the Roman army than anything else in the four centuries that Britain was a Roman province. The inability to date pottery to more closely than a few decades, and the capacity for coins to circulate for decades after they were struck, becomes a good deal less problematic once we lose any detailed historical accounts of campaigns.

The Garrison

Britain had never less than three legions, and dozens of auxiliary cavalry and infantry units. Their forts, and frontiers, dominate the remains of the Roman period but the impact spread way beyond the military zone. Some towns like Cirencester, Gloucester, and Lincoln had had military phases. Inscriptions from these military periods, lasting only a few decades, form a disproportionately large part of the surviving record (**2**). The inscriptions from the Hadrian's Wall zone constitute nearly half the recorded inscriptions from all of Britain. Add on the Antonine Wall and the other forts of northern Britain and Wales, and almost all known Romano-British inscriptions are accounted for. What this

2 *Tombstone of the Frisian Sextus Valerius Genialis, trooper with a Thracian ala. Found at Cirencester, the stone belongs to a fort erected on the site before the town was founded. RIB 109*

means is that Roman military inscriptions dominate the epigraphic record, even in the civilian zone. They are the most fertile sources of additional historical detail, a certain type of art and representation, and even of the actual people who lived in Britain. A single detailed epitaph provides more precise data than any scientific analysis of skeletal remains.

In the Eastern Empire, Rome rode on the back of existing urban Greek culture and the same even applied to some extent in North Africa. Filled with admiration for the sophistication of Greek culture, literature and art, Roman administrators wallowed in the aesthetic and physical pleasures of the Greek world. In Britain there was no urban culture to synthesize. The Romans had to create it, but this could only follow conquest. The army was the conduit of economic development, not just by creating the routes along which Roman goods could enter Britain but by introducing them to the goods in the first place. This differs from other provinces where we have large amounts of evidence for the army. In Egypt, for example, the garrison is well attested in an abundance of papyri but it never exceeded around a quarter of Britain's and operated within an established urbanized society and economy. Much of what the Egyptian garrison and its veterans could take for granted had to be brought into Britain.

The new fortresses and forts acted as markets through which goods, and coinage, passed and were dispersed. Pottery, that most basic of all artefacts, was radically altered by the army, not just in its demand for imports but also in how it provoked local British industries. Even the physical appearance of civic buildings suggests that Roman soldiers might have been personally responsible for, or involved in, designing the structures for the local urban government.

19

3 *Altar from Vindolanda dedicated to Cocidius by Decimus Caerellius Victor, prefect of cohors II Nerviorum. Often conflated with Mars, Cocidius was a popular deity in the military zone. The fort at Bewcastle was even named* Fanum Cocidii, *'The shrine of Cocidius'.* RIB *1683*

The influence of the army remained throughout Britain's history as a Roman province. The garrisons were permanent features of the landscape though factors changed. By the late second century the army was supporting British-based usurpers and in the fourth century this became endemic. In the end, it was the cessation of coinage imports to pay the army, which coincided with the collapse of everything else we associate with Roman Britain.

This book is about that army: how it came and fought and was dispersed amongst Britain's lowlands and highlands and adapted to the landscape. It is in the writing tablets, inscriptions, altars, sculpture and artefacts of the Roman military world in Britain that we find the clearest evidence for this strange hybrid provincial culture. The veneration of Mars with British Cocidius in the hills of Northumberland symbolizes this above all (**3**). Here a classical god from the depths of Roman tradition found expression in a warrior god from a place on the edge of the known world. This army brought the classical world to Britain and when it went, or dwindled, so the classical world went with it. The great villas of the south may have had little or nothing to do with the garrisons of Hadrian's Wall, but when the troops of the frontier ceased to receive their pay and left their decaying forts to the elements, the world which supported those villas went with them.

The summer of 43

To the soldiers crossing the Channel in the late summer of the year 43, the prospect of invading Britain must have meant a mixture of fear and promise. Caesar's invasions of nearly a century before had entered Roman popular lore. The Romans were never great seafarers though in this part of the world there will have been many men for whom the waters of the North Sea were familiar. A large proportion of the forces involved, particularly the auxiliaries, will have had origins in northern Europe or at least spent part of their military careers there. Even so, the sea was a desperately unpredictable factor in any plans. The terrible storm in the year 16 which wrecked Germanicus' fleet was a prime example of how the most powerful military force in antiquity could be destroyed in moments. Some of the soldiers were washed up in Britain and were sent back by tribal chieftains, unfortunately unspecified by Tacitus (A ii.24).

Soldiers, however, sign up for a variety of reasons. War was a fast track to glory, status, wealth and honour. Some of the land won would be granted them as veterans, and provide them with farms and an income into their old age. Whatever the dangers were of crossing that treacherous narrow stretch of water, the prospects for the lucky ones were magnificent, though at the time many seem to have been content to scupper the project. Few will have given much consideration to why they were there. Soldiers exist within a regime of routines and discipline. So long as the orders were fair, and the money regular, these armour-clad time-servers will have grumbled along the way, regardless of whether it was to glory or the oblivion of a frontier garrison. For the officers clambering their way up the greasy poles of senatorial and equestrian careers, legionary and auxiliary unit commands were relatively brief affairs, compared to the working life of an ordinary soldier, and this was a golden opportunity to be present on the stage of one of the great events in imperial Roman history rather than having their eyebrows plucked and skin oiled in some effete eastern garrison post. Whether all of them relished the chance they had been given is another matter. The opportunity to leave the known universe was not one they welcomed.

These troops were about to bring the Roman world with them to Britain. It was not unknown to the Britons, with whom Rome had traded for generations already, but exposure to the Empire was limited. That fact is plain enough from the archaeology. Roman artefacts existed in Britain but in isolated pockets and clearly accessible only to a few, though they must have been visible to many more. Britain was not a classical vacuum. The archaeological and literary evidence shows that Roman goods were already being shipped in and British goods shipped out. Tacitus observed that, a generation before, in Germany, traders and camp followers from Roman provinces had been lured into enemy territory by the prospect of trade, enhanced by privileges conferred in a treaty. Once established, they had made the place their home (A ii.62, for the year 16 under Tiberius). We do not know that this occurred in Britain but it seems likely. The native trading settlement at Sheepen by *Camulodunum* (Colchester) could well have thrived on the commerce operated by resident traders and their contacts across the sea.

Less unequivocal, but more intriguing, is the evidence of coinage. Issues of Cunobelinus, king of the successful and dominant Catuvellauni, resemble some official Roman coinage. The same applies to the coinage of Juba II of Mauretania, a more overtly Romanized client king of Augustus whose issues are remarkably similar to some of the Catuvellaunian types. This may not be coincidence. Perhaps these men, their associates, and sons, were being deliberately subjected to Roman ways through education and training in Rome. We know this to have been the case with Juba.

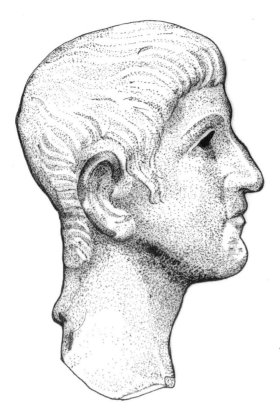

4 *Bust of Claudius (41-54). Found in the River Alde at Rendham, Suffolk. The raised profile indicates it may have come from an equestrian statue displayed in a town. The findspot makes it likely it was deliberately vandalised and disposed of in a totemic way, probably during the Boudican Revolt. Height 34cm*

The coming of the Roman army was a completely different influence. Not only were the numbers greater than scattered traders, but a colossal infrastructure came with them to provide and supply the goods and food which they took for granted. The army brought goods and craftsmen. It also brought money: a means to buy local goods and skills. In the hands of individual soldiers it could be spent on anything. Even if that included activities like prostitution it still meant cash filtering into local economies. The critical difference with many other parts of the Empire was that much of this was new — at least in terms of quantity.

The reasons for the glorious venture are varied and often rehearsed. One thing is almost for certain: there was no 'grand strategy' to conquer Britain. Instead, power and politics were essentially the tactical consequences of personalities and opportunities. This does not mean Britain had not presented some sort of long-term challenge, but it does mean that the decision to invade Britain devolved out of the conditions present in the early 40s AD. But an invasion provided Claudius with the chance to consolidate his personal prestige amongst the senatorial class at Rome (**4**). The mere fact that writers such as Tacitus measured emperors by their military achievements, together with the devices of triumphs, the adoption of military titles by the emperor, and the need to exceed a predecessor's conquests, shows how the power of an emperor was legitimised. Conquest provided dynamic actions in which the senatorial and equestrian class as military commanders and officers could win their own glory, create new provinces for the Empire

5 *Gold stater of Cunobelinus of the Catuvellauni. Although the images were of importance to tribal peoples, they drew on Roman models, while the lettering is pure Latin, recording the king Cuno(belinus) and that it was struck at* Camu(lodunum). *About AD 10-40*

in which they served as governors and garrison commanders, and produced new opportunities for making money.

In short, the emperor as a man and leader was defined by his actions and those actions were military. The art was choosing the right place and time. It was said that a man called 'Berikos' fled from Britain to Rome after a rebellion and implored Claudius to embark on an invasion to set matters aright. Sadly, we do not know anything about this man's origins or why he felt inclined to seek help from a Roman emperor though his own education may already have provided him with contacts. He is probably the man named as Verica, son of Commius, on coins associated with the Atrebates tribe in southern Britain. It is conceivable that there was a family link with 'Commius the Atrebate' who was involved with Caesar as a pro-Roman, though the 'Commius' was probably a different man — perhaps his son. The coinage itself is interesting because it expressed tribal identity and relationships within a Roman and Latin idiom. Thus Verica was VERICA COMMI.F for *Verica, filius Commii*, on the obverse of one silver unit, which named him as REX on the other. This can hardly be adduced as evidence for an automatic pro-Roman stance though it does show that the British tribes had to borrow concepts and words from the classical world in order to express themselves (**5**). Either this was because they lacked the mechanisms themselves or found this an expedient, perhaps even prestigious, alternative. What matters is that this was the choice they made, and it even extended to standard Roman numismatic motifs such as *cornucopiae*.

The distribution of the coins, and their estimated dates, have been used to argue a reign for Verica roughly between *c.*AD10-40, or 30 years. This was no mean feat (if accurate) for a tribal leader in a world where territorial disputes were manifested as swaggering tribal wars conducted by greedy chieftains and their cronies. Thus divided they would be ruled, as Tacitus himself so memorably observed, 'individually so they fight

23

and thus the whole lot are conquered' (*Agr* 12). In our own time, these tribes are sometimes presented as noble savages ensconced in a Paradise about to be soiled by the corrupt horrors of the urban Roman world. This image, a projection of European imperial guilt, ignores the chronic instability of the tribal world in which 'freedom' was the freedom to be despoiled by one's own betters, and where fate hung on the whims of a few personalities who were already privately enjoying Roman benefits. Into this the Roman army would project a hitherto unknown sense of order, new varieties of corruption and oppression, and thus perpetuate their impact.

For Verica, the problem seems to have lain north of the Thames. If the coins are anything to go by — and to be frank, they are not much — the Catuvellauni, then on a roll, were busy absorbing Atrebatic territory and were making headway into the lands of the Cantiaci in Kent. We cannot know what this really entailed. What matters is that it presented Claudius with a 'legitimate' reason to invade Britain. How much this was Dio's spin on events is anyone's guess. The relevant passages in the *Annals* of Tacitus are lost, and Suetonius just tells us that Claudius viewed Britain as an appropriate place in which to justify the senatorial award of a triumph. Given the circumstances of his accession, this was not an indulgence and helps explain why he decided to do something Augustus had implicitly rejected by stating that the frontiers should not be extended. Tiberius had followed suit, and only Caligula had considered the invasion to be a possibility — though in his case it was merely a vanity.

The invasion was *modicam* ('middling') as campaigns went, in Suetonius' opinion, but this of course was a judgement made in comparison to the exploits of Augustus, Vespasian and Titus, and, more significantly, his contemporary Trajan. But he does allude to the fact that Britain had not been invaded since the days of Caesar, and this was not the only time that Claudius sought to match or exceed the achievements of his forbears. His efforts to build the harbour at Ostia expressly associated himself with a project Caesar, for all his successes, had considered impossible.

Suetonius does add that Britain was in a state of *tumultuantem* ('rebellion'), attributed to a refusal to return deserters. If this is a reference to an event he recorded under Caligula then the mists start to clear. The Catuvellauni were not enjoying an entirely easy ride. Cunobelinus was powerful enough to be called by Suetonius *rex Britannorum* ('king of the Britons'), though his coinage indicates that he controlled what we call Hertfordshire, Essex, and parts of Kent. The latter is supported by Dio's reference to Catuvellaunian control of a tribe called the 'Bodunni' who seem to have lived somewhere in the south-east. He struck coins at Camulodunum (**5**), but tells us he was 'son of Tasciovanus'. The latter were struck at Verulamium (coins marked VER) allowing us to deduce that the Verulamium-based Catuvellauni had taken power over the Trinovantian territory in Essex. Power means power struggles, and Cunobelinus expelled his son Adminius during the reign of Caligula. Adminius surrendered to Caligula, who was at the time indulging himself with a military expedition to Germany. Delighted by this unexpected turn of events, Caligula presented the occasion to Roman senate as the full capitulation of Britain.

Even if Cunobelinus had the power to expel his son, it did not bring him immortality. By 43 he was dead, as Dio tells us. Thus, the Claudian invasion may have been occasioned by a British power vacuum. Cunobelinus had at least two more sons:

6 *Vespasian (69-79), on a brass* dupondius *struck at Lyons in 71. Vespasian won some of his military reputation while leading* II Augusta *in south-west Britain. The Lyons mint produced most of the base-metal coinage used in Britain in the late first century*

Caratacus and Togodumnus. Whatever their willingness to help repel the Romans it is as likely that prior to the coming of the Roman army they were engaged in disputing their father's will. None of this will have mattered to the Romans for whom any squabbling was simply a convenience, though it seems the brothers combined their energies to confront the Romans.

It was into this high tribal tension that the Claudian army was despatched. The invasion of Britain has always been a fertile source of speculation, not least the confident claims about which parts of the army were involved. The normal statement is something on the lines that *II Augusta, VIIII Hispana, XIIII Gemina,* and *XX* were involved, together with a similar number of auxiliary troops, making a combined force of some 40-45,000 men.

It is as well to state from the outset that the only unit specifically testified in the invasion of 43 is *II Augusta*, and that comes in a retrospective commentary on Vespasian's career (*H* iii.44). At this date, Vespasian was the legion's legate and he would win the kind of respect and esteem on campaign that helped his bid to become emperor more than 25 years later (**6**). Ever inconsiderate of his modern counterpart's needs, the Roman historian rarely bothered to record in detail the units involved in campaigns. So, the invading army of 43 is one that is unknown to us either in detail or quantity beyond Tacitus' statement that it was made up from *legionibus auxiliisque*, 'legions and auxiliaries' (*Agr* 12.2) and was *quantulum*, 'how small', compared to the Britons had they only counted the Romans (*ibid* 15.3).

We can infer, from later deployments, that *VIIII Hispana, XIIII Gemina* and *XX* were probably involved in part or in full, while the career inscription of G. Gavius Silvanus, sometime *primus pilus* in *VIII Augusta*, and decorated in the British war under Claudius, suggests it also participated. As for the auxiliaries — well, apart from a unit of so-called 'Celts' (usually translated as Germans) described by Dio — we cannot say. The fact remains also that the invading force may well have been made up from legionary vexillations, and that the legions, which eventually found themselves permanently garrisoned in Britain, may not have been here in full for several years after the invasion. It is almost certainly the case that most of them will have operated in vexillations for many years after the invasion, and we know from much later inscriptions that vexillations of other legions occasionally arrived in Britain to reinforce the garrison.

The army was commanded by Aulus Plautius, a man testified in several references to the invasion. The fact that he enjoyed a considerable military reputation was not enough to sway the troops who were reluctant to cross the water. Britain's exotic obscurity placed it firmly in the swirling mists of legend and lore. It is difficult for us to appreciate the psychological context. Content in our knowledge of the geographical limits of the world, the only way for us to understand this is to consider how many of our soldiers would be willing to take part in an expedition to Mars. This is no idle comparison. Britain was, literally, as unknown — if not more so. We, at least, have highly-detailed maps of Mars and few suspect it now to have a hostile population.

Things ancient soldiers shared with those of later ages were superstition and the fear of humiliation. The latter proved more compelling than the fear of what lay beyond the sea. Claudius despatched his freedman, Narcissus, to address the troops. This humiliating experience caused an instant change of heart and they immediately accepted Plautius. This had not been a short-term problem because the invasion was delayed until late in the summer. The 'three divisions' in which they were despatched remain an enigma. Does this mean that they sailed to separate places as the Allies did on D-Day, or landed in three different waves at the same location? We cannot know. The enthusiastic association of 'early military structures' on Britain's south coast with this monumentous event is understandable but unsupportable, though it is scarcely unreasonable to assume that the army landed somewhere in the south-east.

The voyage was far from uneventful and shows that the soldiers' reluctance to set sail was well-founded. A contrary wind confounded the initial course but they were invigorated by a bolt of lightning, interpreted as guidance for the route to be taken. Nevertheless, the chaotic events of the preceding days and weeks had caused the defenders to pack up and disperse. The landing was unopposed, but once the Britons had the measure of what had taken place they wisely disappeared into the landscape with the intention of carrying on a guerrilla campaign.

This account is derived almost exclusively from Dio. It is tantalisingly short on detail. We learn nothing about the route, the landing spot, or the bases which must have been established. Excavations have revealed installations at Richborough in eastern Kent, and at Fishbourne in West Sussex, which are compatible with this date, but compatible is not the same as a demonstrable association. There are good cases to be made for a major landing in the vicinity of either (see for example Hind 1989, and Black 1998).

What looks like a narrow gap in archaeology could easily be five or even ten years, a long time in history. So, an 'early military installation' is just as easily associated with a slightly or significantly later phase of the campaign. Given the narrowness of the Channel from Gaul to eastern Kent, this seems a reasonable location to suggest but nothing precludes the possibility of coastal reconnaissance once in British waters to seek additional landing spots.

We have no choice therefore but to return to Dio, though it is Tacitus who tells us that Britain's reduction to a province was only achieved *paulatim*, 'gradually' (*Agr* 14.1).

Plautius was initially confounded by the reluctance of the Britons to fight a pitched battle. In such scenarios a Roman victory was generally a certainty if for no other reason than that numbers and technology operated in disciplined waves were bound to overwhelm chaotic and indiscriminate unilateral action. Plautius seems to have been able eventually to engage forces led by Caratacus and Togodumnus, one after another. They fled, leaving their erstwhile vassals, the Bodunni, to the Romans who garrisoned the territory and proceeded inland. Their foes decided to wait across a river. Naturally the river is unspecified. It may have been the Medway, though a more recent suggestion (based on the idea that the invasion may have occurred in the Chichester area) is that it was the Avon. Either way, it was wide enough for the Britons to assume the Romans needed a bridge, overlooking apparently that if they had been able to cross it then so would their pursuers. This was where the 'Celtoi' came in. Presumably these men were of Central or North European origin, perhaps Germans. They were trained to tackle rivers in full kit and did so with enough presence of mind to take the Britons by surprise and then to engage in the equivalent of shooting at tyres: they wounded the horses which pulled the British chariots forcing the charioteers to bale out and engage in the kind of fighting which Romans generally won.

The rout of the charioteers created chaos, which the Romans readily exploited. Vespasian, and thus we can assume *II Augusta* was present, took his forces across the river too (**6**). How he did this was a mystery to Dio but he had perhaps scouted for a ford, or obliged a local to provide the information. The battle lasted that day and started again the following morning, which shows how resilient British resistance could be. On one hand this could be interpreted as legitimate and admirable British defence of their land. On the other, it needs to be remembered that the tribal warriors lived and breathed battle and probably relished their chance to compete with the Roman army. A glorious death in battle was infinitely preferable to idling time away, especially if it meant that the survivors would tell tales and sing songs about their dead compatriots' valour. Equally, the chance of a victory against the mighty Romans might mean a spectacular reputation. Many will have been fighting over territory they had stolen from other tribes. In essence, the Romans just represented another episode in the endemic warfare of the age. Ultimately the battle ended with a Roman victory so compelling that it won a participant, Gnaeus Hosidius Geta, the *ornamenta triumphalia* at an unusually early point in his career.

Perhaps this was when a soldier buried his savings at Bredgar, a little to the east near where Sittingbourne is now. The 34 *aurei* do not post-date the period 41-2 and the substantial value of the pieces, equivalent to 3.75 years pay for a legionary (then paid nine per annum), make it likely that these belonged to someone of high rank though whether he was Roman or even a quisling Briton is a moot point. It is also not impossible that the coins were deposited a generation later. Nero's gold after 64 was of reduced weight and it is an observed phenomenon of hoards that the hoarder will usually prefer older, better, coin for his savings. This hoard might have been forgotten but it is a timely reminder that the time of the invasion meant not just soldiers but their money too.

The battle was only a lull. The Britons fell back on the Thames and once more assumed that the water would provide them with a barrier. This took place, according

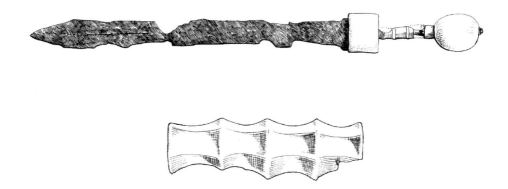

7 *Above:* gladius *found at Caernarvon. The iron blade has partially corroded away, and the bone grip has cracked and crumbled. Length 46cm. Below:* gladius *bone handle, found in a first-century ditch at Aldgate, London. Length 86mm. The locations make it quite possible that neither item was used by a legionary, and shows that military equipment was probably issued as required rather than only to specific units*

to Dio, near the estuary and where at high tide a lake formed. It is of course quite impossible now to assess where that might have been with any precision, though we can take it that it was somewhere in the London area. A *gladius* and scabbard found in the Thames at Fulham make an attractive, but unproven, association (**7**). The interesting possibility has been raised that this battle, and that on the 'Medway', are actually one and the same. The argument is that they ended up in Dio thanks to this source's survival only in the form of an epitome, and because Dio had perhaps had access to two different accounts of the same battle, probably on the Thames, and failed to distinguish them (Black 1998). This certainly helps the case for a landing in the Chichester area.

Either way, the location was easy work for those who knew their way amongst the sandbanks and pools. The Romans did not, but their unit of Celts repeated their previous success and swam over. Meanwhile other units crossed by a 'bridge' upstream, which means that either the Romans built one — something they were more than capable of — or made use of some sort of crossing already in existence. This made it possible to attack the Britons from several directions, an advantage nearly thrown away by chasing fleers away through the mud — a mistake, which meant losing a number of men.

At this point, the invasion was effectively halted. Togodumnus was dead — presumably in the fighting, because the Britons are said to have been all the more determined to avenge him, thus elevating the tension and their resistance. Plautius ordered a halt and waited for Claudius. Well, that is the story but of course it was an expedient way of allowing Claudius the opportunity to preside over, and thus benefit from, the march on Camulodunum. He joined the 'foot soldiers' waiting for him near the Thames and proceeded to Camulodunum where he accepted the surrender of various tribes. This was recorded later on his arch, erected in Rome in 51-2, which commemorated the submission of 11 British kings. This event is of great significance and highlights the variable reaction by the British tribes to the coming of Rome. While we cannot identify the kings involved, subsequent events and other references to client kings allow us to make the inference that the Cantiaci, the Iceni, the Atrebates, the Dobunni, and at least one faction amongst the Brigantes were involved.

Only one of these tribes is specified in the sources as having capitulated. Dio calls them the 'Bodunni' (lx.20.2), and tells us they were ruled by part of the Catuvellauni. This presents an obvious problem. The Bodunni are otherwise unknown. Given the fragmentary nature of the sources this should not be surprising but it has been treated as such. Normally the suggestion is that this is the Dobunni, a tribe whose heartlands lay in the Cotswolds far to the west. The geographical incompatibility with the account of their apparent proximity to the invading force is explained by arguing for a foresighted embassy trundling across Britain to make a peace. However, this makes it harder to understand how the Catuvellauni had managed to control them.

'Bod-', however, is a perfectly normal prefix to a British name, though it seems odd that what must therefore have been an insignificant tribe was worthy of mention. Dio of course may have conflated two incidents: the surrender of an unknown local tribe and a later surrender of the Dobunni. Unfortunately, tribal coinage provides no clues. The Dobunni coinage is attributed on distribution — the name does not appear and no coinage of the 'Bodunni' is known. One more complication is that coinage in the Dobunni tribal area includes issues in the name of a king called Boduoc[us?], and another called Corio(…), giving rise to the suggestion that the tribe had split between pro- and anti-Romans.

The whole issue is an intriguing example of the scholarly love of fabricating unresolvable debates, or should one say 'bedates', where nothing more sinister than a mishearing or misreading is probably involved. One need only try spelling the name over the telephone to see what happens. The conundrum is insoluble but does not affect the point that here we can see how the coming of the Romans caused different reactions.

The same subject helps us consider how to interpret the identification of Claudian military establishments. It is too simplistic automatically to see these as the result of military engagement in the immediate vicinity. Forts and supply bases are initially better located in reliable areas, or to the rear of the theatre of war, for obvious reasons. The Chichester area is one of the most conspicuous. Military-type buildings and equipment have been found in the area and this has also led to the theory that part of the invasion force landed here. That an inscription recording the client king Togidubnus has been found at Chichester, seems to emphasise the probability that the zone was one occupied by a pro-Roman tribe, probably part of the Atrebates which we already know to have been where Verica came from.

Something of the process can be seen at the hillforts in south-west Britain. This is one of the areas which where we have a specific description of the campaign. Suetonius states that Vespasian, 'fought 30 battles against the enemy, conquered two powerful nations, more than 20 towns and the island called *Vectis*' (Suetonius, *Vespasian* 4). From the *Histories* of Tacitus (iii.44) we know that he commanded *II Augusta* at this time. The reference to *Vectis* and the eventual arrival of *II Augusta* at Caerleon in south Wales more than 50 years later allows us to infer that this campaign was in the south-west, perhaps with the vast Iron Age hillfort at Maiden Castle, Dorset, set against it in a futile gesture

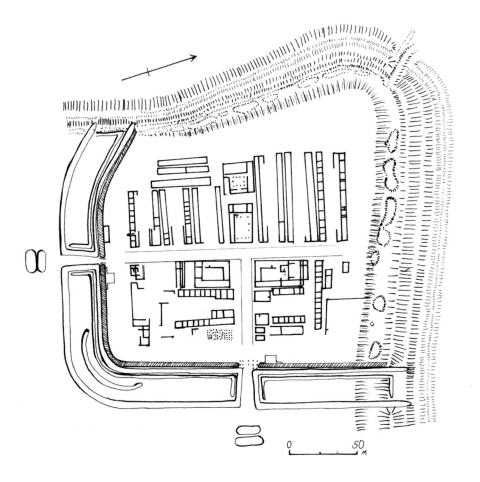

8 *Plan of the Claudian fort at Hod Hill, Dorset. The fort was built in a corner of the Iron Age hillfort, utilising some of the old defences in doing so. It is likely that the hillfort was taken during Vespasian's campaign in the mid-40s*

of resistance (**colour plate 2**). Early Roman forts located within the hillforts in the territory of the Durotriges (Dorset) at, for example, Hod Hill (**8**) and Waddon Hill, are very unlikely to date from the actual campaign for the simple reason that an ongoing series of battles will scarcely allow a commander to lose troops to unlimited fort building and garrisoning though they are likely to have fallen in the same onslaught that wiped out the defenders at Maiden Castle. The forts probably belong to the immediate post-campaign phase, perhaps by as much as three to five years, a period which is generally invisible in archaeology. The forts and facilities to support the actual campaign are probably those to the rear, in the area identified as the Dobunni heartland and further back at Chichester-Fishbourne.

All this lay in the immediate future. For the moment it was still the year 43. The Roman army in Britain is, as yet, unknown to us apart from the fact that *II Augusta* and a unit of 'Celts' were involved. But the account makes it clear that while the advance had been rapid, it had exposed the Roman forces to the problems of an enemy composed up of tribes inclined to make and break alliances with one another. This diffused them as a target, the classic frustration for a developed army trying to make sense of a scattered and ill-defined foe. The landscape was also not straightforward. The Medway and Thames are significant tidal rivers, the latter being particularly substantial and surrounded by troublesome low-lying land inclined to floods and swamps. This was a presage for the future. Britain might be small but the diversity of terrain is impressive, and much of it is a gift to forces disinclined to engage in set-piece battles.

Claudius withdrew, his reputation enhanced, and ordered Plautius to conquer the remaining territory. His great achievement was eventually commemorated on gold and silver coins issued at Rome and Lyons several years later, which included a depiction of the triumphal arch erected in Rome. The occasion was also proclaimed in the East, where silver *didrachmae* of Caesarea in Cappadocia were issued between 46-8, and at Aphrodisias where a stone relief of Claudius with Britannia has been unearthed. But imperial interest in the new province had all but expired. Claudius had other things to worry about.

Whether Claudius had meant that all of Britain be conquered, or only the lowlands, is beyond assessment. In the *Agricola* Tacitus tells that the Britain which was gradually reduced to a province was the *proxima pars*, 'the nearest part', but he was bound to draw attention to this because the prime purpose of the work in hand was to emphasise Agricola's achievements in conquering *the rest* of Britain. This concept of the 'nearest part' gave rise to the idea in earlier modern times that the Fosse Way represented a provincial boundary. Not only was this a concept generally unknown at the time, but it would also have exhibited a complete failure to understand Britain's political geography. If the Romans had not realised it before 43 (and they probably had), Britain was not 'Britain' as we understand it, but a diffuse mass of independent tribal groups whose existence was only defined by their lack of definition. In a perpetual state of flux, these tribes rose and fell on the whims of their mercurial leaders. Each tribe regarded its neighbours differently, and had its own attitude to Rome.

New friends and enemies

By 47, when Tacitus picks up the story in the *Annals*, Rome had acquired *socii* ('allies') in Britain (*A* xii.31). These were presumably tribes in the south who had accepted Roman power, probably made up from those who had already sided with the Romans before 43 and those who decided it was the sensible solution thereafter. It is unfortunate that Tacitus does not tell us who they were. The only clue comes from elsewhere in his writings. Togidubnus was awarded 'certain cantonal areas' to rule as king (*Agr.*14). The inscription apparently naming him, in Chichester, is our only evidence for where part of his client kingdom lay, though even his title is a matter for dispute as the inscription is damaged at the crucial part. He was either a king, or a legate, depending on the two restorations though his adoption of the names Tiberius Claudius shows precisely where his allegiances lay. The reading of the critical line 5 is complicated by inversions of letters, ligatured letters, and compressed formulae.

[N]EPTVNO.ET.MINERVAE
TEMPLVM
[PR]O.SALVTE.DO[MVS].DIVINA[E]
[EX.]AVCTORITAT[E.TI].CLAVD.
[TO]GIDVBNI.R[EG.MA]GNI.BRIT.
(or [TO]GIDVBNI.R[.LEGATI.AV]G.IN.BRIT.)
[COLE]GIVM.FABROR.ET.[Q]VI.IN.EO
[SVN]T.D.S.D.DONANTE.AREAM
[…]ENTE PVDENTINI.FIL
(Chichester, *RIB* 91)

We only know that Togidubnus was still apparently alive, and loyal, around the time Tacitus was writing in the late first century and that this was considered to be of note. This is far from impossible though there are many historians of Roman Britain who have considered it so. Higher death rates in pre-modern times have never precluded the possibility that people might live to ripe old ages — it is merely the case that fewer people managed it, but plenty did. At Caerleon, much later, Julius Valens, a veteran of *II Augusta*, lived to be 100 (*RIB* 363). If Togidubnus had been an impressionable and compliant 21 in 43 he could easily have survived to Trajan's reign at the age of 76.

Prasutagus, who died in 59/60, ruler of the Iceni, was another client king. Whether he and Togidubnus were both operating in this capacity in 47 is unknown. Tacitus tells us that the Iceni had accepted client status by 47, without having been defeated in battle. It would be interesting to know to what extent this client status involved a military presence. The Chichester and Fishbourne area is one of the few to have been considered. Our first problem is whether Togidubnus actually ruled from the vicinity. The Chichester inscription does not settle the matter and his association with the 'palace' at nearby Fishbourne is, frankly, an understandable convenience for those who have explored and presented the site to a modern public. Nevertheless, more recent excavations have confirmed the nature of early timber buildings on the site, which seem to bear a distinct resemblance to certain military models.

Another possibility, particularly given the extravagant developments in the 60s and later here, is that Fishbourne was where the governor wintered. He would have enjoyed a military staff of officers and troops detached from their respective units, well known at a later date from various inscriptions, and the facilities for rapid transit to the continent. We may safely assume that London became the governor's home by the late first century, where there was certainly a fort. Perhaps Togidubnus played host to the governor and his escort in the first century. This would certainly help explain several of the inscriptions from Chichester. None is explicitly military in content, but the Togidubnus stone, and another dedicated to Nero (*RIB* 92, now lost), are both so early they must have been produced by expert immigrant masons.

Ostorius Scapula 47-51

The loyalty, or acquiescence, of the British clients in 47 was under threat. Publius Ostorius Scapula had become governor and, interestingly, he seems to have had an *exercitu ignoto* ('untried army'; *A* xii.31). This can only mean that some of the invading force had been replaced with fresh troops, perhaps vexillations from the same legions but left behind on the Continent until then, or stationed in Britain well to the rear of the actual fighting.

Some of the tribes attempted to exploit this window of opportunity and entered the client kingdoms. It is interesting to speculate whether this was intended to expel the Romans or simply take advantage of their tribal rivals being off their guard. It is too simplistic to presume that the Romans were automatically regarded as the enemy. For some of the tribes the Roman presence may have been seen as a chance to disrupt the status quo and settle old scores, without ever seriously considering the likelihood of a protracted Roman sojourn. In Eastern Europe during the Second World War, some countries initially welcomed the invading Germans. Indeed, the siege of Stalingrad in 1942 saw more than 50,000 Soviet citizens fighting with the German Sixth Army (Beevor 1998, xiv). Many had been provoked to change sides either because of ideological differences or because they found the brutal discipline of the Red Army unacceptable. For some Russians the Germans represented a chance to bring order, for others they provided a chance to indulge in local (often anti-semitic) genocide. Once it became clear what invasion and occupation meant though, attitudes changed, as perhaps they did in Britain too under the Romans.

Ostorius recognised the importance of blooding his troops hard and fast. The initial fighting went with the Romans but the follow-up iron-fist policy seems to have backfired. Tacitus specifies that this occurred in an area *cis Trisantonam et Sabrinam*, 'on this side of the Trent(?) and the Severn'. The translation of *Trisantonam* as the Trent makes geographical sense but it is improbable that Tacitus had much idea of what he was referring to. But it seems likely that territory approximating to some of what we call the Midlands and East Anglia was involved. The Iceni, evidently aggrieved by the arrangements, led the resistance. The archaeological evidence from the mid-first-century vexillation fortresses of Longthorpe, Rossington Bridge, Osmanthorpe and Newton-on-Trent is not incompatible with this. The vexillation fortress was an important device. Larger than a standard auxiliary cavalry or infantry fort, it was smaller than a legionary fortress, and seems to have been devised as a facility for what are now called 'field army groups', made up of *ad hoc* detachments from a variety of units, auxiliary and legionary. Equally, this makes it impossible to identify what the group might consist of at any one time, especially as the Roman army probably made no distinction.

Ostorius confronted the rebels in their fortified base with only a force of auxiliaries, which included cavalry and infantry. This may be a statement of fact, or it may be Tacitus' way of enhancing the perception of the governor's achievement. But the implication is that the legions were otherwise engaged, presumably in consolidating their own and other bases. Had it been another war, Tacitus would have been more interested in them than the auxiliaries. The outcome was successful, but it was a close-run thing.

Despite the narrow margin of victory, Ostorius confidently diverted his troops against the Deceangli, a northern Welsh tribe, thanks to the reluctance of the lowland tribes to try their hand at any more fighting (for the meantime). This took him into the highland area, a risky business but he presumably had his eye on conquering new territory — suppressing already-conquered land was not going to enhance his personal reputation.

9 *Text from the tombstone of the centurion M. Favonius Facilis of* XX *(see also* **colour plate 1***). The stone, found at Colchester, was erected by his freedmen, Verecundus and Novicius.* RIB 200.

The campaign illustrated his haste and poor judgement. The Brigantes, whose territory crossed northern Britain, had become *discordiae*, 'seditious' (*A* xii.32). Although this involved only a small number of men, it was an interesting foretaste of this tribe's internal strife which illustrated the dilemma facing all tribes as the Romans encroached: to fight them or join them. Despite the speedy suppression of this problem Ostorius found himself fighting on two fronts. In Wales, the Silures proved intractable opponents and were now led by Caratacus. This much might have been predicted from the nature of the terrain favouring small groups of tribesmen stealing into the hills and narrow valleys. Caratacus' actions are perhaps the main reason why the conquest moved into the highlands. It has never been clear whether there was a policy only to take the lowlands, 'the nearest part', to begin with. This may be asking too much — the idea may never seriously have been discussed in great detail. It hardly matters. Within four years of the invasion the Romans were heading west — and stayed there.

The solution to the logistical problem seemed straightforward enough. A legion was brought up to the Welsh front. Sadly, Tacitus does not tell us which legion, or where it went. He does tell us that it was made available by establishing a colony at Colchester (*A* xii.32). That tells us that a legion had been left in the rear at Colchester during the first four or five years of the campaign. The only evidence for which legion that was, is the tombstone of M. Favonius Facilis, a centurion of *XX*, found near Colchester (**9, colour plate 1**). The style is mid-first century but, strictly speaking, the tombstone is undated and the possibility of his detachment to another unit, or on other business, does not mean that it follows *XX* was there while he was. Even if *XX* was at Colchester, the evidence of vexillations elsewhere would support the contention that part or much of the legion may already have been long since sent west with Ostorius. Similarly, circumstantial evidence suggests the Gloucester area as the eventual location for the legion.

Either way, that the colony was at Colchester is not in doubt, though which soldiers were settled there is not known — it certainly need not have been just those retired from *XX*. The device of a colony was a simple solution to several problems. It provided rewards for veterans, at minimal expense if the land was in conquered territory, and gave them a purpose in life other than turning into brigands and landless chancers trying to make good a life without legionary pay. Conveniently too, a colony could serve as a trained reserve while at the same time providing a mechanism for familiarising locals with the obligations incumbent on being part of the Roman Empire. This is especially important to us here because it is an emphatic statement that retired soldiers were specifically used as the mechanism of Romanization. The fact that élite tribal burials seem to have continued up to *c*.60 in the vicinity of the tribal religious and ceremonial centre near to Colchester at Gosbecks implies that some tribal leaders were either obliged to stay on, or chose to be quislings.

However, setting up a colony was not straightforward. Just after the accession of Tiberius in 14, a legionary called Percennius started a mutiny amongst the troops stationed in Pannonia. One of his gripes, and that of his colleagues, was the prospect of forced settlement on retirement in a far distant country in a waterlogged marsh or an uncultivated hillside (*A* i.17). If this was how legionaries could treat the chance to be a member of a colony, it is hardly surprising that their attitudes were not necessarily going to include looking forward to peaceful co-existence with locals. Not only that, the implication is that a place like Colchester might very well have also been settled by ex-soldiers from almost anywhere in the Empire, and thus many will have had no interest or personal investment in the invasion of Britain. Unfortunately, tombstone evidence from Colchester is far too limited to draw any conclusions about who was involved.

The archaeology at Colchester has been revealing. It has emerged that the early phases of the colony made use of redundant military facilities. In other words, far from clearing away the legionary fortress it would be more accurate to say that the colonists moved into some of the vacated barracks and adapted them as they stood. Some buildings were replaced, including those identified as tribunes' houses, but broadly speaking the new town preserved the orientation and layout of the fortress (**10**).

Apart from an extension to the east (probably in fact across a fort annexe) the appearance of the new colony can scarcely have differed much from the earlier fortress — except of course that it was probably less well defended. In this respect we can see more clearly than anywhere else just how the military infrastructure was translated into town form. Although we know that by the year 60 this settlement had a theatre, a senate house, and a vast temple to Claudius, Colchester was effectively presented to the Britons as a town built out of a fort and lived in by ex-soldiers.

Despite the problems with terrain, the battle to deal with the resistance in Wales went the Roman way. Caratacus was attributed with having rallied all opponents to a Roman consequence. He made the fatal mistake of establishing a fortified base in Ordovician territory and preparing himself for a set battle. The Romans initially struggled against the barriers placed in their way, the river and a stone embankment, but their equipment and armour proved decisive in hand-to-hand fighting. Caratacus fled to the Brigantes, which turned out to be a misjudgement. The Brigantian queen, Cartimandua, handed him over to Ostorius leaving him an admired, feted, but defeated, leader who was granted a pardon by Claudius.

In Silurian territory, one of the legions was divided. The camp prefect was left with several cohorts to start building forts. An easy target, they were attacked, with the prefect, various centurions and other soldiers killed. Help sent on the summons of a messenger was routed. Ostorius initially sent auxiliary cohorts to help stem the flow though Tacitus

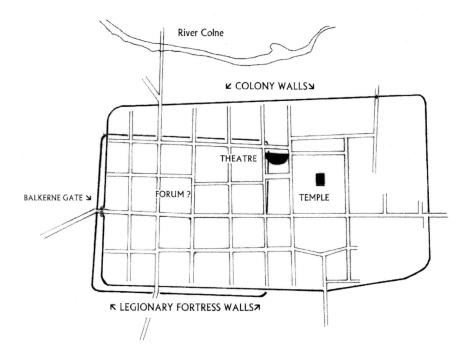

10 *Colchester,* Camulodunum. *This plan shows the Roman colony laid out over the short-lived legionary fortress. Part of the fortress defences seem to have been adapted, as well as some of its grid. But the colony builders had no qualms, it seems, about erecting the theatre across part of the eastern wall. (Based on plans by P. Crummy)*

attributed the turn in the Romans' favour only to the moment when the legions were sent in. Even so, the battle seems to have dwindled with daylight rather than come to any decisive close and it was followed by guerrilla-type fighting.

The Roman army, at this stage, illustrated the arrogance of conquerors and started to make serious mistakes. Extermination of the Silures was expressed as a desirable prospect and, armed with this approval, some of the units started to ransack settlements for goods and prisoners. Of course, all this did was provoke more resistance. Two auxiliary cohorts were cut off by the gathering resistance. In the middle of this, Ostorius died. Tacitus attributed the death to his worries over the conquest. Reading between the lines, this is not impossible. The conquest of Britain had been underway for eight years, and yet even the rearward parts of Britain were not secure, while the client kingdoms exhibited traces of erratic loyalty. Perhaps more significantly, the Roman army was not enjoying unequivocal success in fighting British tribes. The army was acting as a proactive tool of oppressive exploitation, something which Tacitus attributed to the whims of individual commanders. While this would have catastrophic consequences in the short-term it seems that the presence of the army and its relentless indulgence in conspicuous Roman consumption had set wheels in motion which would last as long as it did.

2
CATASTROPHE AND RECONSTRUCTION

After nearly ten years of almost constant fighting, the Roman army found itself still very far away from total conquest of Britain, though whether that was the plan is beyond us to know. The time was equivalent to nearly half a legionary career. Many of the troops who had fought in the invasion will have retired, died, been wounded or been transferred elsewhere. Others had joined up. Just as the British, Dominion, and American soldiers who marched into Berlin in 1945 were almost entirely different from the men who had landed in Normandy in 1944, so the Roman army in Britain was in a state of constant flux.

In the 50s events conspired to create a scenario in which the province came close to being lost. The background seems to have lain in an entirely complacent exploitation of the new province. Some of the problems in understanding how to relate the archaeological evidence for the Roman army to the history have already been discussed. If anything, the picture has become more confused. It was once the case that archaeologists would happily reconstruct the movements of units based on inscriptions recording, say, a centurion of *XX* here, an ordinary legionary of *XIIII* there, and so on. Now we know that we cannot necessarily draw such conclusions.

In a time when military units were constantly on the move, bases were short-lived and occupied by different units as and when required. The evidence of the vexillation fortresses, marching camps, military equipment, and documents from later in the century, shows that the Roman army was not deployed in readily identifiable units. Instead, units were broken up into sections, mixed and matched, and dispersed as needed while individual soldiers were variously detached on special duties here and there (see chapter 8). Consequently, the type of troops based in any given location is practically impossible to distinguish, quite apart from the fact that whoever was there one month or one year, might be replaced by a completely different garrison in the next campaigning season.

There is no better instance than the vexillation fortress at Longthorpe near Peterborough. Large enough to hold around half a legion, the excavations on the site have only served to complicate the picture by showing that auxiliary units may have formed part of the garrison, from the evidence of auxiliary cavalry horse trappings. At Hod Hill, built in the corner of the old Iron Age hillfort during the mid-40s, duplication of some facilities means that two or more units could have formed the garrison (**8**). Longthorpe seems to have been built by the year 48 at the latest and remained in commission for up to 13 years afterwards (**colour plate 23**). It would be nice to be able to draw a reliable conclusion, but instead the most we can say for certain is that there is no certainty. It is even impossible to demonstrate continuous occupation within this period. Instead, we have to conclude that the comings and goings of units of the Roman army are beyond archaeology's ability to resolve, though such excavations have at least shown how the neat picture of legions moving around must be a false one.

11 *Text from the tombstone of Longinus Sdapeze, duplicarius of ala I Thracum, who served 15 years (see also **colour plate 5**). Note the wasted space, which suggests Longinus' heirs purchased a standard stone. Found 0.75km south-west of the west gate of Colchester. Mid-first century. RIB 201*

In any case, the detailed niceties of which legion or *ala* was doing what, where and when, will have been of little concern to the British tribes, apart from those who saw the chance to settle old scores with territorial rivals. Roman soldiers will have been perceived in different ways: infantry or cavalry, good soldiers or bad soldiers. The mounted auxiliaries, so keen to preserve a potent image on their tombstones, may have been especially feared, or at any rate regarded with considerable respect (**11**). The arrival of these units, with their administrative and support machinery, will have had a devastatingly potent impact on their enemies. Longthorpe, replete with facilities for manufacturing metal goods and pottery, cannot have failed to leave the locals with long memories about what the Roman army could do.

Aulus Didius Gallus 52-7

Didius Gallus was governor for five years, long enough to make Tacitus' disparaging comments about his policy of limited fort-building in *ulteriora*, 'remote territory' (*Agr* 14), difficult to accept. Tacitus accused him of doing this in order to appropriate glory from his predecessors. Didius had earlier served as governor in Moesia, recorded on an inscription, which also testifies to his command of cavalry, though whether that was earlier in the British campaign is not stated (*ILS* 970).

When Didius arrived he found that 'a legion', commanded by Manlius Valens, had been defeated in the interregnum by the Silurians (*A* xii.40). Tacitus was sceptical about the claims made by either side for the severity of the event. The Britons stood to intimidate the Romans if the affair was exaggerated, whilst Didius could either benefit if he defeated the legion's assailants, or plead mitigating circumstances if he failed. The legion's identity remains unknown. It seems probable that it must have been the one brought forward from the east, but given the appearance of *II Augusta* in Wales later, the possibility subsists that the unit defeated here was either *II* or *XX*. Didius succeeded in fending off the Silurians, who had been capitalising on the opportunity provided by the lack of a governor to carry out widespread raiding.

The Silurian rejection of the Roman world is an interesting, and sustained, feature of their attitude. This probably reflects the manner in which the tribe was governed. The

Iceni, the Atrebates, and the Brigantes, were drawn into a Roman orbit principally by their leaders, men and women who found in the Roman way of life the idiom and trappings of power and luxury which appealed to them. They were also actively courted as participants, because by creating an identity of interest the Romans drew their provincials into a system from which all were believed to benefit, and which greased the wheels of exploitation. While we can only guess at the political machinations within the tribes, Verica had fled to Claudius for help and thus presumably represented a pro-Roman faction within the Atrebates. It is perfectly feasible that such factions saw the potential aggression facing more remote tribes as a highly satisfactory consequence of their acquiescence. Lacking the recorded history we have, for example, no idea whether the Silures had simply transferred their antagonism from the south-east tribes to the Romans.

That the Silures comprehensively failed to play the game by Roman rules must reflect a structural difference in the way they lived. Firstly, their leaders are opaque to the point of being invisible in the sources and, secondly, the relative lack of Romanized goods found in their territory suggests that little or nothing was finding its way there prior to the Conquest. By its very nature this type of society is all but untraceable to us. To the Romans this was pure barbarity, a frustratingly uncooperative type of community whose perceptions and rules were beyond the fringe. One might consider the uncomprehending frustration of the explorers who made landfall on mainland Australia from the late seventeenth century onwards. While the Polynesian peoples generally lived in monarchical social structures comprehended by Europeans, the Aboriginal peoples of Australia did not and regarded, or more accurately disregarded, Europeans and their ships as irrelevant to the extent that initially they frequently simply ignored them. Explorers like William Dampier and James Cook were bewildered by them. No doubt the feeling was mutual.

Didius Gallus was faced with a more pressing problem in the north. The erratic loyalty of the Brigantes had already caused problems and Roman diplomacy was now becoming embroiled in the internal politics of British tribal hierarchies. But the latter illustrated how easily exploited British tribal feuds could be: the Brigantian nobility were conducting their disagreements within a Roman idiom. Even in northern Britain, Roman living of a sort was becoming normal — at least for the tribal élite. Stanwick (N. Yorks) has long since been recognized as a Brigantian equivalent of the pre-Roman settlements of the south, replete with defences and a vast enclosed area. The site has produced unequivocal evidence for a tribal lifestyle, which was giving itself over to the Coca-Cola culture of the Roman Empire. Whoever lived here was enjoying the chance to consume the goods shipped in amphorae, and eat off fine Roman wares from Italy and Gaul, under tiled roofs as tribal further south had been doing for decades (**12**).

Now, in a drama worthy of Shakespeare, the marriage of the Brigantian king, Venutius, and his queen, Cartimandua, broke down. Venutius' skills in warfare had already given Tacitus something to talk about, as he reminds his readers. Unfortunately that reference is lost, though elsewhere he explicitly points out that Venutius hated the Romans (*H* iii.45). Perhaps the Roman goods found at Stanwick had helped provoke his rage at a quisling wife. The divorce had occasioned a Brigantian civil war. Cartimandua's pro-Roman policy, manifest in handing over Caratacus, meant that Venutius regarded his ex-

12 *Italian amphorae and other imported pottery from a rich tribal grave found at Welwyn Garden City. The social and economic power wielded by tribal aristocrats allowed them to indulge in protracted dynastic wars over territory. By the time the Roman army arrived in 43, the Catuvellauni (in whose lands this grave lay) controlled much of south-east Britain*

wife and the Romans as paired opponents in war. Her initial successes against Venutius led to his supporters attacking her. That, in turn, led to Roman military help being supplied for Cartimandua. The tribal infighting seems to have continued until 69 when events took a dramatic turn for the worse (see below, and Braund 1984).

For the moment, the battle was another Roman victory. This time, Tacitus castigated Didius for being a backseat general while his *ministros*, 'subordinates', conducted the affair. It can equally be interpreted as an occasion in which a legate trusted his officers and gave them the opportunity to flex their muscles without his interference. Clearly, he was not required but Tacitus seems to have been only concerned with running Didius down, attributing his laziness to age and the weight of his 'honours'. The legion involved this time is also not named though we learn that the commander was a man called Caesius Nasica. From subsequent dispositions, *VIIII Hispana* seems probable.

At this distance we cannot unravel why Cartimandua was pro-Roman. It may simply have been a cynical realization that Roman backing was likely to guarantee her own greed for power, and an alliance formed purely to further her own domestic ambitions. The Romans played CIA to her Third World dictatorship. There may have been more to it. The possibility exists that she or her forbears had benefited from Roman education of a sort somewhere in the past and had therefore already been inveigled into Roman ways. But neither she nor her estranged husband, nor their predecessors, seem to have issued coinage even though the Corieltauvi, just to the south, had produced a wide range of coin types, some of which used Roman lettering to record names. Even if the Brigantian leadership had escaped Roman education they will certainly not have escaped traders in Roman goods, quite apart from witnessing the Roman army whose administrative machinery provided the conduits along which these traders will have passed.

The evidence of a diploma of the year 80 suggests that Britons started entering the Roman army as auxiliaries as early as this governorship (see chapter 8). It counterbalances the evidence for such turbulence in the new province, particularly given the catastrophe now brewing on the horizon, and is an important reminder that many Britons were content enough to accept the imperial shilling and abandon dreams of a tribal golden age, if it had ever existed.

Q. Veranius Nepos 57-8

This governor is exceptional in Romano-British history for his tombstone's survival, which announces that 'he was made governor of Britain, the province in which he died' (*LAC* 8.30), and is thus one of extremely few instances of epigraphic confirmation of first-century British history. He lasted just a year in his governorship. From this stone we also learn that while Plautius and Ostorius were labouring in Britain he was engaged in mountain warfare in Cilicia, qualifying him for the testing opportunity to fight a similar war in Wales. He had a great reputation for being a man of initiative but, in a surprising revelation of his personality, he boasted to Nero that two years would be enough to lay the province of Britain at the emperor's feet. Whether this means the existing province, or all of Britain, is unresolvable, and irrelevant. His short tenure deprived him of the chance to clarify the claim. Tacitus discarded his achievements as a few trifling raids against the Silures. Doubtless, Nepos' ego was enhanced by the fact that a contemporary Greek military writer called Onasander dedicated his treatise on 'generalship' to him.

G. Suetonius Paullinus 58-61/2

Paullinus succeeded Veranius and, with his personal experience of suppressing a revolt in Mauretania, embarked on a campaign to conquer the island of *Mona* (Anglesey), a place considered to be a Druid stronghold and a haven for refugees. As such it was a powerhouse of resistance to Roman power, and an inevitable target. The crossing was made in barges, or by swimming. Considering the general Roman tolerance of religious activities and beliefs, their approach to the Druids needs a little more explanation. Caesar provides one of the first accounts, and recalled the general view that Druidism had been born in Britain before being exported to Gaul. His description concerns the Druids in Gaul, but it is unlikely that there was much difference with the Druids in Britain.

> The two classes of nobility are the Druids, and the knights. Druids are involved with everything sacred, and deal with public and private sacrifices and any theological questions. Many young men cluster about them in order to be educated and hold them in great esteem. Actually, it is the Druids who settle almost all disputes, whether public or private. They take decisions on crimes committed, murders, and arguments over boundaries and wills, deciding what the compensation or punishments will be. Anyone who does not abide by their decisions is excluded from attending sacrifices, the greatest penalty they can

impose. People who are banned this way are considered to be impious and criminal. Everyone gets out of their way and fear their society and debates, terrified they might be harmed by coming into contact with them.

Caesar, *Gallic War* vi.13

It is immediately obvious that the intense political and social control wielded by Druids was going to be unacceptable to the Roman high command. It was one thing to be a priest organising an exotic and intriguing cult. It was quite another for that priest to exist within a separate social and legal order. In some respects the conflict resembled that which Henry VIII had with the Catholic Church, and his solution was not perhaps so very different. The Roman army was the means by which the Druid obstruction to Romanization could be erased with ruthless exactitude. Initially transfixed with horror at the spectacle of the Druids engaged in ritual incantations in a crowd of men and women waving firebrands, the Roman army overcame itself and wiped out the opposition. The work included a deliberate policy of suppression and destruction. The sacred woods were destroyed and the area garrisoned. Whether this really suppressed Druidism or caused it to retreat into the groves from where it had come, and then gradually resume something of its influence, is unknown.

Any sense of success was wiped out by the news that the south-east was in flames. Once more, the advance Roman forces had been surprised by rebellion in supposedly controlled zones, and once more Roman exploitation had provoked outright hostility. The event is a reminder that the Roman army was not the overwhelmingly powerful force it has often been described as. It was impossible to garrison Britain with decisive blocks of troops stationed everywhere. There were simply not enough. In any case, Roman imperialism ultimately depended on compliance, not force, and the semi-independent operation of local government. In the end, where Rome succeeded, permanent success was always as a result of cultural, not military, victories. The assumption had been made that the south-eastern tribes, including East Anglia, had accepted Roman rule and thus could be awarded this essential independence. This was what had made the advance west feasible, by leaving the south-east only sparsely garrisoned.

The will of Prasutagus, king of the Iceni, occasioned the conflagration though it is improbable that news from Anglesey was unconnected. Prasutagus had left his kingdom to Nero and his own daughters in the hope that this would protect it from plunder. Unfortunately, his precautions were futile. Tacitus describes the miscreants as the centurions who ransacked the kingdom while slaves made what they could out of his household, an interesting indirect reference to the unilateral way in which units and individuals in the army could behave. His wife, Boudica (incidentally, never called a queen in ancient sources) was flogged and the daughters raped. It is scarcely surprising that the Roman officials felt they could act with impunity. In Rome, Nero was busy shaving his beard and celebrating the fact, prior to instituting public games in which he performed as a lyre player.

This was political suicide for the Romans. But there was more to it. Claudius had lent large sums of money to prominent Britons, which we can assume meant tribal leaders and their friends. In the year 60 the incumbent procurator, Decianus Catus, had recalled the loans, as had Seneca, Nero's advisor, who recalled his own personal loan of 40 million sesterces and sought severe ways of enforcing the recall. This provides a different angle to Tacitus, whose emphasis on the pillaging of Iceni territory was a spin which helped illustrate Roman decadence — a popular topic with him, and for which he constantly sought analogies. There is likely to have been truth in both versions. The money must have been provided as a means to allow the Britons to indulge in more Romanization — not unlike the practice of Western countries loaning cash to poorer countries so that the latter can buy arms and goods from their 'benefactors'. The calling in of the loans suggests that either the scheming had not worked, or that creditors lost their nerve as Britain turned out to be more recalcitrant than planned.

Either way, such behaviour left the Iceni with nothing to lose by rebelling, though Romanization worked best when the subjected peoples had everything to gain. The Iceni found ready partners in the Trinovantes who harboured a festering resentment at the legionary veterans installed at Colchester. Here the colonists had dispossessed locals, helped by serving soldiers who expected to do the same when they retired. This is an interesting angle as it suggests that serving legionaries were still operating in the Colchester area, which in turn suggests that the legions themselves were divided into vexillations across Britain. As we shall see later, this relieves the archaeologist and historian of Roman Britain from the obligation slavishly to explain the movements of the legions, as whole units, across Britain to their final garrison bases. At the same time it also leaves us with the clear impression of active troops operating in the 'civilian' zone and thus remaining an integral part of the process of Romanization.

The most prominent feature of the colony at Colchester was the temple to the divine Claudius (**13**). Not only was this regarded as visually offensive in the sense that it looked like a tactless display of domination, but it also served as another arm of exploitation in compulsory priesthoods for natives who were forced to spend their fortunes on fulfilling their duties. A further characteristic of the over-confidence of the Romans was the apparent failure to build defences. This is slightly difficult to understand, given that we now know the colony had been adapted out of the old legionary fortress. Perhaps the expansion of the colony had levelled part of the defences, while the remaining fortifications had been allowed to fill with rubbish.

This complacency seems to have poisoned the Roman invading force from the outset, in spite of the setbacks, which afflicted men like Ostorius Scapula. Soldiers who had invaded Britain in 43 would either now be experienced men in the latter part of their careers or who had retired altogether. Some will have taken a right to plunder for granted. This must reflect a sense of physical isolation in Britain, and also a sense of isolation from any sense of fair play or decency. Similar patterns of behaviour were noted in Vietnam in the 1960s, when an isolated and demoralised US army was engaged in a protracted and seemingly endless war of attrition. The comparison is not entirely fair — the US was not engaged in a war of conquest, but perhaps the answer lies in the state of mind of individuals for whom the details of grand strategy are neither here nor there. We need also to remember that the Roman army was not necessarily filled with hardened and committed troops. Many of them were eking out

13 *Façade of the Temple of Claudius at Colchester,* Camulodunum, *as it may have appeared in the mid-first century. The size and proportions can be calculated from the extant podium core and vaults, preserved under the Norman castle*

their contracts in order to retire quietly to a farm somewhere, or to run a business, not lie bleeding to death in a raid-sodden wood in Britain. The addition of retired legionaries from elsewhere will not have helped. Mutinies over conditions and pay were far from unknown. Even so, with the analogy still in mind one might consider the potent cultural impact of the US forces on the Vietnamese. The war might have been catastrophically futile but the Americanization of South-East Asia marched on regardless, if anything invigorated.

When the war in Britain broke out, Colchester fell easily to the rebels. The town garrison and the 200-odd soldiers sent by the procurator were hopelessly handicapped by their numbers, and the lack of defences. It seems the veterans were quite unable to provide the trained reserve, which they were intended to. Even so, *VIIII Hispana*, then commanded by Petillius Cerealis, arrived on the scene only for the infantry to be reportedly wiped out in a very disastrous engagement. There is a contradiction in the account. When the revolt was over, 2000 legionary reinforcements were sufficient to fill the gaps — yet a legion had around 5000. Tacitus must have been referring to a vexillation of *VIIII* being annihilated.

Petillius fled with his cavalry back to their fort. In the meantime, Suetonius marched south and abandoned London and Verulamium to the rebels in order to give himself time to regroup. He had with him *XIIII Gemina*, a vexillation of *XX*, and enough auxiliaries (eight cohorts-worth) to make up a force of 10,000. Suetonius also summoned *II Augusta*, but the legion failed to join him. Having bought some time, he spent it on selecting the battlefield and waited for the rebels to come to him. He thus provoked them into a set piece battle which he had a good chance of winning. The battle itself was bloody, horrific, vengeful and decisive. It terminated armed rebellion in southern Britain.

For the legions there were mixed results. *XIIII Gemina* seems to have added *Martia Victrix* to its name (**14**), and *XX* might have added *Valeria Victrix* to its, a slightly curious name which has defied easy explanation. 'Victorious Eagle' is a possibility from one suggested translation of the word *valeria*, though an origin in *valere*, 'to be powerful', seems more likely and parallels *XIIII*'s 'warlike and victorious', and the alliterative appeal of the two words is obvious (see Appendix 1 for a more detailed discussion of this).

Either way, *II Augusta* hung its head in shame and the camp prefect, Poenius Postumus, fell on his sword. That no legate is mentioned can only mean there was an interregnum or perhaps he, whoever he was, was away with a vexillation. For the Britons, the outcome was initially devastating. Any tribe, which had contributed to the rebellion, was subjected to more oppression though this paled into insignificance in areas where the rebellion meant agriculture had been ignored. Starvation followed quickly on the heels of failure.

The army was kept *sub pellibus*, 'under tenting' (*A* xiv.38), meaning that it was kept mobilized on campaign. The part-restored fort at Baginton may belong to this phase, though it remained in commission for another 20 years (**15**). Restored to

14 *Tombstone of the* signifer *Marcus Petronius, who served 18 years with* XIIII Gemina *before dying in Britain at the age of 38. He came from Vicenza, here* Vic(etia), *in Italy. Found at Wroxeter. About 50-65. The lack of the titles* Martia Victrix *may place it before the Boudican Revolt but this is not diagnostic as some demonstrably later examples from elsewhere in the Empire lack them too. However, it cannot post-date the legion's permanent transfer out of Britain by 69.* RIB 294

full strength with the reinforcements, the probability is that this mobilization included building forts throughout the territories where tribes had risen. One of these has only recently been identified from aerial photography, lying across the Peddar's Way in Norfolk — an interesting exercise in policing movements down traditional pre-Roman trackways.

Suetonius apparently found his plans confounded by the new procurator, Gaius Julius Classicianus, a thoroughly Romanized Gaul. Classicianus' father-in-law, Julius Indus, had helped the Roman suppression of a rebellion in Gaul in 21. Like the British tribal chiefs after him, Indus had found the Roman army a convenient device with which to pursue his own tribal disputes. So even here, the conciliatory procurator owed his career and position in part to Romanization borne out of military affairs. The personal relationship between Suetonius and Classicianus was not good and Tacitus blamed the latter for encouraging everyone to wait for a new legate. This seems to have been because Classicianus was alerting Rome to the idea that the tension and violence would continue while Suetonius was in post. If correct, Classicianus had a point. Oppression had provoked all of Rome's setbacks in Britain. Tacitus of course tended to favour decisive military action but his pejorative description of the next governorship suggests he had his doubts about the suitability of Suetonius for staying in post, in spite of his qualifications for suppressing the revolt.

An imperial enquiry followed, headed by an imperial freedman called Polyclitus. It was an official whitewash, which left Suetonius in position but fatally wounded. When a few of his ships were lost along with their crews it provided a face-saving pretext for a transfer of power.

15 *Reconstructed timber buildings at The Lunt, Baginton, near Coventry. The fort lasted only 20 years c.60-80, and went through at least two structural periods, the second being of reduced size. Although atypical in layout, the fort was one of dozens of turf and timber forts used during the first-century campaigns in Britain*

16 *The west gate of the colony at Lincoln,* Lindum. *The wooden blocks mark the posts of the late first-century military gate to the legionary fortress*

P. Petronius Turpilianus 61-3

This governor's policy was straightforward. He *non irritato hoste*, 'did not irritate the enemy' (*A* xiv.39), with the result that he avoided confrontations. If he did anything militarily Tacitus ignores it and rejected the governorship as a time of gutless inertia. This contradicts his admission that Suetonius might have indulged in ludicrously provocative punishments (*Agr* 16). This is a time to which some archaeologists attribute an adjustment to legionary dispositions, with the founding of Lincoln for *VIIII* and the relocation of *II Augusta* from Exeter to the Gloucester area (**16**). While there is a probability that movements on these lines took place around this time, they cannot be so tightly dated. Having said that, fort building is easily something Tacitus might regard as 'gutless inertia' except where his father-in-law Agricola was concerned.

M. Trebellius Maximus 63-9

This man seems to have been a curious choice for a governor of Britain. He lacked military experience and one of his recent jobs had been overseeing a census in Gaul rather than controlling truculent provincials. Tacitus thought him ineffectual and handicapped by greed, meanness, and a lack of military experience. This is probably Tacitus seeking to elevate the achievements of Agricola though he repeated the allegations in the *Histories*. But there may be some truth in it because Tacitus adds that the army mutinied under Roscius Coelius, legate of *XX*, and forced Trebellius Maximus into hiding. By then the Roman world was fragmenting into civil war in the catastrophic years of 68-9. It leaves us wondering whether Trebellius was no more than a place-man on a career ladder, or whether his civilian background was a deliberate device to divert the engine of Romanization and provincial development away from the army. In this sense he may have been a worthwhile and successful incumbent, but thanks to Tacitus' own bias, we are deprived of the evidence for it. Either way events in the next few years reverted to military conquest.

Trebellius fled from Britain and joined sides with Vitellius in one account by Tacitus (*H* lxv.2). In another he made a pact of mutual non-interference with the British garrison (*Agr* 16). Trebellius Maximus had a relatively long period in the governorship between 63-9, which seems odd given his failings. But the background is the deterioration in imperial power during the last four years of Nero's rule, the diversion of imperial resources and interest into self-indulgence, the emperor's descent into vice, followed by the civil wars of 68-9 which may have made Maximus' replacement impossible.

During this period one of the biggest changes was made to the garrison of Britain. The change was short-lived though later it became permanent. This was the withdrawal of *XIIII*, which Nero regarded as his favourite legion for its performance in the Boudican Revolt. All we know for certain is that it was fighting for Otho by 68, though an inscription from Rimini of the year 66 records a tribune of the legion (*ILS* 2648). Otho was defeated in 69 and Vitellius ordered the legion home to Britain where it waited until 70 to be recalled to the continent by Vespasian, then emperor (*H* ii.11, 66, 86). The legion was ordered to crush a rebellion by the Batavian chieftain Civilis (*H* iv.68). The legion never returned. Its activities in this period, entirely undetectable in the archaeological and epigraphic record show the absurdity of trying to unravel the detailed dispositions of the Roman army from potsherds and aerial photographs of marching camps.

Paradoxically, this was also the time that the Roman army in Britain and elsewhere experienced a sudden return to reliable coinage (**colour plate 4**). Until 64, coinage of all types and denominations had been in short supply. The last four years of Nero's were marked by vast strikings, with the west being largely supplied from the revived mint at Lyons. Soldiers who had had to make do with degenerate local copies of Claudian coins were now paid in the new coin, which was rapidly dispersed into the wider provincial communities.

The North

During the last 30 years of the first century, and on into the second, settlement of the northern part of Britain seems to have become the principal preoccupation for those who governed and garrisoned the island. The practical effect of this was gradually to withdraw the bulk of the military forces from the southern part of Britain. By the early second century the permanent legionary bases had been established at Caerleon, Chester and York (**colour plate 32**), leaving behind short-lived bases at Exeter, Usk, Wroxeter, and Lincoln as well as various numbers of vexillation bases. Some of the auxiliary forces found themselves devolved from legionary escorts and independent units into the frontline garrison.

M. Vettius Bolanus 69-71

In 69 Vitellius appointed Vettius Bolanus governor of Britain. Vitellius, like Galba and Otho before him, discovered that a violent end was the usual price for imperial opportunism and the consequence to set one part of the army against another. He was murdered by the late summer that year. Their short-lived careers created a pattern of instability to which the Empire would return a little over a century later. Right now though, the circumstances of the civil war compromised the new governor's plans. The victory of Vespasian over Vitellius in 69 was followed by a period in which the new emperor consolidated his power, leaving Vettius in post until about 71.

Tacitus considered Vettius Bolanus' style of government to be too placid for a violent frontier province like Britain, supposedly forcing Agricola, then legate of *XX*, to moderate his ambitions. In a further device to elevate the achievements of Agricola, Tacitus said that Vettius Bolanus never achieved peace, a harsh judgement on a man who was in post so briefly. We have no idea what this man was sent to Britain to do but it is obvious that Vettius had limited military resources at his disposal, thanks in part to the removal of *XIIII*, unless *II Adiutrix* arrived during his time. It is also quite possible that he sensibly opted to remain relatively inactive rather than pose as the commander of an active provincial army, and thus as a potential threat to those competing to remain as emperor. Vettius may simply have been acting reasonably within a very broad general remit for governor. Tacitus creates the impression that ongoing conquest was some sort of long-term directive and that governors like Trebellius Maximus and Vettius Bolanus were inadequate. It is quite possible that policy was vague, and that governors were allowed considerable free rein. After all, the holding of the post at all was as much to allow governors to add that tag to their own personal resumés.

Around this time (or so it seems), and perhaps partly as a result, Brigantian politics went out of control. During the governorship of Didius Gallus, Cartimandua and Venutius had fallen out creating a period of political strife and feuding lasting from the mid-50s until 69 (see Braund 1984 for a discussion of Tacitus as a source on this). Now it seems that Cartimandua made a fateful decision by taking Venutius' aide, Vellocatus, as her lover. This occasioned a rebellion amongst the Brigantes. Vettius Bolanus provided Cartimandua with a military escort, leaving the area to Venutius for the meantime. Vettius Bolanus was only able to use auxiliary cavalry and infantry units. This probably reflects the participation by vexillations of the legions in the civil war theatre and, perhaps, their suspect loyalties.

The outcome is ambivalent. A poem by the poet Statius was dedicated to Vettius Bolanus' son and describes a British war in which forts were built and a breastplate won from a British king. On the other hand, Vettius seems only to have removed Cartimandua from danger, leaving the volatile Venutius with his violent ambitions intact. For Rome, the strategic implications were clear enough. The secure buffer zone in the north disappeared in an instant, and Cartimandua's fragile position was exposed for what it was.

Q. Petillius Cerialis 71-3/4

Petillius Cerialis, governor of Britain between 71-4, was legate of *VIIII Hispana* during the revolt of Boudica in 60-1 when he came close to losing the whole legion. His performance

17 *Tombstone of the soldier Titus Valerius Pudens who served with* II Adiutrix *for six years before dying at the age of 30. The foundation of* II Adiutrix *during the civil war of 68-9 means this should date to the mid-70s, unless he was a later recruit. From Lincoln.* RIB *258*

in suppressing the revolt of Civilis in 70 restored his reputation and he was installed as the first Flavian governor of Britain, though family connections helped his promotion — he seems to have been related to Vespasian, and possibly Caesius Nasica, a legionary commander in Britain under Didius Gallus. Petillius Cerealis' dates as governor are provided by the sequence listed by Tacitus and the consulships he held in 70 and 74. The governorship must lie between those years.

Petillius Cerialis may or may not have brought the newly raised *II Adiutrix* with him to replace *XIIII* (**17**). There is no doubt that it was in Britain at Lincoln by 76 where it presumably supplanted *VIIII*, though it is also perfectly possible that vexillations of both legions went on campaign with Cerealis, leaving elements of both behind at Lincoln until *II Adiutrix* went to Chester. Unfortunately, there is no unequivocally dated stone from Lincoln to confirm exactly when *VIIII* was there. But evidently, the garrison of Britain was restored to the pre-civil war four.

It was left to Cerialis to deal with the Brigantian problem once and for all, which meant a permanent move of Roman forces into the north. The prospect was intimidating — the Romans believed it to be the most populous tribe in Britain. It is questionable whether Roman policy had ever been to conquer the north, but by this date it must have been obvious that the client kingdoms had by and large remained intractable problems. It was also true that soldiers, on the whole, were better occupied fighting wars of conquest than sitting about grumbling and supporting would-be usurpers. Rome was being drawn further into the net. Once she started to garrison northern Britain she would be stuck with sustaining those garrisons for the next 300 years. But it may also have been the case that the insidious effects of Roman commerce created a climate in which it looked as though conquest might be more successful. The evidence from Stanwick, already mentioned, shows that part of the Brigantian leadership at least was already thoroughly involved in being Romanized.

Tacitus passes over the campaign rather briefly. There were *multa proelia*, 'many battles', and he adds that sometimes these were *non incruenta*, 'not bloodless' (*Agr* 17). The implication is that there was a significant, and uncharacteristic, loss of Roman (or at least auxiliary) blood. Due to his earlier career with *VIIII* it has been assumed that the legion formed the backbone of Petillius Cerialis' campaign. This is not testified and is merely a reasonable inference. The foundation of York as a fortress for *VIIII Hispana* is usually attributed to this governorship but there is no epigraphic or literary confirmation of this. The earliest and only dated confirmation of its presence comes with a later inscription found near the south-east gateway for 107-8 (*RIB* 665).

The campaign itself is to all intents and purposes undetectable now for certain, though forts like Castleford, certainly in existence by the early 70s, may owe their initial foundation to this time. The site represents an important crossing point at the confluence of the Rivers Aire and Calder (which feed into the Humber) on the main eastern route into northern Britain. Roughly equidistant from York and Lincoln, but further inland, it secured a diversion around the obstacle of the Humber Estuary, and served as a springboard for forces moving north-west to where Carlisle would be founded, perhaps as early as 72 on the evidence of tree-rings.

The reference by Tacitus to there having been many battles sounds as if there was no defining set-piece engagement, leaving the Brigantes crushed. It seems as if Petillius and his troops found themselves scattered across the north, dealing with a variety of strongholds. There is more than one candidate for places to attack such as Almondbury, close to Huddersfield, as well as Stanwick. The only moderately satisfactory association of archaeology with history is the straggling series of undatable marching camps at Catterick, Rey Cross, Crackenthorpe and Plumpton Head which lead the map-viewer neatly from north Yorkshire past Stanwick and across the Stainmore Pass up to Carlisle. Were it not for tree-ring dating there would be little to conclude from this, but the dates of timbers used in the primary fort at Carlisle have been set in the early 70s. If this is correct, the evidence shows the effectiveness of the Roman army in consolidating its control of remote regions in pursuit of a mobile enemy. The outcome was that the greater part of Brigantian territory was annexed, and in a manner that allowed Cerialis' successor to focus his attention on Wales. Many forts and camps traditionally interpreted as belonging to Agricola's campaigns, thanks to Tacitus' eulogy, perhaps well into southern Scotland, could belong to this campaign.

S. Julius Frontinus 73/4-77/8

Sextus Julius Frontinus succeeded Petillius Cerealis in about 73 or 74. His time in Britain merits only a few sentences by Tacitus, who was probably keen to move on to his glorious son-in-law. Even so, Frontinus was credited with the comprehensive defeat of the Silures, which would have made a fuller account interesting.

The campaign represented a temporary total change in direction. The Silures may have forced the Roman hand, rising while Cerialis was engaged in the north. Or, the campaign may have been considered a necessary preamble to a sustained northern campaign. But it is obvious enough that Cerealis' campaign had ceased before all the Brigantian territory had been conquered. So, on balance, the likelihood is that the Welsh tribe had returned to the resistance last heard of prior to the Boudican Revolt.

The probability is that this was the time when the consolidation of Caerleon and Chester as permanent legionary bases began (see chapter 7). Tacitus does refer to Frontinus' success in getting a handle on Welsh territory and this probably reflects reconnaissance, control and garrisoning of the valleys and hills of south Wales. What this means is that, after 30 years of more or less continuous fighting, the military control Roman Britain was starting to take on some of its permanent and settled form.

Gnaeus Julius Agricola 77/8-83/4

Agricola was another of the specialist governors sent to Britain. Like Petillius Cerealis, he had already served in Britain. His first post was as a military tribune under Suetonius Paullinus on the governor's staff. Within a decade he was back, but this time in command of *XX*. Agricola was Vespasian's man, and *XX* had hesitated to swear allegiance to the new emperor. The previous incumbent, Roscius Coelius, had associated himself with Vitellius. Of course it is also true that no one in 69 had particularly good reason to assume that Vespasian would be more successful than his immediate predecessors. So the legionaries of *XX* were probably more inclined to distance themselves from these machinations rather than ally themselves with another disastrous prospect.

That Agricola was Tacitus' father-in-law is invariably pointed out as a reason to treat the *Agricola* with caution. That is reasonable, but the fact remains that much of what this vital source covers is probably true even if the credit need not be entirely accorded to Agricola. Agricola is the only governor for whom we have any sort of significant evidence for civilian policy. He is also the only governor from this period for which we have physical evidence in the form of epigraphy (**18**). The reference to Agricolan building policy is discussed in more detail in chapter 7, but if we can take it at face value it means that he took time out to focus his mind on developing the province as an institution. There is some reason to think that there might be some truth in the tale. Titus was so popular in Britain that the island was widely decorated with statues of the man who lived for only two years as emperor (79-81) during Agricola's governorship. While it is not impossible that Titus was tremendously popular as an individual, thanks partly to his own earlier military career in Britain, it is more likely that the popularity also derived from works. So, perhaps Agricola was able to benefit from being the incumbent during a time in which imperial policy was proactive in the civilian zone.

For the moment, Agricola was a smart appointment by Vespasian to the command of *XX* in 69 because his personal background with the legion will have made it difficult for the soldiers to reject Agricola. His time will have been spent under Vettius Bolanus, and Petillius

18 *Lead pipe from Chester,* Deva, *bearing imperial titles for 79 and Agricola's name.* RIB 2434.1-2

Cerealis, providing him with useful experience of dealing with northern affairs, or so we might assume if it were not for the fact that Tacitus is thoroughly opaque about Agricola's role. A governorship in Gallia Aquitania followed in *c.*74 before he returned to Britain in the year 77 or 78, this time as governor. The debate about exactly when he arrived is not particularly important. As a province without a garrison, Agricola's activities will have been entirely civilian, providing something of a balance to his military experiences.

Although it is possible to engage in a year-by-year analysis of Agricola's campaigns and civilian activities that would not be particularly useful here. Agricola's activities spanned three reigns: the last year of Vespasian, the whole of Titus, and the first three years of Domitian. That he remained in post throughout probably reflects the important remit he had been given. There can be no doubt that this was essentially to propel Roman power through what is now northern England and into Caledonia, following an initial campaign into Wales to suppress the Ordovices.

In general Agricola succeeded, and tracking what seems to have been his path through archaeology bears witness to his, and his delegates', capacity for selecting suitable routes, and locations for forts. The most conspicuous relic of all is the fortress at Inchtuthil (**19**). The victory at Mons Graupius in 83 or 84 may have been the occasion for awarding *XX* the titles *Valeria Victrix*, though the evidence is frankly very ambiguous. The recovery of a writing tablet from a primary level at Carlisle, recording Agricola and a trooper of the *ala Sebosiana* detached to his staff, helps confirm the association of places like this, Corbridge, Newstead and other bases with this governorship. Another tells us of a debt between two soldiers of *XX* at Carlisle on 7 November 83, a prosaic piece of daily business, evidence at least that part of the legion seems to have been passing through. Given the movement of individual blocks of soldiers, and the time of year, it cannot be concluded that this is evidence for the battle having taken place a few weeks before, or being yet to come (Tomlin 1992). These individual legionaries might have been engaged in supply or administrative business during the winter season, involved in police duties or associated with the governor's staff (see chapter 8).

Overall, the Agricolan campaign shows us the capacity for the Roman army organization to engage in the kind of modern warfare, which made it the premier force of antiquity. That this led to an eventual set-piece battle, following various setbacks like the ambush of *VIIII*, was to some extent inevitable and almost a rhetorical requirement of prosecuting a high-profile Roman campaign. But bringing the recalcitrant northern tribes to a battle at all, something they usually (and wisely) tried to avoid, was a very considerable achievement. More than a century later (see chapter 4), the failure of the Severan campaign to do just this characterized an ill-starred campaign leaving the Roman army foundering in the bogs.

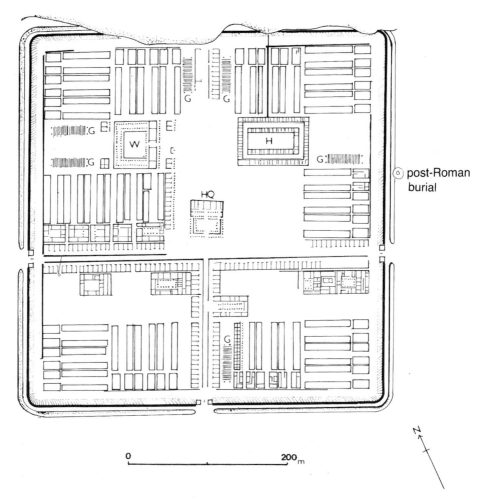

post-Roman
burial

19 *Plan of the Flavian turf and timber legionary fortress at Inchtuthil, Perthshire (after Richmond). Built and operated c.83-6/7. The short-lived nature of the site explains the small size of the headquarters building (HQ),* and other open spaces, though essential facilities like the workshop (fabrica) (W), hospital (valetudinarium) (H), and granaries (horrea) (G) were all provided

It was also ultimately logistically irrelevant. What matters is that much of northern Britain as far as what we call southern Scotland was incorporated into the system of Roman Britain. Just as the railways of North America brought previously isolated and parochial settlements into the commercial and social orbit of the East, so the military roads of northern Britain created a new world. Although the new forts would have varied fortunes, some remained in commission and were frequently rebuilt until they were consolidated in stone many decades later. But once they existed at all they attracted civilian settlement, commercial traffic, Roman deities, and the cultural convergence that generated the Romano-British identity (**20**).

20 *Dere Street on the route north from Corbridge to Risingham. The road is attributed in its earliest form to Agricola's campaigns and it remained a major route into the far north throughout the Roman period and beyond*

Built by Agricola and perhaps his predecessors and successors, the Flavian military roads made Northern Britain, every bit as remote as the foothills of Nebraska, a seamless component of a universe which stretched across to London and beyond to Asia and Egypt. Agricola himself was credited with circumnavigating Britain and thus establishing the island as a physical and unitary concept. That it was an island was long since known but his voyage seems to have created a more vivid recognition of the fact. It was one thing for traders to report, and geographers to note, but once Agricola had done it, the place became formalized just as New Zealand did when Cook set out to map it in the eighteenth century. Agricola's feat seems to have been fortuitous — according to Dio the reason had been that a group of mutinous soldiers had inadvertently done this when they made off in boats. Tacitus mentions the mutiny but does not connect the two. Either way, it reflects the power of the army as an institution that it had the resources to do this at all, whether at the hands of mutineers or those under orders from the governor.

As it happens, Domitian seems to have been content to let Caledonia go. Inchtuthil was systematically dismantled and levelled — a normal Roman military routine when abandoning a base. The effects spread much further south. Domitian had no real choice. He had lost two armies in Germany and the German frontier was of far more vital significance to him than the prospect of Caledonians who, at the very worst, could get no further than the white cliffs of Dover. Tacitus, subscribing to his view that all tyrants were the same and all tyrants were guilty of the same crimes, attributed this withdrawal to

Domitian's jealousy. Dio said much the same and said Agricola was murdered as a result. That Domitian was Agricola's co-heir and that Agricola, shortly before his death, had the choice between the governorship of Asia or Africa, makes some of this rather implausible. For Britain, Agricola's fate was irrelevant. Sadly, we have no idea who came after him and from hereon we lose Tacitus or anyone like him.

3
THE NORTH AND THE WALLS

Agricola to Trajan

The years after Agricola, right up to the end of Trajan's reign in 117, are not exactly a blank — archaeology has seen to that — but for a student of the Roman army in Britain, the situation is very different from those illustrated by the pages of Tacitus. And that means that judging the impact of the army is more difficult. There is no tantalising description of a campaign to associate with forts, and scarcely any inscriptions. The ill-starred career of Gaius Sallustius Lucullus illustrates the point. He is the only governor of Britain known to us after Agricola until 98, but this is only because Domitian had him executed for designing a new spear and naming it the *Lucullean* (Suetonius, *Domitian* x.3). Nothing else whatsoever about his tenure was considered worth mentioning, though we could indulge in the pointless speculation that the new spear was needed because of exacting military requirements in Britain, or because demands on his time were so light he had the opportunity to work on his design. Some Trajanic governors are known from diplomas (**21**), Pliny's letters and the Vindolanda tablets but there is nothing in them to tell us what was going on.

There is a great deal of archaeological evidence for extensive building in stone at all the legionary fortresses in the last quarter of the first century, with some particularly unusual structures being begun at Chester (**22**). But there are no inscriptions to confirm the fact, or context, until the beginning of the second century with one of 99-100 at Caerleon and 107-8 at York (*RIB* 330 and 665). Neither stone identifies the buildings on which they were displayed so we can only assume that they were part of the programme. In truth, we do not even know if they were really programmes. The evidence from Chester is for a thoroughly disrupted sequence of building involving delays and abandonment — right up until the third century (see chapter 7). Whatever had caused the commencement of building in stone, *XX* and the other legions soon had other fish to fry.

The extended institution of the army in Britain around this time found homes in new colonies. Unlike Colchester we have no certainty about when this occurred. Instead we have to fall back on inferences. Gloucester was home at least to one soldier, Marcus Ulpius Quintus, of *VI Victrix*. His name, and the fact that *VI* did not arrive until the reign of Hadrian, does not get us very far but he was also a member of the Nervian voting tribe, while his personal name suggests he or an antecedent gained citizenship under Trajan. Nerva (96-8) was Domitian's successor and at the very least it seems that the permanent abandonment of Gloucester as a full-time military base must at least date from this time. The theory also goes that Nerva appropriated inscriptions and dedications to Domitian, because Domitian had been subjected to *damnatio memoriae*. So, it is possible that Gloucester became a colony earlier. With Lincoln we are on even less certain ground. The

21 *The Malpas diploma. Found on farmland at Malpas, Cheshire, in 1812, the diploma belonged to one Reburrus of* ala I Pannoniorum Tampiana *(visible on the left-hand panel, three and six lines from the bottom respectively). Apart from another diploma of 122, the unit is otherwise untestified in Britain.* RIB 2401.1

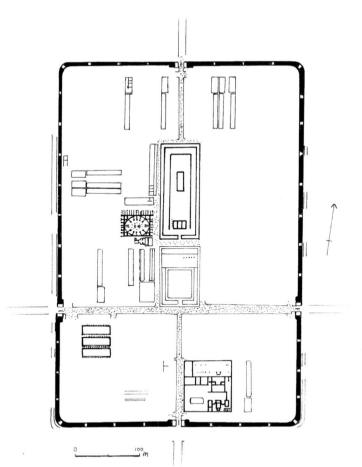

22 *(left) Chester, Deva, fortress of* II Adiutrix, *and* XX Valeria Victrix. *In the centre is the headquarters building, above the large enclosure, and to the left the elliptical building (see* **102***). (Based on various sources)*

23 *Stamp of* VIIII Hispana (here IX) *on a vault tile. From Bainton, Northants, near Longthorpe, but thought to come from a tomb. The stamp matches those made at York c.70-100, making the provenance difficult to understand as it postdates* VIIII'*s possible occupation at Longthorpe. Perhaps used in the tomb of a veteran.* RIB *2462.12 (iii)*

earliest inscription telling us it was a colony is dated to 237, and no use to us here. But if *VIIII Hispana* was at York by 107-8 at the latest the probability must be that Lincoln had been given up to a colony before then (**23**). York is a different case altogether. It remained a fortress — its colony lay across the river from the military base, and its establishment as a colony could have taken place at almost any time between *c*.100 and 237.

At the very least though it seems that Britain's military cornerstones were matters of fact by the time that Trajan ruled (98-117). Not only did the average Roman Briton know that three legions were installed in major permanent fortresses, but that veterans were also established in at least three colonies at Colchester, Gloucester and Lincoln. This effectively made six major military power centres, quite apart from London where a fort was certainly in existence by the 120s (**24**). As almost the entire infrastructure of the province fanned out towards these settlements and the array of other forts scattered across the north and west it is fairly plain that Roman Britain was part of the Roman army world, and that the army was making Britain what it was.

So it is particularly frustrating to have so little idea of the administrative decisions lying behind this turn of events. The period between Agricola's recall in 84 and the coming of Hadrian in the 120s covered almost two military generations. The troops who could show scars earned by feats done on their Crispin's day in Caledonia with the legendary general will have been, for the most part, aged warriors by the time that the Wall was begun. Between those times lay decades of infrastructure, skirmishes, and imperial indifference. Under Trajan Britain excited not even the slightest comment in the meagre sources we have. Had things of note occurred then we would have heard about it — instead Trajan's coin designers and his chroniclers preferred to record his wars in Parthia and Dacia and the expansion of the Empire to its greatest extent.

The question of the Trajanic frontier along a road strung out between Carlisle in the west, through Corbridge and out to the east somewhere, has occasioned much debate

24 *Tombstone of Vivius Marcianus of* II
Augusta, erected by his wife Januaria Martina.
Found in 1669 at St Martin's, Ludgate Hill,
London during the post-Great Fire rebuilding.
The explicit reference to wife, coniunx, *may or*
may not indicate a post-197 date (but see **40***).*
RIB *17*

amongst the archaeologists of the army of Roman Britain. In truth we do not know whether the infrastructure of this zone was deliberate, incidental, piecemeal, or even exactly contemporary. But we do know that this was a world of military movement and casual engagement at the end of colossal supply lines. This much comes from the documents found at Vindolanda, one of the Stanegate forts. The documents do not come from the stone fort visible today (*see* **103**) but from the deeply buried remains of one of the succession of timber forts that stood here from the latter days of Domitian until well into the second century.

To us, these documents are like the pages of Samuel Pepys' diary of the 1660s. They represent a window flung open for a brief period, allowing us to catch a glimpse of Flavius Cerealis, prefect of *cohors* IX *Batavorum* at Vindolanda, his contacts, staff, hangers-on, family and friends. This emergès as a world where unit commanders engaged in bouts of upland hunting, where their wives indulged in social occasions, and where their troops malingered from sickness, were deployed in blocks or as individuals here and there, even as far as London. Gone in a trice is the neat world of military dispositions so fondly imagined by the archaeologists of former generations. If anything is clear enough it is that archaeology cannot, apart from producing these documents in the first place, create this information out of potsherds.

Broadly datable to the period 90-105, the documents are a fabulous find and they are rightly celebrated as one of Roman Britain's greatest treasures. What they reveal more compellingly than anything else is the essential Roman-ness of the world the military had created on the edge of Empire. The observation has often been made that these people had achieved what the British created in the colonies. They had 'turned a savage wilderness into a glorious empire' (Edmund Burke, 1775). And, if this was what the Roman army had created at Vindolanda by 100, then it had done so everywhere else in the military zone and not only now, but before then — right back to 43.

The documents include the oft-quoted 'strength report' for *cohors I Tungrorum* at Vindolanda. The unit is listed at 752-strong, but anyone making assumptions about the available firepower would be mistaken. As it turns out, 337 of the soldiers alone have been detached to Corbridge, with another 119 elsewhere including London. The London reference is important because it reminds not only that this premier commercial settlement was almost certainly the capital of the province by now, and probably had been since the 60s or 70s, but that its fort may belong to this time too. As the governor's headquarters, the constant movement of troops detached to his staff and personal garrison will have provided London with a permanent sense of the military, reflected in some of the inscriptions found there though these only commemorate legionaries.

Once the sick and wounded have been accounted for, Vindolanda's Tungrians turn out to be only 265, perhaps consoling themselves that the fewer men, the greater share of honour. Inscriptions from elsewhere provide further clues to gaps in strength. A building stone of a generation later from Hadrian's Wall near Birdoswald records work by the 'century styled *Probiana*' of the fourth cohort of an un-named legion (*RIB* 1930). Had the centurion Probus been in post then the normal protocol would have been to call it the 'century of Probus'. It seems that he had died or moved on, leaving his post unfilled. His former soldiers called themselves after him in the interim. There is plenty of other evidence for sustained dispersal of all types of units across Britain. If we read for everywhere else what we now know to have been the case at Vindolanda it becomes quite obvious that not only was the Roman army's day-to-day availability impossibly different from what we might hope to assess from merely the names of units listed in diplomas, but also that the soldiers were widely dispersed across the province — just from one minor auxiliary infantry unit.

This means career soldiers constantly in institutional transit across the military and civilian zones, a situation perhaps not repeated until the days of the Jacobite rebellions of the eighteenth century, the Napoleonic Wars, and the Second World War. There are plenty of other clues to this complex picture, ranging from the debt arrangements in late 83 between two soldiers of XX at Carlisle (Tomlin 1992), to the bronze *trulla* from the fortress of *II Augusta* at Caerleon which bears the stamped name of *ala I Thracum* (Zienkiewicz 1993, 106). Perhaps no more than a souvenir, it could just as easily be evidence for the auxiliary unit's association with the legion — which would not be surprising, given the late first-century tombstone of a member of the unit at Cirencester (*RIB* 109), and is a conclusion reinforced by finds of horse harness fittings.

This kind of information is ultimately frustrating because it makes assessments of the garrison of Britain, or assumptions of the implications of movements impossible. Clearly, the Vindolanda tablet cannot be a model for anywhere else, or even Vindolanda a week later, apart from telling us that every day and every place was different. Frere states that 'heavy fighting in Britain both in Domitian's reign and in Trajan's is certain', and cites as part of his evidence the movement of *cohors II Asturum* from Germany to Britain between 89 and 105 (from diplomas). The Vindolanda material does not exactly contradict this, but the documents show that movements were constant and strength perpetually variable. As it happens there is other evidence to suggest that the Asturians were involved in fighting in Britain at this time, as one of their former commanders was decorated for a British war at some time between 89 and 128, but the movement of the unit is not of itself evidence for this.

None of the documents refer to ongoing campaigns or battles. This is not surprising. Had anything of great import occurred in the period we might hope to have heard about it from somewhere else. Instead we have to be satisfied with a single reference to the *Brittunculi*, an insulting and derogatory racial term of the type illegal today. The passage is not easy to understand.

> The Britons have no protection from armour. The many cavalry make no use
> of swords and nor do the wretched Britons settle down in order to hurl spears.

> *TV* ii.164, *c*.90-105

The last phrase is particularly difficult. Either it means that the Britons did not climb onto horses to throw their spears, or they did not kneel down in a fixed spot to do so. The latter seems more likely, given the writer's irritation, which seems to suggest that they were inconveniently elusive. Either way, it is plain that the soldiers were familiar with skirmish fighting, so we must assume that violence occurred on and off. But whether this was founded on attempts by the Britons to expel the Romans or, as seems just as likely, attempts to steal food and *materiel* from the alluring prospects of the new forts, is something we cannot discern.

Nevertheless, it would be entirely a mistake to assume that the fighting concerned the officers all the time. Flavius Cerealis would have been a career equestrian working his way through a series of posts which could have included military commands as well as civilian administrative posts (see chapter 8). Whatever level of fighting was involved the Batavians and Tungrians at this new timber and turf fort were well served by the quartermaster. Innumerable references to food and goods, payments, receipts, debts, and transportation, all show that Vindolanda (and thus all the other forts) were integrated into the system of military commerce. The physical remnants of Gaulish samian ware show that this most ubiquitous of all high-quality goods found its way to the mess tables — and in sufficient abundance for damaged goods to be summarily hurled into pits and ditches on arrival.

Compared to Vindolanda, most of the other forts of the region like Carvoran or Hardknott are comparatively sterile relics, lacking records of the day-to-day inconveniences and surprises of real life. When the Vindolanda documents cease, the window is shut and it remains closed for the rest of Roman Britain's history. Together with the archaeology of the period, the documents illustrate the process of Roman Britain being formalised into the permanent arrangements of the next three centuries. The military character of the province was fully established, though one of its features was yet to be built, let alone conceived. This is in contrast with almost everywhere else in the Empire, which had nothing like this density of military strongholds, except the Rhine and Danube frontiers.

The lead-up to the Wall

With the lack of any adequate epigraphic or literary evidence for what went on in Britain under Trajan and the first few years of Hadrian's reign, it is impossible to be certain how much Hadrian's Wall came in the aftermath of a significant bout of warfare, or whether it was the product of a more general frustration at a resilient problem. A tombstone from Ferentinum in Italy names Titus Pontius Sabinus, sometime *primus pilus* of *III Augusta* amongst other posts. It adds that he had commanded vexillations of *VII Gemina*, *VIII Augusta* and *XXII Primigenia* on the 'British expedition' (*ILS* 2726B). A reference in the text to his decoration by the deified Trajan makes it probable that the expedition occurred in the latter part of Trajan's reign or under Hadrian.

Of course, we have no idea what the troops were needed for, though this is useful further evidence for the perpetual dispersal of Roman military units across provinces as and when needed. It also shows that Britain did not have to rely on its existing garrison when circumstances arose to compromise the situation. These legions were not strangers to Britain and would return as vexillations again. In the meantime, the frontier zone in Britain was shortly to change out of all recognition.

The Wall

It is usually said that Hadrian made the decision permanently to cease the expansion of the Roman Empire. This is true but he was, to a great extent, acknowledging what was largely already the case. Britain exemplifies that. The withdrawal from the deep north was a decision now nearly 40 years old. The scattered forts of the so-called Stanegate frontier testify to the reality of a military zone in the area between where Newcastle and Carlisle now lie. It is easy to imagine a sense of complacent resignation setting in, with a cycle of long winters and erratic summers, on the northern frontier. The peace was probably only broken by routine, and futile, incursions by bands of northern tribesmen sustaining a posture of resistance to manufacture their own sense of parochial esteem and peer respect. As they raced off with stolen weapons, and a hostage or two, their own feelings of frustration will have been momentarily admonished while the Roman army perceived them as a source of casual inconvenience and occasionally the stimulus to ruthless revenge on a hapless local village.

Perhaps both communities somehow developed a symbiotic dependence for a sense of purpose. Northern tribes will simply have substituted the Romans for their own former tribal rivals. For the Romans, the chance to win battles was a way of breaking up the monotony and winning a little glory. When Hadrian started touring the north-western provinces in 121 he was determined that stabilising the borders would not mean diminishing the army's readiness. In Germany he restored the routines and practices of an army on campaign into the permanent garrisons, and diminished corruption. From here he sailed to Britain. What he did on his arrival is not completely clear. He was said to have 'put right many things' (*SHA* xi.2) which may or may not mean that he reformed the British garrison in the same way. We also know that *VIIII Hispana* left Britain around this time for an uncertain fate — it more or less disappears from the record hereafter — and was replaced by *VI Victrix* (**25**). The new legion is first testified at Haltonchesters on Hadrian's Wall between 122-6 (*RIB* 1427) but the fact that it came from Lower Germany,

the same place as the governor of the period, Aulus Platorius Nepos, means it probably escorted him.

That Hadrian instituted the building of his Wall is beyond doubt (**26**). Whether he designed it or not is unknown, though the likelihood is great given his interest in architecture. Certainly the scheme as initiated looks very much like a paper plan being laboriously executed on the ground. The stone curtain was broken only at roads and rivers, except that the milecastles, little more than elaborate gatehouses, provided crossing points (**27**). A couple of turrets at one-third-mile intervals, with the occasional extra tower in zones of restricted visibility, allowed troops to keep an eye on every spot. West of the river Irthing it was built of turf, with turf milecastles and wooden turrets. Along its way the gates of the forts provided further crossing points but these were only sited every six to eight miles along its length, with the forts themselves being added only after the other work was well underway. By the end of the second century the turf section had all been rebuilt in stone. Evidence from numerous locations shows that whatever the plans had been, the curtain was built of variable thickness

25 VI Victrix. *Altar from the Tyne at Newcastle, dedicated by the legion to Neptune and found with another dedicated to Ocianus (sic). Probably from a shrine on the Roman bridge after which the fort here,* Pons Aelius, *was named. About 125-60.* RIB 1319

(*see* **105**). No stretch survives to full height, but it is likely that this varied as well. It is also quite possible that the Wall was not completed at some points until perhaps much later — if ever.

In front of the Wall the crags provided defence, and where the crags gave way to gentler slopes a ditch was dug. Behind the Wall a more substantial ditch, flanked by mounds, ran approximately parallel far enough to provide a significant ribbon of military zone, but close enough to be reached in moments and remain visible. This, the so-called Vallum, was dug regardless of the terrain while the forward ditch was abandoned where rocks proved too tough. The Vallum was built after the forts, which it skirted (except Carrawburgh, added later in Hadrian's reign, or possibly even after that, and built across

26 *Granary inscription from Benwell,* Condercum, *on Hadrian's Wall, naming Hadrian, the governor* Aulus Platorius Nepos, *and what can be restored as* classis Britannica, *the fleet. c.122-6.* RIB *1340*

27 *Hadrian's Wall milecastle 39, 'Castle Nick', looking east. Here the epigraphic evidence is lacking, but the style is considered to be attributable to* VI Victrix *by a process of elimination as inscriptions of* II Augusta *and* XX Valeria Victrix *are associated with different styles*

28 *Building stone from the north wall of the Hadrian's Wall fort at Benwell,* Condercum, *naming* II Augusta *and depicting its Capricorn emblem. Probably Hadrianic.* RIB *1341*

the Vallum). Many inscriptions confirm the Wall's date, and the involvement of all the legions, as well as the fleet (**26, 28**). All those, which can be read with certainty, belong to the governorship of Aulus Platorius Nepos, dated by diplomas to *c.*122-6. None tells us anything about the operation or success of the Wall which makes the next stage in the process all the more difficult to understand. The Wall did not function in isolation. The Stanegate forts remained in commission and to the south, other forts were built, or now consolidated in stone, for example at Hardknott (**29**).

The Antonine Wall
The building of the Antonine Wall was recorded by the biographer of Antoninus Pius. He announces that 'through the legate Lollius Urbicus he defeated the Britons, and built another wall, of turf, having driven back the barbarians' (*SHA Antoninus Pius* v.4). This terse, but explicit, comment leaves us in no doubt that a *second* wall had been built and that it was a matter of note that it had, this time, not been made of stone. An inscription from High Rochester names Urbicus, and shows that the developments were not confined to the new wall (*RIB* 1276) (**30**). The context was memorably recorded in 143 in the first explicit major series of coins depicting Britannia, and announcing that Antoninus Pius had been declared *Imperator* for the second time. The style and imagery of these coins is discussed in chapter 6 but they were remarkable for being struck in significant numbers and types. No previous military event in Britain was so widely publicised this way (**colour plate 15**).

That the new wall was built to a reduced specification — it had no Vallum or turrets for instance and was only held for around 20-25 years — makes it an ideal subject for excited and heated archaeological debate. This tends to centre on whether it was conceived as a permanent replacement for Hadrian's Wall or held alongside, and whether its abandonment occurred once, or was followed by reoccupation and then permanent abandonment. With no historical or epigraphic evidence to answer these questions, solutions have been optimistically sought in the distribution of Gaulish samian name stamps. One study concluded that a diminished overlap in names found on both Walls was evidence that they were not held together (Hartley 1972). But it can be shown, with ease, that the distribution of names is mathematically linked to the size of samples compared to the total number of potters operating rather than having any chronological implications. As no samian potter can be more tightly dated than within a couple of decades it becomes obvious that ceramic evidence is not up to making good the gaps in historical data (de la Bédoyère 1987, and 1988, 62).

Overall, it is easy to see the time the 37-Roman-mile- (59km-) long frontier was in use as brief and inconclusive. But this time covered a whole imperial reign and a generation of troops as well as several governorships. It was also commemorated with pride by the units concerned (**31**). The minutiae of circumstances, changed policies and personalities

29 *Hardknott,* Mediobogdum, *looking west across the fort platform. Internal buildings, including a granary are visible*

30 *High Rochester,* Bremenium. *Dedication slab of Antoninus Pius, naming the governor Quintus Lollius Urbicus and cohors I Lingonum. Preserved by reuse in antiquity as part of a fort water tank.* RIB 1276

IMP·C·
T·AE·HADRIA
NO·ANT·NN·AVG·PI·P·P·

VEX
LEG·XX
VV·FE

P·P·ĪĪĪĪ   CƟXI

31 *Antonine Wall at Ferrydyke, near Old Kilpatrick. Dedication slab naming Antoninus Pius,* XX Valeria Victrix, *the distance-built of 4411ft. Thought to have marked the western end of the Wall. The design features a Victory in the main field, and a boar, symbol of* XX, *in the ansate panel at the bottom. c.139-61.* RIB *2208*

make this insoluble. If the new wall was conceived as a permanent replacement then minds were changed. If not, then we can only assume it was devised to serve as a solution to a problem without any serious concern for its use or validity 30 or 50 years hence.

Whoever designed the new frontier had undoubtedly spent time considering the specifications, and changes of plan, so evident on Hadrian's Wall. Whatever the Vallum's role it had either been too much trouble or too ineffective to bother with again, a fact which is reflected in the crossings thrown across the Vallum when the old wall was reoccupied. The value of more forts to the rear was not forgotten. A Flavian fort at High Rochester became the basis of a new stone fort. The undated, but Antonine-style, inscription from Birrens which names *VIII Augusta* and *XXII Primigenia* may mean Lollius Urbicus brought vexillations with him to build there and elsewhere though this may not have been until the 150s when *cohors II Tungrorum* was building there (B 1992, 318, *RIB* 2110). *XXII Primigenia* also turns up on an inscription from an unknown site in Scotland (*RIB* 2216). Hadrian's Wall itself was not left to the elements, but it is unlikely a stretched garrison could have done much more than keep things ticking over. Perhaps the idea that one or other had to be abandoned is another example of an over-simplistic interpretation by us. The evidence from Birdoswald is that parts of the fort were still unfinished and remained so during this period. Even so, some soldiers were present at Hadrian's Wall forts intermittently during the reign. Visits were made to the temple of Antenociticus at Benwell, and inscriptions of Pius went up at Chesters in 139 (*RIB* 1330, 1460-1). But given what we now know about constantly mobile units it is quite possible that both walls were held more or less simultaneously, even episodically and intermittently.

As we have no idea what the Antonine Wall was *intended* to achieve it is difficult to measure its success or lack of it. That it was given up is an unalterable fact, but withdrawal need mean no more than that it had served its purpose. If the Roman army ever exhibited anything it was a capacity for flexibility. Giving it up in the 160s might be a reflection of the difficulty of sustaining frontier warfare at such a distance from core control centres at York, Corbridge and perhaps Carlisle. The issue of Britannia coins in 154 (**colour plate 16**) is usually interpreted as evidence for renewed warfare, and we know that at the beginning of Marcus Aurelius' reign in 161 'a British war was threatening' (*SHA Marcus Aurelius* viii.7-8). Although the Antonine Wall was never reoccupied on a permanent basis this is not the same as the idea that it *never* might have been. Had circumstances been different there can be no doubt that the Antonine Wall would have been recommissioned, or even rebuilt in stone, if it had seemed appropriate.

The long-term impact of the Wall and forts

So much evidence of Roman culture survives in the vicinity of Hadrian's Wall that it dominates the available record. Items and aspects of the Wall recur throughout this book with unavoidable frequency. In some senses this must be a distortion, borne out of the survival thanks to remote locations and the fascinated attention paid the straggling ruins by armies of academics for centuries. But it is also a reflection of the Roman military world and its extraordinary durability combined with relentless practicality. Many parts of the Wall area have never been as thickly populated since the Roman army and its hangers-on operated there. So it is worth briefly considering its impact on ancient consciousness.

Once the Antonine Wall was given up, Hadrian's Wall was eventually all built in stone. So were all the forts of the north, at least those to be kept in commission. The Wall was the most sophisticated of all these installations. Excavations at many of these places have revealed an intensely variable degree of operational readiness, depending on the period. Many of the turrets were eventually demolished. The milecastles fell into differing degrees of usage, with the gates blocked up or abandoned. The forts themselves were similarly treated (*see* **122**).

The Wall thus bears all the hallmarks of a textbook plan, executed only in part before practical experience changed everything. The ten-foot Wall became eight foot within a year or two of commencement, built on the carefully prepared ten-foot foundation. The forts themselves were an addition around this time and required the demolition of new turrets, and sections of the Wall. Then the Vallum was dug, before someone decided the gap between Chesters and Housesteads forts was too big and introduced a new fort at Carrawburgh. Here the nice new Vallum had to be filled in, and the fort built over it. At Limestone Corner the ditch diggers gave up and left the blocks where they lay. Birdoswald fort seems to have been half-finished and then left for an unspecified period before the fort was completed.

What this means is that we seem to be faced with a Roman army bumbling around with a plan they were told to change, or found they could not always execute. Part of this perception is based on modern expectations that the Wall ought to be conforming to a regimented plan. Eric Birley for example recorded the unsuccessful search for milecastle 11 in 'its calculated position' (1961, 96). More recently, the identification of a new milecastle within Newcastle at Westgate Road was only unexpected because it was not in a location that fitted the pattern created by modern interpreters to fill in the gaps (Harbottle *et al.* 1988). But variations and changes are really scarcely surprising. In the aftermath of the First World War, the government found it financially and politically expedient to give up some of its new airfields. Within a few years it was busy re-requisitioning the land and rebuilding them. There is no suggestion here that the motive was the same on Hadrian's Wall but merely to illustrate that however plans are conceived, their execution is subject to variables and unpredictable developments of such broad potential that unless we know what they were it is impossible to reconstruct them.

For all the changes, and the crumbling, and the rebuilding, the fact is that the Wall was there and it remained. There is little or no evidence at all that it affected the consciousness of the civilian south, even though we know that at some point, probably in the fourth century, urban communities contributed working parties to repair sections of it. So, the evidence initially points to a fundamentally local social influence, and by extension we might assume that perhaps that applies to the other forts of the northern frontier.

Today there is no more potent symbol of the Roman army than the remains of Hadrian's Wall. In fact, much of what is visible has been restored, cleared or even rebuilt. Vast swathes of the Wall have been cleared away and reused in numberless farmhouses, field walls and road foundations. But the excavations which have continued here on and off for the last two centuries have exposed so much, and been so subject to research, recording and recondite debate that a colossal amount of information has emerged.

None of these aspects mean that the Wall is settled as a subject. Despite the inscriptions testifying to the Wall's inception under Hadrian between the years 122-6, and the historical references providing a tantalisingly thin glimpse of Hadrian's policy, we know nothing about the Wall's day-to-day operation. But we do need to look at what the Wall was and how it affected the vicinity and, more importantly, all of Roman Britain. It would not do to separate out the Wall and consider it in isolation. The Wall was just part of the vast permanent military garrison of the north and forts like Hardknott, Maryport and South Shields (**32**) were as much a part of it.

First and foremost it created a vast, permanent, military zone straddling Britain. Not only did this mean that local movements of trade and people were permanently affected by this obstacle to free movement, but it also meant that the general economy of *Britannia* was affected by the need to service it. Yes, it is true that forts like Vindolanda and Corbridge were already effectively permanent parts of a military zone but the Wall took it into a new level by effectively obstructing a whole part of Britain. This ribbon of troops was also an unbroken display of Roman architecture, engineering, imagery and identity.

Secondly, the Wall and its garrison created a new type of military community. The existence of permanent garrisons elsewhere in Britain had already created something akin to Britain's great naval and military depots of the seventeenth and eighteenth centuries. Essentially supported by the wages paid to troops, places like Roman Chester and Corbridge, or Georgian Portsmouth, were state-supported towns which acted as channels for state finances, social status, national pride, the sale and consumption of goods, and the absorption of resources. Hadrian's Wall added to this by creating a variant, which was effectively a 73-mile long unfolded fort. Its permanence, and isolation, together with the longevity of the units on the Wall must mean that serving soldiers in the third and fourth centuries were often able to trace their origins to soldiers who arrived here in the second century and made their peace with local women — so to speak.

32 *South Shields,* Arbeia. *Building stone naming* VI Victrix. *Found in situ built into the front wall of the headquarters, and since removed to the site museum.* RIB *1061*

But it needs always to be remembered that the garrison of the Wall and all the other forts was primarily made up of auxiliaries, working alongside legionaries and legionary vexillations. This began as the land of ethnic Thracians, Sarmatians, Gauls, Tungrians, and a host of others who in time merged seamlessly into the local communities over successive generations. This mixture is no better symbolized than by Nectovelius. He was of the 'Brigantian nation' and served in *cohors II Thracum* at Mumrills on the Antonine Wall (*RIB* 2142). Perhaps he was a local man who had found himself a military career by signing on with the local unit. Britain's garrison was disproportionately large, and that created problems of recruitment and retention — even for the legions. The only sensible policy, in the long-term, was harnessing local people. The problem in Britain is identifying them (see chapter 8).

The impermanence of the Antonine Wall demonstrates how the absence of the army seemed to preclude the possibility of sustained Romanization. Its brevity meant that the civilian communities, which developed round the forts of Hadrian's Wall and the Stanegate strongholds to the rear, simply did not emerge. And while Roman goods and money trickled out into Caledonia in a piecemeal fashion it was only in that direction. Caledonia remained largely what it had always been: a wild and untamed place where urbanization was beyond comprehension and the Roman world a distant, flickering, intractable behemoth lurking behind torches and walls to the south, as Septimius Severus would discover in 208.

Conversely, to the Roman army the territory north of Hadrian's Wall was *trans Vallum*, 'beyond the frontier', memorably described thus in an inscription found at Kirksteads near Carlisle. To an unknown god, Lucius Junius Victorinus, legate of *VI Victrix*, dedicated his thanks for his 'successful exploits beyond the frontier' (*RIB* 2034). It cannot date to after *c*.208, because by then the legate of *VI* was also governor of Britannia Inferior (northern Britain), the province having been divided into two in order to dilute the power of the governor of the island. The short text is unequivocally an 'us and them' statement, though whether men like Junius Victorinus treated the area north of the Wall as a kind of playground or as a terrifying leap into the unknown is another matter. The official name for a chain of outpost forts was *praetentura* or *praetensione*, apparently recorded on an incomplete inscription from Corbridge (Speidel 1998).

33 *Plan of the fort at High Rochester,* Bremenium

The presence of scattered forts in this zone, like Bewcastle, Birrens and High Rochester, show that it was symbolically regarded as a Roman domain. But High Rochester in particular is emphatically a military stronghold, the Romano-British equivalent of a cavalry base in Indian land in the unorganised territories of western North America in the mid-nineteenth century (**33**). Inscriptions from the site itself show that this was an artillery installation on a grand scale while a sculptor amongst its garrison fashioned a crude representation of Venus (**77**). To the west, the fort at Bewcastle was named *Fanum Cocidii*, 'the shrine of Cocidius'. Cocidius was a Romano-British warrior god, usually given form and coherence by associating him with Roman Mars. So, here we find Roman Venus and Mars, those unequivocal images of the classical world, in their own different frontier forms. Scattered finds on the moorland beyond show that the veneration of these deities extended beyond the forts themselves.

Much of this, including the completion of the Wall itself, and the innumerable repairs and alterations, stretched across the rest of the second century and across the third into the fourth. Circumstances changed beyond recognition as the frontier moved round to include the English Channel, and new forts were built around the south coast. But the Wall remained. Whatever happened in the Severan campaigns, or in the suppression of pirates, the Wall and its military zone had come to define Roman Britain itself not just at the time but also to us.

4
THE LATER ARMY

The occupation(s) of the Antonine Wall will remain a problem for the foreseeable future, though the detail tends to obscure the fact that it was permanently given up. By the 160s at the latest Hadrian's Wall was being recommissioned, and that was the way things remained. Writing a few decades later, Dio Cassius called it 'the cross wall which splits the island in two' and said that of Britain's territory, 'we hold a fraction less than half' (lxxvii.12.1, 5). An inscription from Heddon records that *VI Victrix ref(ecit)*, 'rebuilt', a section of Wall in the year of the consulship of Tertullian and Sacerdos (*RIB* 1389). This places it firmly in 158, three years before the death of Antoninus Pius in 161. On one hand this illustrates the ongoing problems with keeping the Wall operational at all. On the other it demonstrates that manpower was still being committed to the old frontier, though there is no need to assume that repairing Hadrian's Wall means that it had been abandoned up till then or that this was the first time any repairs had been done.

The governor responsible will have been Julius Verus, testified in the post between 157 and 158 on a slab from Birrens (*RIB* 2110). The context has not really been clarified by the inscription from the Tyne at Newcastle with its enigmatic and cryptically-abbreviated reference to vexillations of *II*, *VI* and *XX* in connection with 'the armies of the two Germanies' (**34**). If the text means reinforcements were supplied from Upper and Lower Germany for the British legions, then a case can be made for trouble in northern Britain of sufficient severity to warrant the provisions. There are several problems with this (Speidel 1987). Firstly, there is no evidence of a war of sufficient severity and had there been one it would seem unlikely that members of *VI* could have been spared to go and repair the Wall in 158. Secondly, it is improbable that reinforcements had been pre-allocated to each of the British legions. It can be equally well interpreted as evidence that the British legions had contributed reinforcements to the Germanies, and that these troops had now returned, sailing into the Tyne. The latter seems more probable, especially taken into account with a revised reading of a inscription from Ribchester (see below).

Sextus Calpurnius Agricola

Under Verus' successor, Sextus Calpurnius Agricola, there is no doubt that war in Britain formed a backdrop to the epigraphic evidence which survives. Calpurnius Agricola was governor of Upper Germany in 158, and a new reading of a lost inscription from Ribchester restores his name along with a reference to a vexillation of cavalry from that province (*RIB* 589 and Speidel 1987).

The *Life* of Marcus Aurelius announces that amongst other military problems in about 162-3, 'a British war was threatening . . . Calpurnius Agricola was sent to face the Britons' (*SHA Marcus Aurelius* viii.7-8). Several inscriptions testify to his presence in Britain, but they add little to the information about a war which we would otherwise know nothing of and which went unrecorded on coinage of the reign. One of the stones naming him

34 *The Tyne at Newcastle,* Pons Aelius. *Panel dredged from the river with a cryptic text naming Antoninus Pius, the governor Julius Verus, and vexillations of* II Augusta, VI Victrix *and* XX Valeria Victrix. *The phrase* ex Ger(manis) Duobus *means that vexillations were arriving from Upper and Lower Germany to reinforce the British legions, or had been sent to Germany and were now returning. The text has been carelessly laid out. Other inscriptions and references date this governor to the late 150s.* RIB *1322*

comes from Carvoran, by Hadrian's Wall. It records no more than a dedication to the goddess Suria by *cohors I Hamiorum* (*RIB* 1792), and shows that reoccupation was underway, or that occupation was continuing. This is reinforced by an altar from Stanwix, fortunately dated to 167 (*RIB* 2026), unless one takes the view that a fort sometimes believed to have been the Wall headquarters would have been left in commission regardless of the state of the rest of the frontier system. Perhaps the case was that it had become obvious the Antonine Wall was over-stretching the garrison of Britain. Calculations of how many, and where, are fairly pointless because the one thing we know for certain is that garrisons were in a permanent state of flux. Frere's observation that 'there were now 33 forts (with 18,500 men) held south of Hadrian's Wall' (1987, 145) is essentially untenable.

In the mid-170s Marcus Aurelius made a peace settlement with a tribe called the Iazyges on the Danube frontier. The deal included a return of Roman prisoners, and also the provision of 8000 cavalry. Aurelius sent 5500 of them to Britain (lxxi.16.2). It is very easy to see this kind of troop movement as a deliberated response to a crisis, or some pressing need. But, it is improbable that troops recruited like this also acquired overnight loyalty to Rome, which makes their despatch to Britain more easily understood. What better place to relocate them while they learned the ways of the Roman army? Apart from the presence of Sarmatians on two tombstones at Ribchester (*RIB* 594-5) there is no further evidence for them. Neither stone is datable, even on style, as they are long lost and survive only as sketched records from the seventeenth century.

Ulpius Marcellus

Thanks to a diploma, it is now known that the governor by 178 was Ulpius Marcellus (**35**), succeeding Quintus Antistius Adventus whose career included service in Parthia and the governorships of Arabia and Lower Germany. Ulpius Marcellus had an unusually long time in post, once thought to be impossible. The confusion which originally reigned over this man, and which led to the postulated existence of a descendant to explain what would otherwise be a theoretically impossibly long tenure, is too arcane to recount here (see *Companion*, 249-50). During his governorship an aqueduct was built at Chesters, but he was still in post in the early 180s, by which time the thoroughly unsuitable Commodus had succeeded his father. The reign began with a number of conflicts:

> However, the most important war was in Britain. For the tribes in the island crossed the Wall which divided them from the Roman soldiers and did a huge amount of damage, even taking out a legate with his troops. In consequence Commodus grew worried and despatched Ulpius Marcellus against the tribes . . . he inflicted serious defeats on the British barbarians.
>
> Dio, lxxiii.8.1-2

The 'legate' must have been a legionary commander, but his identity and the legion, probably only a vexillation, are unknown. The 'Wall' concerned must have been Hadrian's. It is not terribly easy to unpick the nature of the opposition the Romans faced,

35 *Chesters, Cilurnum. Inscription recording the bringing of water,* aqua adducta, *by ala II Asturum during the governorship of Ulpius Marcellus, who served c.177-84. Fifty years after the building of the Wall, auxiliary units were now engaged in building projects rather than the legions.* RIB 1463

and we need to work backwards. When subsequently describing the year 208 Dio was able to describe the peoples in the vicinity of the Wall as the 'Maiatai', Latinized to Maeatae, and those further north as the Caledonians. These tribal names, he said, had absorbed the names of other tribes (lxxvii.12.1). In 197 the Caledonians had defaulted on a deal with the Romans, and had started offering help to the Maeatae (lxxvi.5). Ulpius Marcellus' victory, celebrated in *Victoriae Brittannicae* coins of 184, might have led to that very deal. As we will see, the problems of the late 190s led to the last great Roman campaign in Britain.

Priscus and Perennis

Underlying the events over the 20-odd years before 178 was a Roman garrison apparently engaged in a certain amount of piecemeal reconstruction of Hadrian's Wall, combined with a retreat from the Antonine Wall. In spite of the victory of 184, the garrison of Britain now demonstrated its lethal potential. In Rome, the recklessly decadent Commodus was busy fulfilling his father's worst fears and delegating power to the prefect of the Praetorian Guard, Perennis. As prefect Perennis was an equestrian which might explain his policy of elevating equestrians to legionary commands, a policy driven by Commodus' pathological hatred of the Senate, whose members he distrusted (Herodian i.8.7-8). An undated tombstone names one Lucius Artorius Castus as serving at one point as prefect of *VI Victrix,* and leading a force which included two legions and cavalry to deal with a revolt in Armorica (Britanny) (*ILS* 2770). The stone has been attributed to this period, and it certainly fits the context because the incongruous office of 'prefect of *VI Victrix*' would otherwise be hard to place until well into the third century.

The British legions were outraged by developments and their volatility led them to take an ominous step. They elected one of their legates, Priscus, as emperor in place of Commodus. Priscus wisely declined this display of loyalty but 1500 members of the British garrison went to Rome to see Commodus and revealed that Perennis was plotting against him. Commodus was frightened by the British soldiers and handed over Perennis to be lynched by his own Praetorians. Soon afterwards he despatched Publius Helvidius Pertinax, a ruthless stickler for discipline and order, to suppress the rebellion, and govern Britain and her recalcitrant garrison. Interestingly, although he was superficially successful in this he clearly failed to persuade the British garrison to abandon its pretences to electing emperors. Indeed they seem initially to have decided that Pertinax himself would make a first-class candidate (*SHA Pertinax,* iii.5-6).

Clodius Albinus

The British garrison remained ripe for rebellion in spite of, or because of, Pertinax. It is improbable that this unsettled state could have been dictated by events in Rome. By the late 180s Pertinax's popularity had waned. One of the British legions even mutinied and he was left for dead amongst the victims. It was in his nature to be a disciplinarian and he dealt with the culprits ruthlessly, a move not likely to restore his erstwhile popularity. So, he asked that he be removed from the post, a move which incidentally made him available to be made emperor anyway but this time by the Praetorians after the murder of Commodus on 31 December 192 (*SHA Pertinax* iii.3.5-10).

His replacement was Clodius Albinus, a man of high birth from North Africa whose military success on the Rhine frontier attracted Commodus' attention to him as a possible heir (*SHA Clodius Albinus* vi.3-4). Albinus, however, contented himself with the governorship of Britain until Commodus was murdered. He then utilised the British garrison to compete with Septimius Severus and Pescennius Niger for the Empire while Pertinax's brief succession to Commodus ran its course. Albinus was double-crossed by Severus who appointed him as his junior colleague, and then dealt with Niger before returning to defeat Albinus at the Battle of Lyons in 197.

Although Albinus was well resourced in his position as governor of Britain to fight a war, he was not as well resourced as Septimius Severus, even though Dio attributes 150,000 troops to each side. From this it has been inferred that he must have seriously denuded the province's garrison to be able to compete at all. It is very difficult to know if this is really true. Frere, for example, claims that 'very few' northern forts have the same garrison testified in the third century as in the second. Movements, large and small, were so integrated into the Roman army's dispositions that we cannot draw such a grand conclusion from so little. Far fewer units can be associated with any fort at all in the second century — much of the evidence comes from diplomas, which do not attribute units to forts. What matters really is that the garrison was prepared to support Clodius Albinus at all. It was a devastating mark of Britain's potential, and one to have far-reaching consequences.

Septimius Severus

After defeating and killing Albinus, Severus appointed Virius Lupus to the governorship, which allows us to meet the Maeatae and the Caledonians. In 197 the Maeatae, who lived in the vicinity of Hadrian's Wall, were causing trouble and had succeeded in persuading the Caledonians to join in. The context must have been the demands made on the garrison by Albinus. Lupus was obliged to buy time by paying off the Maeatae. The appearance of African-type ceramics at York in the early third century has been attributed to the introduction of legionary reinforcements from North Africa. Unfortunately, there is no inscription specifically testifying to any troop movements at this time, or even any tombstones from York to support the contention.

A period of sustained rebuilding on the northern frontier and elsewhere in the military zone seems to have begun at this time, or at any rate, recording it became more common. At Ilkley an unspecified building was rebuilt and at Corbridge a new one erected (*RIB* 637, 1163). At Bowes a more explicit altar stated that 'Virius Lupus . . . restored the bathhouse, burnt by the force of flames' (*RIB* 730). This unusually dramatic description might be taken as firm evidence of enemy action but, for a start, no enemy action is mentioned and secondly, the very nature of bathhouses was that they were more likely than most buildings to be burned down by fire in the normal course of events and rebuilt. Perhaps this is why more bathhouses are recorded in this way than any other military building. It is as possible that Virius Lupus was charged with the duty of improving fort facilities and seeing that damaged facilities needing repair were dealt with in the interests of improving morale. A stone which probably originated from Brougham fort and which undoubtedly belongs to the general period reflects this. It records the repair of a bathhouse which had also been burned and subsequently *[in rui]n(am) dilabsum*, 'fallen into ruin' (*RIB* 791).

The picture is certainly not of emergency rebuilding and smacks as much of remedial work to put right casual dereliction. Archaeologists have detected repair work on Hadrian's Wall but it is interesting how a generation or more ago this was usually interpreted as following deliberate destruction by the 'enemy'. That sort of view failed to recognize that the type of wall used for the frontier was prone to decompose, thanks to building it with a rubble and mortar core and restricting use of dressed stone to the facings. Vitruvius (ii.8.7-8) said only men in a hurry used this method and its disintegration was inevitable. Milecastle 37's partially collapsed north gate was inevitably seen, in the great archaeological tradition of assuming malice aforethought, as the results of someone's attempt to 'lever [it] over' (Frere 1987, 156), rather than acknowledging the possibility that it might have suffered partial subsidence. It is not really possible to attribute damage to such specific motives, given the ambivalent nature of the evidence.

Lucius Alfenus Senecio

Just as the Wall itself may originally have made work for idle hands, so repair of the curtain and that of the northern forts may have served the same purpose now. It also allowed for making hay while the sun shone in the form of the peace deal with the Maeatae. Virius Lupus' successor was Gaius Valerius Pudens, named on an inscription recording the building of barracks at Bainbridge (*JRS* 1961, 192). This time there is no question of 'restoration' — the text simply refers to the work that had been done, and this is what is found in the Wall forts under Senecio. The slab from Birdoswald specifies a granary, while others from Benwell and Chesters are merely dedications of unspecified structures, and there may be another from Housesteads (*RIB* 1909, 1337,1462, *JRS* 1967, 205).

The picture then starts to emerge of building work that could be no more than reverting to complete half-finished building programmes on the Wall, and perhaps even further afield. This is particularly interesting when one considers the evidence from Birdoswald for large areas of the Hadrianic fort being left open until later in the second century, not unlike the longer hiatus at the *XX*'s fortress at Chester throughout much of the second century (Wilmott 1997 and Strickland 1999). The latter has also produced part of an inscription, which may be a building dedication though it belongs to 194-6 (*RIB* 465). It has always been assumed that forts were built until finished but it now seems more likely that changes of plan could result in certain places being unfinished, while other buildings which had been damaged by accidental fires could be left untended for decades.

At Bainbridge, work continued under Senecio, now involving a rampart (*RIB* 722). Slabs from Bowes and Greta Bridge are again mere dedications and do not specify exact buildings, or repairs (*RIB* 740, 746). Only at Risingham do we find repair work, this time a gate with walls, described as being *vetustate dilapsis . . . a solo restit(uit)*, 'decayed through age . . . restored from the ground up' (**36**). Of course, it would be easy to refute this as a euphemism for destruction by the enemy, but then why should it simply not be true? Further south, rebuilding work for the same reason is testified at Caerleon and on the aqueducts at Caernarvon (*RIB* 333, 430).

Unusually, the imperial procurator seems to have been involved in this work. Normally the procurator was concerned with the financial administration of the province

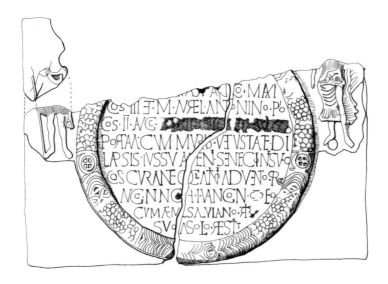

36 *Risingham*, Habitancum. *Inscription from the south gate, of an unusually elaborate variety. The text includes enough to restore the titles of Septimius Severus for c.205-7, and names the governor Alfenus Senecio as well as the procurator Oclatnius Adventus. The slab commemorated the restoration of the gate and walls from ground level by* cohors I Vangionum. RIB *1234*

including army pay, in a division of responsibilities intended to narrow the spread of the governor's control. Marcus Oclatinius Adventus is mentioned on the Risingham slab and the one from Chesters (*ibid*), as well as turning up in Dio, where he is described as a man who had risen through the ranks of mercenary 'spies and scouts' before reaching a procuratorship, and then proceeding to be made a senator (lxxix.14.1). It has been suggested that the reason he turns up on the northern frontier is that his particular pedigree made him ideal for planning the Severan campaigns as well as conceivably organising the unit of scouts, ambitiously but not unreasonably restored as *expl[oratores Habitancenses]*, based at Risingham and restored on Caracallan inscription there of 213 (*RIB* 1235, and Speidel 1987).

The Severan Campaign

The overall picture then, from the beginning of Severus' principate, is of Britain's military infrastructure being steadily repaired, improved or completed and, conveniently for us, recorded on a large number of surviving inscriptions. There is no epigraphic proof that he made any significant contribution at all to Britain's civilian settlements, though there is some archaeological evidence that he may have been responsible for building projects at London and York, either by him or in his honour. He had brought a considerable amount of ready cash with him as well as his wife, Julia Domna (Dio lxxvii.11.2).

At some point around now Britain was split into two, Superior and Inferior, though we do not know when. It was certainly the case after 213, though there is no epigraphic confirmation until an altar from Bordeaux of 237 naming Britannia Inferior (Herodian

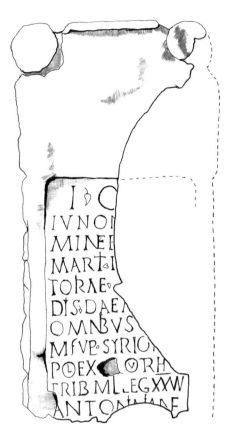

I Ɔ C
IVNOI
MINEI
MARTɑI
TORΛEᵥ
DISₒDΛEΛ
OMNBVS
MꜰVEₒSYRIO
POEX◁ORH
ꞱRIB MLₗEGXXₗᵥ
ANTONIᴧₗANE

37 *Carlisle,* Luguvalium. *Altar dedicated by Marcus . . . Syrio, a tribune with* XX Valeria Victrix Antoniniana *(and thus datable to c.212-22), to Jupiter, Juno, Minerva, Mars and Victory.* B *1989, 331-3*

iii.8.2, *JRS* 1922, 102). It may be that Severus thought of it, but that it was not enforced until Caracalla's reign. *II Augusta* and *XX Valeria Victrix* were in Britannia Superior, and *VI Victrix* was in Britannia Inferior (Dio lv.23.2-6). This was obviously a precaution against a governor of Britain ever again exploiting its large garrison to threatening the emperor, though in fact Severus made a general overall increase in the army, recruiting three more legions and several auxiliary units, and provided improved privileges and remuneration for its ranks. The division could also be seen as an integral part of military reform in Britain, of which the extensive building work was another aspect, and illustrates once more how military conditions and requirements dictated the form of Roman Britain. What we now call northern England, and the southern uplands of Scotland, had become a separate zone.

The governor of Britannia Inferior was synonymous with command of *VI Victrix* and thus implicitly subordinate to the governor of Superior. However, the virtual absence of *II* and *XX* from the northern military building inscriptions of the late second century onward probably means an effective cessation in that role for those legions in the north, with auxiliary units absorbing responsibility for their own bases. A centurion of *II Augusta* was near Old Carlisle in 255-9 (*RIB* 913). A military tribune of *XX* was in Carlisle between 213-22 and the legion may have been working at Maryport in 238-44 (*RIB* 854, and **37**). The latter, however, is a tenuous restoration and the former, like the Old Carlisle centurion of *II*, was only an individual, quite possibly on attachment. More convincing is an altar from milecastle 52 on Hadrian's Wall, dedicated by soldiers of *XX* between 262-6 though this was under the Gallic Empire (see below), when different conditions probably applied. Not surprisingly, *VI Victrix* continued to make occasional appearances, for example at Corbridge in *c.*197-202, and Ribchester and Stanwix between 238-44 (*RIB* 1163, 583, 2027).

It is around Senecio's governorship that Herodian reports a 'dispatch' arrived from an unnamed governor of Britain to say that a barbarian rebellion was wreaking havoc in the province (iii.14.1). This does not fit the archaeological or epigraphic context, and nor does it match Dio's account which instead tells us that Severus was 'winning the wars in Britain' through 'others', but had found it extremely difficult to suppress a robber band in Italy himself (lxxvii.10.6) (**38**). Both Herodian and Dio agree though that Severus wanted to remove his sons from the decadent appeals of Rome and toughen them up in a northern war. Dio adds that Severus also considered that the army was suffering from enforced idleness.

The plan was to conquer Caledonia. Of course, given that so much rebuilding work had been underway in Britain for around a decade it could be argued that he had planned this all along. On the other, having done the work at all might have sown the seeds of an idea. The substantial building works at South Shields are most easily attributed to this general period and unlike other sites, such as the so-called stores building at Corbridge, do seem to represent a major decision to alter the fort's function. The interior was remodelled to increase hugely the quantity of granaries available, but it is possible that this scheme was actually part of a long-term revision of the supply arrangements for the northern frontier. The most convincing evidence for Severan use of the compound is a series of lead sealings depicting Severus with his sons and successors, Caracalla and Geta with the legend AVGG (*RIB* 2411.1-16). The device indicates two emperors by doubling the G and dates them to 198-209. Geta was at this time a junior colleague and remained so until 209 when he was elevated to Augustus as well. Others have been found at Chesters, and London (including an example with a triple G, and thus dated to 209-11). Such sealings will have been attached to parcels or sacks of freight, presumably discarded when opened. Imperial seals are not common, so this unusually large concentration cannot be regarded as purely coincidental.

Severus took the precaution of arriving in Britain with vexillations from the continental legions. A soldier of one of the legions possibly involved, probably of *XXII Primigenia* (of which more later), was subsequently buried at Amiens by his colleagues who had served with him on the *expedi[t(ionem)] Britan(n)icam* (*ILS* 9123). Strictly speaking, the text is not automatically datable though the lettering style is compatible with the period. Herodian is slightly ambiguous about how the force was made up. He describes Severus reaching Britain and holding a 'general levy of the army' (iii.14.3). A tombstone from Rome records Gaius Cesennius Senecio, a centurion with *cohors II* of the Praetorian Guard, whose body had been brought from Britain. The text includes the Praetorian title *pia vindex*, awarded by Severus, making it likely that Cesennius Senecio had died on Severus' expedition. A vexillation of cavalry from Upper Germany may have been at Ribchester about this time, though this relies on a good deal of restoration of a highly fragmentary inscription (*RIB* 591, see Stephens 1987, and Tomlin in *RIB* 95, 767, where this possibility is rejected). The public-relations requirements of the expedition were fulfilled by a large issue of coins of all denominations, in the names of Severus and both his sons, with variations on the legend *Victoriae Brittannicae* (**38**).

Severus was wrong-footed when the opposition instantly sued for peace, and had to pack them off so that he could still fight a war. He made a mistake: the campaign led the Roman army into the kind of fighting which confounded it. Helped by swamps and minimal equipment, and tolerance of appalling conditions, the Britons engaged in constant tactical retreats, drawing the Romans ever deeper into a trap (**39**). Dio's account of the war is a vivid description of the intolerably difficult landscape with its marshes, forests and rivers, populated in the Wall area by the Maeatae and, beyond, the

38 *Bronze* as *issued by Septimius Severus with the reverse legend* Victoriae Brittannicae, *struck c.210-11. Reflecting the propaganda nature of the campaign, these coins (of all denominations) represent the most substantial numismatic commemoration of a British war*

Caledonians. These warriors were at ease in their own territory, exploiting the swamps and terrain to evade set-piece battles, thereby confounding an elderly and sick emperor bent on a last stab at glory.

The Britons were content to bide their time lurking in the cold water, but it left the Roman troops half-crippled from exhaustion and exposure. Split up into scattered groups, they made easy pickings for the tribes. This makes it very easy to understand why, Severus' campaign apart, the Romans had already abandoned any attempt to control significant tracts of land beyond Hadrian's Wall, and how the Wall zone settled down to a permanently static frontier garrison. Severus continued to follow the retreating Britons and the army eventually reached the north-east tip of Scotland.

Caracalla

Ever happy to make promises they had no intention of keeping, the Maeatae and Caledonians agreed to a peace in 210 and promptly revolted again, forcing Severus to renew the campaign in the winter of 210-11. Worn out with ambition, age and exhaustion, he died at York in February 211. Caracalla had no interest either in continuing to prosecute a campaign in Britain, or ruling jointly with Geta. He made peace in Britain, withdrew his forces and abandoned the forts in their territory (Dio lxxviii.1.1). In 212 he murdered Geta.

A paroxysm of paranoia pervaded the administration of Roman Britain and the garrison. In 213 the governor was one Gaius Julius Marcus. His full name is only known from a long-lost milestone found near milecastle 17 on Hadrian's Wall (*RIB* 2298), but a large number of other inscriptions belong to the same year. Most seem to have had Marcus' name erased. Caracalla's name was also usually excised after his death in 217 thanks to his murderous regime, in a routine Roman cathartic practice. It is likely that a similar sense of paranoia, if not an imperial directive, led to the legions identifying themselves smartly with Caracalla. *II Augusta*, for example, had *Antoniniana* added to its titles, utilising Caracalla' official name, Antoninus Pius (*RIB* 19) (**37, 40**). The title could refer to Elagabalus (218-22), who also used this name, but Caracalla is much more likely.

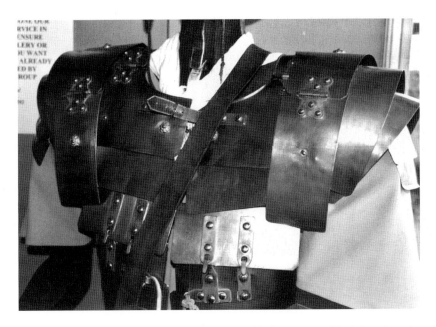

39 Lorica segmentata. *A modern restoration of the segmented body armour used by legionaries and possibly by some auxiliaries, based on excavated fragments. The numerous buckles and straps made it high maintenance. Although ideal for protection in pitched battles, it was unsuitable for troops engaged in pursuing tribal warriors into treacherous marshy terrain because it weighed them down*

It is not clear whether this was a global edict imposed on pain of death or whether Caracalla generously bestowed it on units earning his favour.

However, in 213 Caracalla had the governor of Gallia Narbonensis murdered. In consequence, 'a great deal of upset resulted amongst everyone involved in governing Gaul' and Caracalla followed it up with 'many measures directed against persons and in violation of the rights of communities' (*SHA Caracalla* v.1-3). There is no reference to Britain but it is impossible to imagine that the incumbent governor could have felt relaxed about his personal security. Julius Marcus must have ordered epigraphic declarations of loyalty, of which perhaps the most impressive known was the 5.72m wide slab from Risingham (*RIB* 1235), but others are known at a wide range of other northern forts (*RIB* 905, 976, 1202, 1265, 1278, 1551, *B* 1980, 405, and 1985, 325-6). Marcus also managed to maintain the building programme, recorded on another slab from Netherby on which part of his name survives (*RIB* 977). Paradoxically, Caracalla's grant of universal citizenship should have led to unswerving loyalty from all those auxiliary troops who had been instantly elevated to the status they craved.

This series of inscriptions represents a peak in all the datable epigraphy from Roman Britain. All the examples come from auxiliary forts, and none names a legion. Together with the Alfenus Senecio series, they are evidence for how auxiliary units above all others seem to have had a particular taste for monumental dedications. It is possible that they are freak survivals but, given that legions are far better represented in the second century, it is much more likely that taste and practice are the reasons. This is discussed in more detail

40 *Tombstone from London of . . . Celsus,* [s]peculator *of* [II] Aug(usta) A[ntoniniana]. *Assuming the expansion is correct, the stone can be attributed to the reigns of Caracalla or Elagabalus, 212-22.* RIB *19*

in chapter 7 but for the moment the texts they contain are amongst the most important source of evidence for military activity in Britain in the early third century.

XXII Primigenia

XXII Primigenia had already been involved in Britain under Hadrian, again on the Antonine Wall and, as we saw above, may have taken part in the Severan campaign. In or around the 190s Quintus Aurelius Polus Terentianus was appointed to command *II Augusta*. This is recorded on an inscription from Mainz, probably because it commemorated a transfer from the command of *XXII Primigenia*, also mentioned on the inscription (Birley 1979, 45). Apart from epigraphic evidence, Dio tells us that *XXII* was in Germany in the early third century (lv.23.6).

Now a centurion from Upper Germany made a dedication at Piercebridge on an altar conveniently dated to 217, mentioning *VI Victrix* and 'the army of the Germanies' (*JRS* 1967, 205). He may of course be referring to units in Britain since Severus' arrival in 208. An undated tombstone from Piercebridge, recorded in the mid-eighteenth century, refers to a soldier from Upper Germany (*B* 1986, 438). Another undated tombstone from Piercebridge records the death of a centurion of *XXII* at the fort (*RIB* 1026). Although one suggestion has been that this man, Gracilis, had retired here to his wife's 'home' as well as rejecting the idea that *XXII* had ever been to Britain at all, the evidence from these and other dedications made at the fort is unequivocally that part of *XXII* was present once more in Britain, for at least the third time (**41**).

41 *Birrens,* Blatobulgium. VIII Augusta *and* XXII Primigenia *recorded on a slab. The reference is presumably to vexillations. The style is that of the reign of Antoninus Pius or Marcus Aurelius (138-61, 161-80), adding to the appearance of these units with* VII Gemina *in Britain under Hadrian (*ILS 2726*), and the possible reappearance under Severus. B 1992, 31*

The third century after Severus

After the Severan campaigns Roman historians ceased to pay attention to Roman Britain. Neither Dio nor Herodian makes any further mention of Britain after Severus' death and Caracalla's withdrawal in 211. Dio and Herodian end in 229 and 238 respectively. Even the *Scriptores* makes no mention of Britain beyond the single, incorrect, reference to Severus Alexander's possible death in Britain in 235 (*SHA Severus Alexander* lix.6). This was a vicious age in which opportunistic soldier emperors seized and lost power with ease. Their coin portraits tell us all we need to know about them (**42**).

At the same time public building in the civilian zone had all but ceased, at least insofar as any recording of the fact is concerned apart from some private religious buildings (see Placidus below), and archaeology has done little to contradict this except for attributing some urban defences to this period. This leaves us with no alternative but to rely on military inscriptions. Fortunately, the predilection to erect them, which had begun at the end of the second century, continued for some time. The short governorship of Gaius Julius Marcus was marked by an unusually active programme of imperial dedications but they only represent another category in the large number which survive from the first few decades of the third century. Some, like that of the governor Modius Julius on the east gate from Birdoswald (*RIB* 1914), are not as specific or as precisely datable, in this case attributed to 219, as sometimes presented though they still undoubtedly belong to this period. Many make no mention of the building concerned at all, or like the altar from Risingham recording a bathhouse there is no means of dating apart from basing a guess on the style (*RIB* 1212).

The picture is as sporadic and random as the record, with many buildings only known to have existed from the inscriptions. They range from the enigmatic *ballistaria* at High Rochester, dated to 220 and 225-35, to an armoury and headquarters, and a baths with exercise hall, erected at Lanchester between 238-44 (*RIB* 1280-1, 1092, 1091) (**43**). Greatchesters, a Hadrian's Wall fort with a minimal epigraphic record, has yielded a record of a granary restoration in 225 (*RIB* 1738), the sole building specifically recorded on any inscription from the site. Vindolanda has also produced only one slab specifically

42 *Maximinus I (235-8), from a silver denarius. Typical of the age, Maximinus I made his name in the army of the Severan dynasty. In 235 the army of the Rhine declared him emperor, and a short and brutal reign followed in which success against the German tribes was matched by his brutal suppression of any opposition. Under him, the rebuilding work on the forts of northern Britain continued, recorded at Birdoswald and Carrawburgh (RIB 1922, 1553)*

recording a building, this time from *c*.223 and mentioning the restoration of a 'gate with towers' (*RIB* 1706). It was not all rebuilding; some projects gathering dust were now dealt with. At Netherby, a cavalry exercise hall 'long ago begun from the ground' was finally completed and dedicated under Severus Alexander in 222 (*RIB* 978). The record is even larger than it at first appears, with some instances of inscriptions being too damaged to specify the building though it is plain from what survives that they once did. Thus, a fragmentary slab from Birdoswald, with a consular date of 236 under Maximinus I, states that something was built *a solo*, 'from the ground up' (*RIB* 1922) (**42**). Interestingly though the enigmatic Elliptical Building in the legionary fortress at Chester, abandoned at an early stage by the mid-80s, seems to have been reinstated at a higher level above the older wall stumps in *c*.230 and this time completed following a wider and long hiatus in building work at the fortress (*see* **102**).

Lanchester presents an interesting case because the governors mentioned on the slabs from there are different, though the unit, *cohors I Lingonum Gordiana*, and its commander, Marcus Aurelius Quirinus, are the same (**43**). The inscriptions concerned are also obviously by the same hand; perhaps some local initiative was involved in this building work. Unfortunately, once Caracalla's attention had wandered away from Britain by 212, we have to all intents and purpose no further usable information about imperial policy towards the British garrison. The distribution is distinctly regional, by auxiliary units and largely restricted to the northern frontier. Caerleon has produced some inscriptions recording rebuilding work but these incongruously belong to much later when epigraphy of any sort had become rare and was almost non-existent in the north (Caerleon barracks 255-60, *RIB* 334, and a temple to Diana about the same time, *RIB* 316).

The Saxon Shore fort system, developed sporadically through the third century and discussed in more detail below, has yielded no inscriptions at all apart from one found at Reculver, also belonging to the early third century (see below). Reculver, along with

Brancaster, has long been recognized to represent an early part of the programme, or an earlier fort subsequently integrated into the Saxon Shore fort system. As building work on these forts continued throughout the third century it must be the epigraphic habit, rather than the building, which was the determining factor behind the inscription record of the early 200s.

The record is distorted by other factors. During the first century, when most forts were built of turf and timber, stone inscriptions seem not to have been used. At any rate, they do not survive but this is more likely to be linked to custom. The great phase of stone military inscriptions in Britain was the second century through to the early third, and even the turf Antonine Wall was embellished this way. Before this, a single tiny piece of an inscription from the turf section of Hadrian's Wall shows that timber panels were also used, which would not usually escape rotting to oblivion, and this may have been the case in the first century (*RIB* 1935, from turf milecastle no. 50). Even once a fort was consolidated in stone, a practice largely restricted to the second century and later, older inscriptions were liable to survive only if they were subsequently reused as handy masonry, or as rubble fill. Exceptionally, the Hadrianic granary inscription from Benwell, for example, was found in the granary portico so the building apparently remained largely intact throughout the period or until it was no longer needed (*see* **26**). Unfortunately, in most cases inscriptions have been chance finds, often hundreds of years ago, in or around the ruins of the forts they once embellished which not only attracted antiquarian or archaeological attention but which were still exposed to view unlike most Roman urban public buildings. The recent discovery of an inscription recording the building or rebuilding of a bathhouse at Wallsend is fairly typical (*B* 1999, 380-1). Modern clearance of the whole site, formerly buried under a mining village, followed by excavation led to it being found in 'unstratified in the area of the south-west gate'. It was only identified by a

43 *Lanchester,* Longovicium. *A stylish dedication slab by* cohors I Lingonum *in the reign of Gordian III (238-44), recording the restoration of the headquarters and the armouries under the governorship of Maecilius Fuscus. See also* **59**. RIB *1092*

sharp-eyed excavation director amongst rubble in 1998, and can be dated on style and content to the first half of the third century.

Despite all these factors, the likelihood is that much of this building work was part of a general response to normal decay on military installations around a century old, and was begun in Britain under Virius Lupus. While the Severan campaign might have accelerated some of the work, and brought in some of the necessary cash, there is no need to assume that this was a short-term concerted plan of action or that it was necessarily associated with the war. Had significant numbers of the buildings involved been identified, and excavated, it might have been possible to trace patterns in design and style, but this has not been the case. The consistency in the content of the inscriptions though might indicate a general instruction to record the work in a certain format. Whatever the truth, the work was not confined to Britain. There are many other instances from the continent, which combine to suggest a general problem with deterioration of static frontier installations after as much as a century or more of continuous use, though sometimes demonstrably less. The problems were dealt with by the auxiliary garrisons rather than the legions which had often been responsible for the original works. At Remagen in Lower Germany, the fort sundial was repaired after it had 'broken down from old age' in 218 by *cohors Flavia* (*ILS* 9363). At Öhringen in Upper Germany, the restoration of one of the fort aqueducts, built in 231, was dedicated in December 241 under Gordian III, having been 'derelict for some time', by *cohors I Belgarum* (*ILS* 9179b).

Only at Birdoswald do we have an inkling of the timescale. Exceptionally, a granary is recorded as being rebuilt between 205-8 and another nearly a century later between 297-305 (*RIB* 1909, 1912). There is no guarantee that the same building is meant, but it is quite feasible that here we have a Hadrianic granary which needed rebuilding under Severus, and then again under the Tetrarchy, after similar periods of time had elapsed.

At any rate, the building work does have the advantage for us of demonstrating an active frontier army in the early decades of the third century, and the testified presence of various units at various places at fairly specific times. There is perhaps no coincidence in the fact that this is the time from which the only datable evidence of individual traders with Roman Britain survives. Lucius Viducius Placidus identifies himself as a trader on his dedication of an arch and gate in York in 221, and conveniently turns up on an altar found at the mouth of the Scheldt at the shrine of Nehallenia in Holland where he specifies that he was a trader with Britain, *negotiat(or) Britann(icianus)* (*B* 1977, 430, no. 18 and note 30). Marcus Aurelius Lunaris, *sevir Augustalis* at Lincoln and York, dedicated an altar at Bordeaux to give thanks for his voyage from York in 237 (*JRS* 1922, 102). He may or may not have been a trader. There is no equivalent evidence for any of the major settlements in the south, so it is not unreasonable to see in these men evidence for thriving commerce with the northern military zone.

Few of these examples of recorded buildings can be associated with any physical remains. Their significance here is that they illustrate how the Roman north was a place in which building works were constantly underway, and that these were recorded on monumental inscriptions, sometimes minor works of art in their own right. The habit was certainly not restricted to recording buildings, though these are often datable and have therefore monopolised the discussion so far. There are many religious dedications on military sites generally dated to the period on style, but they are less easily dated exactly.

The dedications of 213 erected by Gaius Julius Marcus typified an age characterised by brutal and murderous emperors, which had begun under Commodus. It was a period of startling instability in which a succession of emperors rose to power, usually as military commanders, and usually by murdering their predecessors. It was normal for military units to associate themselves personally with the current ruling house, and to record this on inscriptions. This was in their professional interests, but it also illustrated that they were liable to transfer their loyalties to commanders from their own regions. The fort of *Derventio* lies under the modern village of Papcastle and has been little explored. Only four inscriptions have been recovered from here, two remarkably from 19 and 20 October 241 (*RIB* 882-3). The latter was dedicated by the *cuneus Frisionum Aballavensium Philippianorum*, 'the formation of Frisians from *Aballava*, styled the Philippians' own', while the former appears to lack the last name in the title. There is a curiosity here because 241 comes from an exact consular date, but Philip I did not accede until after the murder of Gordian III in 244 for which he may or may not have been responsible. It must be that the second altar was retrospectively inscribed, adding the new emperor's name to make sure the appropriate loyalties were maintained. *Aballava* is known to be the fort of Burgh-by-Sands on Hadrian's Wall. The date was a festival of Mars and the only explanation can be that there was perhaps a shrine at Papcastle, which the Frisians visited.

In some senses the detail is fairly useless. It is, after all, impossible to piece this into a greater picture. But it highlights the sporadic nature of the record while at the same time introducing us to a lesser auxiliary unit which otherwise goes unmentioned in the records unless it is one and the same as the formations of Frisians testified at Housesteads in 222-35 and Binchester (*RIB* 1594, 1036). It also shows us that this obscure unit was engaging in formal commemorations of Roman military ceremonies, recording the fact on altars with explicit references to consular dates established in Rome, and allying itself with the incumbent regime.

The building inscriptions do rather tend to create a picture of a settled garrison. *Ala Augusta ob virtutem appellata* is testified at Old Carlisle on a number of inscriptions specifically dated from the 180s right up to 242. But it also apparently appears on a dedication made in 238 in Noricum, indicating that it had been sent briefly abroad (Alston 1995, 166), while *cohors Bracarum*, known from North African inscriptions, turns up on one prefect's career inscription as *in Britannia* some time back in the 160s, but is otherwise unknown in Britain (*ILS* 9002). This reminds us that the record, although improved for the early third century, still lacks an enormous amount of detail.

The Gallic Empire

The legions were remarkably silent throughout this period, as mentioned above, which seems strange considering the babble of voices from the auxiliary epigraphists. A sole dedication by a *primus pilus* of *II Augusta* in 244 marks its presence at Caerleon (*RIB* 327). A couple of inscriptions from the middle of the third century show that the legions in Britain were expected to contribute to imperial wars elsewhere, just as their predecessors had themselves been reinforced. While *II Augusta*'s seventh cohort had its barracks rebuilt at Caerleon in the late 250s, *XX* contributed troops to an expedition under Gallienus in

255 (*RIB* 334, *CIL* xiii.6780). The expedition included *II Parthica*, one of Septimius Severus' new legions, and it has been argued that Septimius Severus had therefore anticipated the demand for a mobile force, stationing it in Italy for the purpose (E. Birley 1969, 78). A dedication to Jupiter Monitor (Jupiter the Guide) from Pannonia for the year 260 refers to vexillations of British and German legions, with 'their auxiliaries', operating there under Gallienus (*ILS* 546). This slightly haphazard arrangement was not particularly efficient and here may lie the seeds of the mobile field army of the fourth century which could be despatched to trouble spots across regions of the Empire, augmenting static garrison and frontier troops. There is some evidence that Gallienus utilised detachments of cavalry drawn from various units to create a centralised cavalry army, later a core feature of the fourth-century army (Southern and Dixon 1996, 12). The contrast though is always rather exaggerated. Ever since Hadrian fixed the frontiers, the army had devolved into relatively static frontier garrisons, supplemented by vexillations sent from elsewhere when necessary. The developments of the later army merely formalised the reality.

The contributions concerned under Gallienus might help explain the apparent reduction in the size of *II* in the fourth century and the eventual disappearance of *XX* because in the 260s Britain had become part of the Gallic Empire, a breakaway subdivision of the Empire that was a consequence of Gallienus' weakness. That not all of *XX* was involved is plain enough from a dedication by 'soldiers of *XX Valeria Victrix*' to Cocidius found near milecastle 52 on Hadrian's Wall (*RIB* 1956), and bearing the names of consuls of the Gallic Empire from *c*.262-6.

Postumus himself was a military commander on the Rhine. Along with his troops he took advantage of the fact that Gallienus was hamstrung by trying to run the Empire single-handedly as well as deal with incursions across the Rhine, while Valerian fought the Persians in the East. The seizure of power in the West was seamless, and reinforced by Postumus' success in repelling German invasions. This was the first time that a military usurper had succeeded in achieving a stable breakaway government in the western provinces and it was symptomatic of the age. With soldiers increasingly static in their garrison bases it was inevitable that they would ally themselves with local commanders. The Gallic Empire proved as mercurial as the legitimate empire. Postumus was murdered in 268 and a brief succession of short-lived successors ended in 273 with the enforced retirement of Tetricus I and II by Aurelian (270-5). The regime does not seem to have affected the normal activities of the auxiliary units in Britain. Some of the inscriptions from Britain's military units show that they were loyal to this passing indulgence in secession. Thus at Birdoswald *cohors I Aelia Dacorum Postumiana* set up an altar and at Lancaster *ala Sebosiana Postumiana*, restored its bathhouse and hall (*RIB* 1886, 605). To what extent this represented voluntary loyalty is impossible to assess, but as it was only Aurelian's efforts, which eventually ended the regime, Postumus or even his successors cannot have been unpopular amongst soldiers who may have seen in them a more reliable (or lucrative) prospect.

The Saxon Shore

The traditional picture of Roman Britain is a civilian south, and a military north. Indeed, the institutionalised separation of the two into Britannia Superior and Britannia Inferior seems positively to confirm the fact. But the south was never entirely separated from the army. Throughout much of the mid-first century parts of central southern and eastern Britain were garrisoned, particularly in the aftermath of the Boudican Revolt. By the early second century the London garrison was established and indeed may have been there a good deal earlier. The amphitheatre outside the south-east corner of the fort, and now under the Guildhall Yard, seems to have had a timber phase as early as *c*.70, and its location makes it highly likely that this was in association with an earlier fort on the same site.

In the Weald of Kent, throughout the second century, the fleet of the province, *classis Britannica*, was engaged (or so it seems) on extensive extraction of iron. Its role may or may not have been any more than simply supervising smelting, and transporting the results out, or — to be absolutely pedantic — just supplying the tiles, but its association is beyond doubt. Not only do stamped tiles at a variety of sites like Dover, Lympne, Bodiam and Beauport Park testify to its presence but remains of a fort of the period have been uncovered at Dover itself (**colour plate 14**). Resembling the forts of Hadrian's Wall in its rounded corners and internal buildings, this fort belonged entirely to a province-wide military infrastructure. The very universality of its form is reflected in the fact that part of the fleet was sent to Hadrian's Wall where it built a granary at Benwell under Hadrian between the years 122-6 (*RIB* 1340). Evidence for its date in the south comes from a once barnacle-encrusted altar found at Lympne in the ruins of the later Saxon Shore fort. It records the dedication to Neptune by one Lucius Aufidius Pantera, prefect of the fleet (*RIB* 66), a position he is known to have held in the Hadrianic period.

Today, south-east Britain is considered so overwhelmingly residential that it often comes as a surprise to appreciate that in the Roman period almost all of southern Kent and inland Sussex was little developed. The main Roman routes to London and on into Britain were across northern Kent from Richborough to London, and across west Sussex from Chichester. Such villas as there were mostly clung to the coast or the valleys of the Medway and the Darenth, reflecting the commercial importance of the Thames. The forts at Dover, and probably at Lympne, if not already part of an extended system were soon to become so. As early as the beginning of the third century, and very possibly before that, a fort was established at Reculver on the north Kent coast. Close by, and in the near future, the monumental archway into Britain at Richborough seems to have been reclaimed by the military and converted into a fortified signal tower. Around the coast at Brancaster in Norfolk another fort was built. Reculver's early third-century date is confirmed by an inscription which mentions a shrine in the headquarters building and which can be dated fairly firmly to the period *c*.210-35 (*Companion* 121, 122). Brancaster can only be dated by type, but the fact remains that the military character of Roman Britain was being extended around its southern shores at the same time as the building works in the north were taking place.

Unlike the events of the northern frontier, the military affairs of the south and east are scarcely referred to by the historians. We are left to analyse the forts of the coastal region from the archaeology. Some are lost or survive in such battered form that it is almost impossible to tell precisely which phase they belong to. Brancaster and Reculver are undoubtedly the earliest, and along the way Burgh Castle near Yarmouth with its part-bonded bastions was added (**44**). By the time the series was finished by the early fourth century, there were other forts at Walton Castle (near Felixstowe and long-lost to the

44 *The walls of Burgh Castle,* Gariannonum, *in Norfolk. A mid-sequence fort of the Saxon Shore, this fort had been begun before the decision to bond the bastions in was taken — unless this was an architectural feature designed to help restrict damage to the walls, should the bastion subside. If so, the policy was later abandoned, and at new forts like Portchester, bastions were bonded from the bottom up*

elements), Bradwell-on-Sea, Richborough, Pevensey, and Portchester, with new forts built at Dover and Lympne. Called the Saxon Shore in the unreliable but indispensable late Roman record of military dispositions, *Notitia Dignitatum*, its purpose seems to have been to guard Britain's southern shores. Some authorities credit Probus (276-82) with the work, though the rebel Carausius (286-93) is thought to have been responsible at least for completing some of it (**45**). In architectural terms (see chapter 7), the new forts illustrate the move to a different type of warfare in which massive walls and projecting bastions for artillery were of overwhelming importance and almost entirely at the expense of substantial masonry internal buildings. The contrast is amply seen at London, where the fourth-century bastions protrude from the city walls, but the much earlier fort exhibits the traditional internal towers (*see* **116**).

The possibility thus exists that the forts of the Saxon Shore were partially developed by the Gallic Empire, conceivably as a line of defence against any maritime assault from the legitimate regime. But even if the Gallic Empire did instigate, or continue, building work in Britain and in Gaul it is as possible that the purpose was to protect the provinces from the waterborne Frank and Saxon pirates which the sources describe (for example, Eutropius ix.21). Unfortunately, unravelling the chronology in detail is effectively impossible because the forts have been subjected to too little and piecemeal excavation, and the lack of inscriptions confounds us. Perhaps that helps. If the Saxon Shore forts had mostly belonged to before, say, *c.*250, then we might reasonably expect some inscriptions of the type found on the northern frontier. Reculver's slab fits entirely that context, placing it before the main sequence.

The pirates were the making of Marcus Aurelius Mausaeus Carausius, whose career ultimately led to the first land battle recorded on southern British soil since the Boudican Revolt more than 200 years before. Carausius was a sailor, born on the coast of what is now Belgium and Holland some time around the mid-third century AD, and relied on the principle that greatness knows itself. In his lifetime Carausius will have become familiar with the raiders who crossed the North Sea from Denmark and Germany to treat themselves to the pickings of southern Britain. We do not know exactly how they did this, but the assumption must be that they operated as the Vikings did 500 years later — swift crossings, a night-time beaching and then a high-speed dash on foot or horseback inland looking for targets of opportunity like a villa, a roadside *mansio*, or travellers, before a hasty retreat and disappearing into the darkness with the tide.

By the 280s the problem had become so serious the Roman high command was looking for permanent solutions. The Saxon Shore forts, matched by further forts along the coast of Gaul, were not enough and in any case, the archaeology suggests they were not complete by this date. Carausius was made commander of the British fleet and ordered to rid the waters of pirates. He was successful, but mostly in selling himself to the garrison of Britain and part of Gaul's. Rebellion lay in his way and he found it. Carausius declared himself emperor in 286 and from then until 293 held out against Maximian and Diocletian (**46**). They accused him of having intercepted the pirates and helping himself to the loot. On one hand that would explain his ability to manufacture the first good quality silver coin for centuries to pay his supporters with. On the other, it is difficult therefore to explain his apparent popularity and, as for Diocletian and Maximian — their reaction was obvious.

The details of Carausius' reign, as reconstructed from the sparse sources and his abundant coinage, need not detain us but it is self-evident that Carausius, or his cabal of supporters, created a warrior hero image in the Roman classical idiom, and blasted the Romano-British public with antiquity. Restoring Rome in Britannia was his unequivocal ambition but it meant that southern Britain became a frontline — all the more so once his narrow power-base in Gaul was lost. One of the central themes of his coinage was military loyalty and he struck a series of coins which made straightforward overtures to a variety of legions stationed in northern Europe and Britain. That *VI Victrix* was not featured originally appeared a mystery, and suggested that perhaps he had no influence in northern Britain, a theory sunk by the only inscription from the reign — a milestone from near Carlisle naming Carausius, and the recent discovery of a Carausian coin naming the legion.

Carausius fell in 293, the consequence of his ill-weaved ambition and exchanged a kingdom for two-paces worth of earth. It is the lot of usurpers and politicians to see their luck changed in an instant. He was murdered by his companion and finance minister, Allectus, who saw in himself a better prince, but seems to have abandoned any attempts to woo the army with coins commemorating military units. Allectus lasted just three years and was defeated in battle by Asclepiodotus, the praetorian prefect in north-west Gaul. The imperial army was led across the Channel in two waves in 296. Asclepiodotus landed somewhere near the Solent, marched inland and confronted Allectus' army. With a tidy victory swiftly achieved, the way was open for Constantius Chlorus, junior emperor to Maximian in the west, to enter London.

45 *Probus (276-82), on a bronze radiate still bearing traces of its silver wash, intended to make the coinage still look convincingly sound. Probus wears the robes of a consul, in an expression of traditional legitimacy*

46 *(below) Carausius (286-93). Bronze radiate coin depicting the rebel emperor, and on the reverse a war galley — the basis of his military power in Britain (see also* **colour plate 19***)*

The late Roman army 'system'

With the Carausian revolt suppressed, Britain was restored to the Empire, 'the eternal light' as a medallion commemorating the event announced. Some forts of the north were restored, though whether the decay was caused by a Carausian or Allectan withdrawal of troops, indifference or destruction can only be guessed at. The forts of the Saxon Shore were continued or completed, and in Pevensey's case perhaps only just begun. In the absence of inscriptions and any other documents we can only turn to the *Notitia Dignitatum* to find any clues as to how this new series of forts was manned — in theory.

Throughout the third century the north and west was governed by the legate of *VI Victrix*. In the fourth a new regime operated. At some point around now, Britain was divided into four new provinces, recorded in the Verona List of 312-14. For the first time the civilian and military responsibilities of the administration were divided. Britain's four provinces were collectively treated as a diocese and overseen by a *vicarius*. The individual provinces had their own governors. Three of these were called a *praeses*, and the fourth was a *consularis*. The latter governed Maxima Caesariensis, while the other three controlled Britannia Prima, Britannia Secunda, and Flavia Caesariensis.

Britain's garrison now came under the command of a *dux*, except for the garrisons of the Saxon Shore forts, commanded by a *comes*, and another *comes* leading a small number of mounted units. The *dux Britanniarum* oversaw the individual commanders of units, legions and auxiliaries across the rest of Britain. The unit names might have been the same but there would have been little sense of distinction by race, equipment or practice. The date of much of the *Notitia*'s information has long since been recognized to be a complicated problem because of inconsistencies. The generally accepted view now is that it represents an accumulation of information on the civilian and military command structure of the Empire drawn together by the early fifth century, but including some obsolete information. So it is far from ideal but it is better than nothing.

The first point to make is that the *Notitia* shows many units where they had been for generations, at least nominally. Thus at Greatchesters *cohors II Asturum equitata* was listed as the garrison. It had certainly been there in 225 (*RIB* 1738) and we know from diplomas it had been in Britain since 105 at the latest, though not necessarily continuously. *Ala I Hispanorum Asturum* turns up at Benwell on the Wall in 205-8 (*RIB* 1337), and again in the *Notitia*, though we know it had been in Britain for a century at least before that. Of course none of this precludes the point that these units were always liable to piecemeal movements to here and there. This would explain the presence of *ala I Hispanorum Vettonum civium Romanorum* building at Bowes between 197-202 for the resident *cohors I Thracum*, while probably based themselves at Binchester (*RIB* 730, 1035). Not all units remained static. *Cohors I Baetasiorum* for example, testified on the Antonine Wall in the mid-second century (*RIB* 2169 and 2170), turns up at Reculver on the Saxon Shore in the *Notitia*.

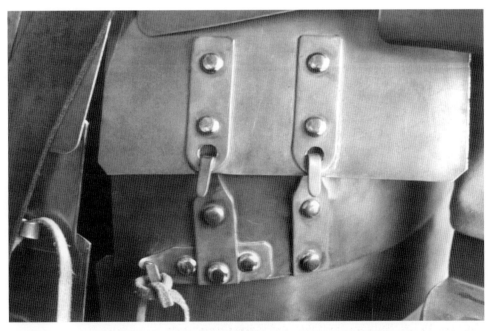

47 *This reconstructed suit of* lorica segmentata *displayed at Leicester Museum includes replica fittings, often recovered as separate individual finds on military and civilian sites in Britain. They help confirm the presence of soldiers, though in towns it is not normally possible to be certain whether they were detached on civilian duties, or with a unit*

Most perplexing of all, Richborough's garrison seems to have been *II Augusta*, a unit last testified for certain at Caerleon between 255-60 (*RIB* 334). It is the reduction in size which is the most difficult to understand. Richborough could not possibly have accommodated more than a fraction of the once-5000-strong legion. This means either that the legion was a fraction of its old size, or no longer operated in a way that required a base capable of housing every man. Using an analogy from the past perhaps Richborough was no more than a vexillation-sized headquarters for a unit now almost permanently dispersed into semi-mobile sub-divisions. Equally likely though is that the title and battle honours were brandished by troops of a type and nature that would have been unrecognisable to their forbears, and which for different reasons are entirely unrecognisable to archaeologists. This, it must be stressed, was not peculiar to Britain. The astonishingly well-preserved remains of Qasr Bsheir in Jordan, a fort built between 292-305, enclosed 0.3ha, and had room for 69 horses and their soldiers. Looking almost indistinguishable from a medieval castle with its projecting bastions, Qasr Bsheir is the vivid evidence for an entirely different form of accommodating and distributing troops.

But, whatever the *Notitia* says, the archaeological evidence for the late presence of military units at any given site is distinctly ambivalent. In the first and second centuries, the appearance of a military unit is normally evident from: military-style ditches, rectangular timber structures of stereotypical design, prolific finds of coinage and imported pottery, fragments of military equipment (usually in the form of buckles and other fittings from armour), and military tombstones or other inscriptions (**47**). When it comes to third- and fourth-century installations the physical structures are usually modifications to existing buildings, either in inferior form or in a style which has no overt military feature, coin and pottery finds cannot normally be distinguished from civilian settlements unless there are enough to demonstrate a statistically significant variation from the average, military equipment is all but non-existent or confined to decorative fittings which are not always definitively military, and inscriptions are no longer a feature of the record (**48, 49**).

Work at several northern forts, for example Housesteads and Wallsend, has shown that accommodation was altered from the original contiguous barracks to so-called 'chalet'-style apartments. How this reflects the nature of the residents is impossible to know for certain, though at Housesteads structures once used for military services like the hospital, and some of the granary storage space, were given over to ordinary domestic occupation. One of the clues lies in the abandonment of the fort *vicus* (see p233). The contraction of the settlement in physical size may just have meant that soldiers now lived alongside their families, traders, and veterans, within the fort walls though small finds from the new barracks are considered to suggest just the opposite. This only goes to show how impossibly difficult it is to draw unequivocal conclusions from such subjective and limited evidence. Given the fact that it is impossible to believe the late frontier garrison had decided to do without women, then they must have continued to maintain families which now had nowhere else to live except in the fort, however improbable that may seem from the artefacts. As attributing artefacts is largely a product of our values, it is fairly obvious where the weak link is. This must represent a reduction in the garrison size, but that reduction may have already been the case way back into the third century.

48 Belt-plate made of bronze, and decorated with enamel from South Shields, Arbeia. Note the animal heads in the centre panel. Exhibiting British influence in technique and style, this piece is much more idiosyncratic and individual a piece of decorative equipment. It is no longer quite so clear whether this is definitively military, despite the find-spot. Length 83mm

Work along the Wall has gradually revealed a much greater range in the type of occupation. South Shields, for example, has yielded a great deal of evidence for a fort being operated by a unit modelled much more on the 'good old days'. Alongside the old-style barracks a substantial Mediterranean courtyard house was built as part of the *c.*300 reconstruction work. It was complete with an integral bathhouse, and an *atrium* entrance hall. Built on a north-facing spur on the south bank of the Tyne, South Shields controlled maritime and river traffic, as well as providing a base for supervising crossings of the river.

Perhaps it is not complete coincidence that South Shields is a fort where the fourth century seems to have seen a new unit installed — the Tigris boatmen. Whether this was an authentic ethnic identity is a moot point, as there is no evidence from the site to support it. Dio's description of the fabricated Batavian cavalry in the early third century is a point to bear in mind (see p211). There is a possibility that the unit once just called itself *numerus barcariorum* at Lancaster, with the more exotic embellishment being added by the commander responsible for the new installations at South Shields (*RIB* 601; and see chapter 8). Conversely, the *Notitia* lists at Housesteads the same unit, *cohors I Tungrorum*, there since at least the third century. The fort is notable for the patching of old facilities in the latter part of the fourth century, whereas at Birdoswald no unit is listed in the *Notitia* at all (Holbrook, cited by Reece 1997, 9). Modern excavations here have exposed occupation of a type which is almost sub-Roman and which lasted on into the fifth century. But the reason for this remarkably convenient match is probably just a defect with the *Notitia*. *Cohors I Aelia Dacorum*, Birdoswald's traditional garrison and testified there in numerous inscriptions, is listed in extant *Notitia* manuscripts as being at Castlesteads, the next fort along the Wall. But Mark Hassall has pointed out (cited in Rivet and Smith 1979, 221) this almost certainly represent a gap with Birdoswald's name, *Banna*, and the Castlesteads unit, *cohors II Tungrorum*, being inadvertently omitted. But a qualification to this eminently sensible suggestion must be that the explicit inscription recording rebuilding work at Birdoswald between 297-305 omits any mention of the unit (*RIB* 1912).

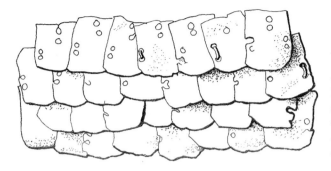

49 *Caerleon*, Isca. *Fragment of* lorica squamata, *scale armour associated with third-century cavalry units and known from paintings of such soldiers at Dura-Europos in Syria (Connolly 1981, 313)*

The *dux Britanniarum* commanded what was effectively a stationary army of resident garrisons, as well as several mounted units of troops whose origins and bases are scarcely known, such as the *equites Catafractariorum* based at the lost post of *Morbio*. The count of the Saxon Shore could reckon a few similar units amongst his number, at Brancaster and Burgh Castle. Both commanders had several *numeri* under their command. These seem to have been casually organised blocks of troops hired as needs required. Such *foederati*, raised from barbarian tribes or simply bands of barbarian warriors following their own commander, had always been hired for campaigns if needed, but the difference in the late third and fourth century and beyond is that those needs tended to be more permanent. Consequently, the *foederati* were liable to be settled across frontier regions, becoming a feature of the Roman military zone. At the same time, it was increasingly common for men of barbarian origin to serve within the mainstream Roman army and rise to positions of high rank. The Vandal general, Stilicho, who controlled the young emperor Honorius (393-423) and married into the imperial family, is one of the most conspicuous examples. However, there is evidence for the unpopularity of this policy amongst existing troops, many of whom could probably now trace a family presence in and around their garrison bases for generations. This friction contributed to the revolt of Magnus Maximus in Britain (see below).

Ammianus mentions the *numerus Alammanorum* in 372 (xxix.4.7). Explicitly a unit of hired barbarians from the Alamanni, the outfit is unmentioned in the *Notitia* reflecting what was probably an easy-come, easy-go, arrangement of ad-hoc provisions best illustrated by the so-called *Areani* or *Arcani*. They turn up in Ammianus in his account of 368-9, described as border patrols or spies, though he tells us they had already been in existence since 'early times' — whatever that means (xxvii.3.8). Given their responsibilities of roaming remote hill country in search of would-be border raiders, they were not surprisingly susceptible to bribes from tribesmen keen to know what the Roman army was up to. As mercenaries their only loyalty was to the pay-chest and it is more than likely that army pay had become unreliable anyway. When it emerged they were accepting gratuities in return for reports on Roman army movements they were promptly sacked and thrown out of their forts. At that point they disappear from the sources, though we can imagine they probably joined the enemy. It is impossible to know where their bases were.

In times of crisis, the army of Britain was reinforced from the Continent by the mobile forces created for the purpose. In 360 a conspiracy of Scots and Picts threatened the provinces of Britain once more. Lupicinus, 'commander of the armed forces', was sent to Britain to deal with the trouble. It is typical of the evidence that this event is undetectable in the archaeological record, but the literary account tells us nothing of any use about the type of forces involved. The much greater crisis of 367, occasioned by a 'barbarian conspiracy', led to a succession of commanders being despatched to help out. First to arrive was Severus, 'commander of the imperial household troops'. For reasons unknown he was replaced with Jovinus who seems to have weighed up the crisis, and returned to the continent to organise the right kind of response. Count Theodosius was chosen to lead the task force, which included various units of 'Batavians, Herulians, Jovians and Victores'. Although he seems to have been successful, this was a far cry from the British garrison of the first and second centuries, which would have been in the thick of the fray, led by the governor and augmented by vexillations from the continent.

Usurpers

Personal loyalties had always influenced military behaviour. In 68-9, Britain's legions took sides in the civil war and in 193-7 they did the same with Clodius Albinus. The Carausian revolt was the most important rebellion and it is obvious from the numismatic and literary evidence that courting the troops was central to the rebellion. During the fourth century, the implicit impotence of the resident garrison and the dependence on imported field units to suppress barbarian revolts was only contradicted by their enthusiastic participation in a succession of in-house rebellions. Diocletian's radical system of imperial government through a college of partners crumbled during the reign of Constantine I (307-37).

Constantine himself achieved a modicum of stability until his death and the division of the Empire amongst his sons: Constantine II, Constantius II, and Constans. In the turbulence that followed, Constantine II was killed by Constans, who seized the Western Empire for himself. Constans was deeply unpopular amongst the troops, and a commander of possible British descent, Magnentius, established himself as emperor in the West. Although the rebellion led to the murder of Constans, Constantius II had defeated Magnentius and driven him to suicide by 353.

The revealing part of the incident is that Magnentius had enjoyed popular support amongst the British garrison. An imperial secretary called Paul was despatched to Britain to operate a purge. This was done with such ruthlessness that Martinus, vicar of Britain, attempted to assassinate Paul in public. What was in it for the garrison in Britain? Perhaps indefinite garrison work was so nihilistic a prospect that soldiers were easily swayed at the thought of war and glory, rather than the frustrating experience of repelling the sustained barbarian assaults of the kind Ammianus reports during the 360s.

Border warfare was not necessarily a passport to obscurity. In 383 Magnus Maximus, a Spaniard, then working as a military commander in Britain, decided to cash in on the kudos earned in his frontier work. Perhaps he saw in himself a new Carausius, enjoying popular support amongst the wider community but critically enjoying the enthusiastic

50 *Late coins. Dates are for the reigns. Top (l-r): bronze radiates of Postumus (259-68), and Tetricus I (270-3), bronze folles of Constantius I (293-305), and Constantine I (307-37). Bottom (l-r): silver siliqua of Constantius II (337-61), gold solidus of Valentinian (364-75), bronze issues of Magnus Maximus (383-8), and Honorius (393-423). See also **45**, **46** and compare with **61***

personal loyalty of the garrison (**50**). If so, he might have considered what had happened to all his role models. The incumbent emperor, Gratian (Augustus 375-83), had tactlessly preferred to promote barbarians from the Alan tribe. Magnus Maximus may also have simply been a more exciting prospect. In 388 Maximus was killed in Italy by Theodosius I (son of the Count sent to Britain in 367) during his campaign to seize more territory.

Each one of these usurpations will have depleted the British garrison, but this was not a world where fewer men meant a greater share of the honour. Of course, the length of time involved was substantial. The soldiers involved in 383 were an entirely different generation from the supporters of Magnentius. But, as we will see in chapter 5, the army was a fundamental component in the distribution of coinage. Coins post-dating 379 are significantly less common than earlier fourth-century issues. Perhaps the demands to be paid, or will to pay, were in decline and there had been no official mint in Britain since 325. Further withdrawals of troops followed in 402 to support Stilicho's campaign against the Visigoths on the continent. After that year no coinage to speak of entered Britain, and even the practice of producing local copies, which had made good earlier shortfalls, was not revived. The final straw was yet another rebellion, which began with a man called Marcus who was murdered, followed by Victorinus who was also killed. They were succeeded by the last of all, Constantine III, who made the final use of what can be regarded as the Roman army in Britain. In 407 he took his household, his general Gerontius, and his troops and set off to the Continent to challenge Honorius (393-423). Constantine III was another failure. By 410 Britain's officials had declared they would take care of their own defence in future. Honorius for his part, instructed Britain's regional governments to look after their own problems.

Perhaps in some senses the position had reversed. The prospect of rebellion, following a leader whose talk of glory, the 'good old days', and a zealous sense of destiny, presented some idle garrison troops who had only ever known Britain with a chance to indulge in the same sort of jingoistic excitement the invading troops had enjoyed so long before.

The archaeology

This summary of usurpations and the references to units and individuals conceals the fact that most are known to us only from single references in the sporadic, unreliable and usually atrociously biased sources of the period. Not one aspect of all of this can be reliably tied to the archaeology. Refuting the history is too easy. The reality is simply that the archaeology of the period is even more diffuse and ill-defined. A modern example illustrates the problems. Hawkinge aerodrome was a frontline fighter airfield throughout the Second World War. An archaeological watching-brief in the summer of 1999 produced not a single artefact associated with aircraft, which would have identified the field's purpose in 1939-45. In archaeological terms, the only identifiable occupation evidence was traces of medieval and Roman pottery. Only the work at Birdoswald and South Shields has started to show how opaque the detritus of the latter phase of military Roman Britain is, with a picture emerging of a gradually dissolving military world in run-down forts lasting on into the fifth century. But this is not the same as a historical picture — the speculation that Birdoswald was manned by a warrior band of soldiers' descendants led by a chieftain-type leader is no more than just that. Whatever the interpretation, the fact remains that the artefactual evidence of Roman-type occupation disappears altogether and the abandoned forts of the northern frontier, bereft even of post-Roman village development, speak for themselves (**colour plate 21**).

Despite the paltry information available to us from the minimal sources, the story is still much fuller than the one available from the civilian zone. The epigraphic record, already tiny, almost ceases (**51**) and there is little trace at all of development in the towns apart from defences. Indeed, there is extremely little positive evidence for sustained urban communities after the middle of the fourth century. Those which subsisted had little time or concern for earlier monuments (**52**). Given that we have so little evidence for whoever the inhabitants were, the possibility is that a large component may have been military, however informally organized. Only the rural villas exhibit a propulsive dynamic in the accelerated enlargement, improvement and elaboration of a significant number of sites throughout the first half of the fourth century, and for another 20-30 years. Here is the evidence for the classical world, or at any rate a half-baked attempt to emulate it, in the mosaics and wall-paintings. But the purpose or motive behind any of this, or even the people responsible, is totally lost to us. Moreover, the proportion of the population represented by these houses was minute. Convincing though the evidence is for the self-image of an élite component of Romano-British society, it ultimately depended on the physical and military security of Britain. As this faded, so it proved impossible to sustain it through its own momentum.

While the units continued to exist, money presumably continued to arrive for pay, and coins remained an integral feature of the Roman systems of taxation and commerce but at a steadily diminishing rate from as early as the third quarter of the fourth century. The

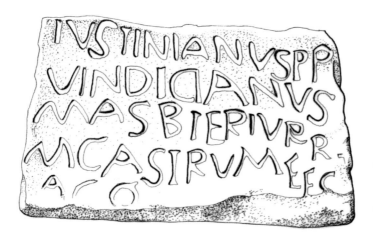

51 *Ravenscar. Inscription recording the* praepositus *Justinianus and the* masbier *(=magister?)* Vindicianus, responsible for the building of a tower and fort. RIB 721

disrupting events such as the barbarian incursion of 367 are, frankly, all but impossible to trace on the ground. But there is no *prima facie* evidence to show abandonment of facilities. Instead we have a small series of inscriptions, undated, which seem to show that civilian communities had contributed working parties to repair the Wall. They include the Brigantes, the Dumnonii, and the Durotriges (*RIB 2022, 1843-4, 1672-3*). The lack of any dating information is frustrating and, in truth, the stones could be attributed to any one of the post-Hadrianic reconstructions or repairs to the Wall. But even if they are not late fourth century, they are still the only clue we have to how the Wall and its importance functioned in the consciousness of the provinces that then went to make up Britannia.

All the time there was a gradual and eventually fatal reduction in numbers before the institution of an army ceased to have any real meaning. Some outpost forts of the later fourth century, such as High Rochester, are said to have been abandoned by now but such an assessment is based on archaeology though, like all the outpost forts, it also goes unmentioned in the *Notitia*. Given the lack of overall examination of the forts the connection cannot really be made, as there is every possibility that while one part of a fort was abandoned, another was still in occupation.

This is at the nub of the problem. The Saxon Shore forts are listed with their units, and by name, in the *Notitia*, rather like the blocks representing the RAF squadrons fighting the Battle of Britain on the well-known map in Fighter Command headquarters at Bentley Priory in 1940. The image is not inappropriate because this is rather how the units of the Roman army are sometimes treated by Roman military historians. Up until the mid-third century there is (just) enough evidence from epigraphy to support the idea that the army of Tacitus and others actually existed. There is practically no way to identify any real connection between what the *Notitia* describes and the physical remains of the forts on the ground. This is partly thanks to archaeology and its limitations. Being coastal installations, some Saxon Shore forts have been either partly or wholly washed away (Burgh Castle, Walton Castle, Bradwell-on-Sea, Reculver), subsided (Lympne), or been extensively reused, demolished or built over (Brancaster, Portchester, Pevensey, Dover). Only Richborough and Portchester have actually been subjected to large-scale excavation and if

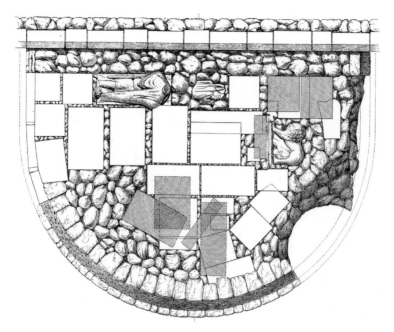

52 *London, Camomile St bastion. Drawing of 1880 recording the bastion as found. Several earlier carved stones taken from tombstones and tombs have been used as hardcore. This reflected the indifference felt in the fourth century when the need to reinforce defences was paramount. The consequence has been the preservation of further earlier evidence for soldiers in the town*

they have yielded anything it has been evidence that the late fort was totally unlike its second-century counterpart, right down to there being virtually no evidence for the sophisticated range of military structures so readily identifiable in earlier establishments. At Portchester and Richborough, despite relentless care, even wooden buildings generally escaped archaeological notice (Cunliffe 1968, and 1975). This can only mean they were not there at all, or that they were so transient they were, and may always be, beyond detection.

In a nutshell, the forts of the Saxon Shore have yielded absolutely nothing to link them to the extant historical record, beyond their existence. To a very large extent, the same problem applies to all the other forts listed in the *Notitia* in the various commands that went to make up the late Roman garrison of Britain. This might be because the archaeology cannot distinguish what we would need to distinguish, or perhaps because the Roman army by this time was so integral with the civilian community that the distinction does not exist. It is worth considering here the provisions made in Gaul a century later by Ecdicius, son of the short-lived emperor Avitus (455-6). His brother-in-law, Sidonius, wrote to him:

> I won't say how you went on to gather a kind of official army with your own personal cash, with minimal external assistance, equipped by great men, and how the enemy — who had until then acted with impunity — found his pillaging attacks, and reckless forays, stopped.

Sidonius, *Letters* iii.3.7

This force, clearly an effective one, would be invisible in the archaeology and would be unknown without the reference.

Though both sprang from different periods, and involved different wall types, the inclusion of bastions linked both forms of defence into late Roman military defensive architecture by the mid- to late fourth century (see chapter 7). Our understanding of the Saxon Shore system is based on the *Notitia*. If we did not have that document, it would be easier to see connections between some of these late urban defences and the Shore forts.

Horncastle, in eastern Lincolnshire, is a case in point. In antiquity the Wash was far more extensive than it is now, bringing the town much closer to the sea than it presently is, perhaps no more than six miles (10km). Not before the end of the late third century, the Roman town had been equipped with an irregular rectangle walled enclosure, with a bastion on each corner at least. At about 2.4ha (6 acres), the area is tiny compared to the straggling evidence for Roman settlement around about. In fact the area *within* the walls is striking for the lack of finds. Closely resembling a Saxon Shore fort, it is easy to see that the late addition of defences at a place like Horncastle was inevitably linked to the extension of the military system to all significant settlements on or near to the coast. Along with other towns, like Caistor (Lincolnshire), and London, Horncastle must have been made part of a sequence of defences which affected every part of late Roman Britain. It is unfortunate that the *Notitia* makes it impossible to know to what extent towns played a role where local leaders commanded bands of civil defence volunteers, or whether these walled compounds served as boltholes for the mobile units stationed, and formally recorded at, the forts listed in the *Notitia*. It is even possible that some acted as temporary prison compounds — under Probus (276-82), 'Burgundian' and 'Vandal' prisoners-of-war seized in continental wars were reputedly despatched to Britain to keep them out of the mainland Empire, later serving as imperial allies (Zosimus i.68.1-3). There is no demonstrable connection with the Saxon Shore forts or places like Horncastle, but it is a useful reminder that the possibilities for them are broader than they at first appear.

Final depletions

Britain's army had been steadily depleted in numbers by usurpations, barbarian revolts, indifference, and a lack of pay. It took generations for this to occur. The troops bundled off by Constantine III will have been a motley crew of opportunist mercenaries, indifferent to Britain and everywhere else, and only interested in who paid them; young British soldiers bent on the main chance, and workaday soldiers following a pay-chest. Unrecognisable to the soldiers who invaded Britain more than 360 years before, they faded into obscurity. They left a Romanized world behind them, but without their presence and the conduit they represented for the induction of the classical world, Roman Britain began to dissolve. That, too, took a very long time but the interruption in the literary, archaeological and epigraphic record is comparatively abrupt. In the rest of this book we will look at the impact the Roman army made on that record and how it illustrates the dramatic effect the Roman army had on Britain.

5

COMMERCE AND MANUFACTURE

Understanding about an ancient 'economy' is almost impossibly difficult because the concept did not exist in antiquity and so many of the criteria needed to recreate it are missing. All we can do is make broad general observations, and explore different facets of mediums of exchange, transport and communications, and evidence of which goods were moved about. Britain was of course primarily agricultural but this is only worth saying because we live in a time when, exceptionally, Britain is not. Like all places at all times except the last century, Roman Britain was a place where most people spent most of their lives working the land.

By being an integrated part of the whole Empire, it is impossible to assess to what extent Britain, or Britain and the Empire, supported the army and the towns. Moreover, like the US military bases of the Far East, Britain or Germany, the army functioned as a kind of extension of more distant economies. Fuelled substantially by imported goods, the power to requisition, and imported cash, a Roman fortress could start out economically isolated from its actual setting. But the army did also demand products locally. As a result pressure on the local environment increased, but with payment following for the goods the local farmers were brought out of a self-contained subsistence economy into a more sophisticated economy.

The Roman army in Britain must have had a significant economic impact but just because it is conspicuous in the record does not mean that it was necessarily as significant as we imagine it to have been. For example, its numbers were small compared to the overall population, regardless of how we extend the 'military community' to include those dependent on soldiers (Allen and Fulford 1996, 252). However, the records of organic produce brought into Vindolanda (see below) bring us to the idea that the army's demands on local suppliers must have impacted on Romano-British farming communities. But did they? Abuses in the system turn up in Agricola's day, but the passage makes it clear a process existed and that the outcome was more efficient management to make sure farmers could deliver what was needed close to the point of demand (*Agr* 19). We can assume that the presence of the army increased the demands on the British farmers, unless the food was imported — though how that could be done would be another mystery. Perhaps more significant than the actual cost will have been feelings of resentment at having to provide it at all. The impact is also likely to have been intensely variable. Poor weather and proximity to a garrison may have combined to make one year in one place far worse then the previous year, while places far to the south and remote from the north and west were perhaps less affected.

However, given the unregulated way in which Iron Age tribal chiefs had handed over Britain's produce to Roman merchants to buy luxury goods before the invasion, perhaps

53 *Housesteads,* Vercovicium, *as it may have appeared in its heyday. The clustering of* vicus *structures along roads outside the fort is testified from physical remains, but this could almost be any fort anywhere in the north during the late second century and on into the third*

in some sense the pressure eased off farmers slightly. The issue will have pivoted around whether Roman demands pushed farmers below the subsistence level or not, either generally or locally. This is not something which we can resolve, other than to note that in Egypt military supplies seem to have been acquired ad-hoc by units as they needed them, rather than through some massive coordinated programme of contracts and requisitions. If this was what happened in Britain, then the way was open for individual officers and units to oppress particular groups of natives, while others could have been realistic and accommodating.

In the fourth century Britain's great villas presumably benefited from the money that could be made out of vast country estates. While we do not know who owned them, how large the associated productive land was, and where their produce went, we can guess that one possibility was providing food for continental garrisons where the problems caused by barbarian incursions were rather greater than they had been in Britain. Being closer to the Channel might have made it much easier to ship produce to the Continent than to northern Britain. The imperial panegyrics of the very late third century laboriously recount Britain's commercial and agricultural importance. This is obviously unreliable to the extent that Britain's recovery from the clutches of Carausius and Allectus had to be justified, but there may very well have been truth in the claim. In any case, the villas speak for themselves — somebody had to have been paying for them.

What we cannot assess is whether growth was achieved by elevating yields from existing farmland through more intensive methods and improved equipment, or whether it was achieved by bringing more land under the plough. Seizure of land for colonies, of which Colchester is the most notorious example, will have had a negative local impact, perhaps forcing some people to become temporarily itinerant. At the same time, the reorganization of land into centuriated blocks around colonies will have largely ignored pre-Roman fields and plots with implications for productivity. By the same token, military exploitation of land in remote areas may have measurably increased productivity. The terraced slopes below Housesteads must have been used for farming and while there is evidence that native farming was already well established (in the form of plough marks beneath sections of the turf part of Hadrian's Wall) it is unlikely to have been as diverse. The subsequent development of the villa estates is probably connected with improved techniques or management, but whether it was because the demands of the army made it essential to combine smaller units into larger ones, or whether this was a social development which translated the pre-Roman hierarchy into a villa-owning Roman form for a very limited section of the community, cannot be answered.

That there is simply no means of assessing any of this just goes to show how intractable a problem the Romano-British economy is. The usual archaeological caveat that 'more work needs to be done' to answer these questions is a deceptive nonsense. The survival of estate accounts and correspondence from the great houses of the eighteenth century should be enough to show any archaeologist that he or she is impossibly removed from the myriad data, which would be essential to understand even a single week in the calendar of a single villa.

The reality is that the Romano-British economy was a million separate economies renewed every year, each wholly dependent on each season's unpredictable figures of demand, supply, yield, weather, equipment and family problems. Unrecorded and untraceable, it can only be said of these countless economic microcosms that they appear to have succeeded in general in supplying what was needed, by being linked into the greater system of roads and rivers, forts, towns, and markets (53). The proof, or what passes for it, is the proliferation of Roman goods with their main concentrations in the forts and towns, and this is all we really have to go on. Some of the surviving material found its way around as part of the overall military system of supply and manufacture, others as personal possessions or goods.

54 *Stanwix,* Petriana. *Tombstone of Marcus Trojanius Augustinus, erected by his wife* (c)oniux, *Aelia Ammillusima. The stone is flanked by a pair of lions holding human heads, considered a symbol of the jaws of death.* RIB 2029

Castleford in West Yorkshire has produced exceptional quantities of artefact evidence, some of which had demonstrably been shipped in from around Britain, such as a Cumbrian haematite whetstone, or from the Continent. Some of the other evidence is directly linked to evidence for on-site manufacture, for example glass, within the fort and *vicus* settlement, and illustrates a scale of production by the Roman army not matched in Britain again until probably the late eighteenth and nineteenth centuries. Here, it has been suggested that the site served as a rearward supply and manufactory base for the forward armies of the north, recalling a description by Vegetius of the need for secure supply bases and routes to service the garrisons (*Epitoma Rei Militaris* iii.8, cited by Bishop in Abramson 1998, 308). Subsequently, this was probably a role fulfilled by better-known sites like Corbridge and South Shields.

One very important consideration to bear in mind is that throughout the period the measurable proportion of *imported* goods declines. If we treat the Roman army as the prime mover of goods and the prime influence in cultural innovation, then this evidence works both ways. On one hand, the decline in imports may be evidence for an increasingly static frontier garrison, reflecting a steady reduction in 'foreign' recruits who might bring in material. That recruits to *VI Victrix* in the early third century might be identifiable in the ceramic record is an important suggestion. Equally, if we start with the assumption that garrisons were increasingly static, then the decline in imports is exactly what we might expect.

The military population

Naturally, there are no figures available beyond those we can estimate for the number of troops in Britain, their pay, and their families (**54**). There is no meaningful way of assessing their financial impact on the province as a whole in a way we could understand it. There are some comparisons though. In 1815 Britain's population was about 13 million. The Duke of Wellington faced Napoleon at Waterloo that year with an army of 67,000, only one-third of which had been drawn from the United Kingdom (Briggs 1959, 160). The costs incurred in financing this war, which of course included paying for the Royal Navy, were so vast that huge loans had to be raised and, eventually, new taxes introduced. In 1871 the United Kingdom's population was 31.5 million and in that year the government raised the standing army from 200,000 to 497,000 (Murphy et al, 1998, 204, 270). In 1815 there was one soldier for every 194 Britons, and after 1871 there was one for every 63, reflecting not only the needs of imperial Britain but also her capacity to support this military power base, which, as an industrialized nation with vast dominions, was considerable.

Roman Britain's population can only be approximated based on medieval figures, and anything between 4-6 million is a likely minimum. This figure could easily be revised upwards to 8 million as new discoveries of Roman settlements proliferate. Her nominal garrison fluctuated around the 40-50,000 mark, which is equivalent to one soldier for every 100-200 people. Most of these soldiers will have spent most of their time in the north and west, and will thus have been far more visible in those areas, in spite of the evidence for high levels of presence in places like London. These figures are only rough and of course, over (and during) time, they will have varied. By the late fourth century the garrison had probably dwindled to a quarter of this, while in 43-69 it may have been nearly half as much again at about 55-60,000. Disease and climate could easily have caused significant fluctuations not only in the whole population, but could intermittently have affected different sectors of the community, causing an imbalance in age distribution. We know nothing of these except that they existed in ancient and medieval times, usually brought from foreign countries and striking without warning. Given the Roman Empire's cosmopolitan nature Roman Britain must have been subjected to epidemics.

The nineteenth-century figures merely help us to illustrate how the British army, very approximately equivalent as a proportion of the population in the early 1800s to Roman Britain's army, had colossal financial consequences for the government of the day. Indeed, as income tax was devised to help fund it, we all live with the consequences. Of course, Roman Britain did not directly pay for its garrison — the imperial state did, using resources gathered from across the Empire to do so. So the comparison cannot be usefully extended beyond simply acknowledging the fact that a standing army cost a vast amount of money.

Soldiers of course did not live in isolation. For every soldier there were several other individuals whose lives will have depended on him: a woman (or perhaps even several), children, traders, artisans, entertainers, and brewers — the potential list is vast (**55**). One only need consider the English towns that grew around the great naval dockyards at Portsmouth, Plymouth and Chatham, to see the effects of a military establishment on a local community and economy.

Supply and demand

When the army arrived Britain will, at the very least, have found itself with two economies. The existing economy, based on feeding the indigenous population and

55 *York*, Eboracum. *Tombstone of Flavia Augustina, aged 39 years, 7 months and 11 days, her son Saenius Augustinus, aged 1 year, 3 days, and (her daughter) [...]a, aged 1 year, 9 months and 5 days. Erected by her husband Gaius Aeresius Saenus, veteran of* VI Victrix. *Saenus seems to have bought a standard slab as the text does not fill the space available, and the children depicted are patently too old for the individuals they represent.* RIB 685

supplying enough to provide aristocrats with resources to trade, will have continued as before but now suffering from two handicaps. The army will have taken a certain amount from it, localised to where it was, and the diversion of human resources into fighting probably diminished its productivity. While it could scarcely be claimed that the Roman army was the sole driving force behind the new Roman economy in Britain, it was probably the most important — certainly to begin with. Even so, the actual numbers of soldiers never constituted more than about one percent of the whole population. However, the effects on society and the economy in Britain must have far outweighed their actual numbers. There is an important distinction to be made here with provinces already operating cash-based economies. In Egypt for example, where estimates of the population in Roman times range from five to ten million, the size of the garrison was around 25-40 percent of Britain's. Not only were their numbers fewer, but they will not have made as much difference as in Britain because Egypt was already a well-established component of Eastern Mediterranean economic civilization.

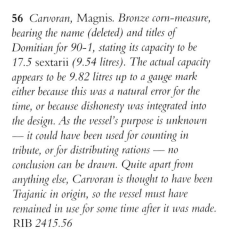

56 *Carvoran*, Magnis. *Bronze corn-measure, bearing the name (deleted) and titles of Domitian for 90-1, stating its capacity to be 17.5* sextarii *(9.54 litres). The actual capacity appears to be 9.82 litres up to a gauge mark either because this was a natural error for the time, or because dishonesty was integrated into the design. As the vessel's purpose is unknown — it could have been used for counting in tribute, or for distributing rations — no conclusion can be drawn. Quite apart from anything else, Carvoran is thought to have been Trajanic in origin, so the vessel must have remained in use for some time after it was made.* RIB 2415.56

Troops were theoretically regularly paid, which meant a constant injection of liquidity into day-to-day exchange. They were also occasionally the willing recipients of substantial cash gratuities. On his deathbed in 211 Septimius Severus exhorted his sons to 'get on together, make the soldiers rich and to hell with everyone else' (Dio lxxvii.15.2). He had himself paid out 1000 sesterces to each man when he took power in 193 though they had demanded 10,000 (*ibid*, xlvi.46, and *SHA* vii.6). Caracalla, Severus' eldest son, murdered his brother Geta in 212 and rewarded the troops for their loyalty with that coveted 10,000 sestertii, and raised their ordinary pay by 50 percent (Herodian iv.4.7). There were numerous other instances throughout the period.

Soldiers were also consumers of resources, whether sourced locally or at a distance, and whether paid for individually, or bought in on state contracts. Cash and prices also came in alongside the concepts of weights and measures and terms of value expressed in abstract units, such as pounds and ounces. While this cannot have been entirely new, the influx of the army will have guaranteed its spread, reinforced by the introduction of Roman taxation. An undated bronze steelyard from Wroxeter seems to have belonged to the site's time as a legionary fortress in the mid- to late first century, and bears the inscription >QVINTI ..., 'century of Quintus ...' (*RIB* 2412.2). A better-preserved item from the short-lived Flavian timber and turf fort at Elginhaugh shows that this was an integral piece of equipment even on campaign. More evocative perhaps is the corn-measure from Carvoran, bearing an imperial date equivalent to 90-1, and the statement *exactus ad S xviis habet P xxxiix*, '17.5 *sextarii* precisely, it weighs 38 pounds' (**56**). There is some debate over the actual capacity, as the measure will take 11.34 litres (9.82 litres to the gauge), whereas the stated capacity is equivalent to 9.54 litres. Perhaps devised as a means of short-changing Britons handing over corn tribute is rather more likely to be due to a missing internal gauge. In any case, there is no means of knowing whether it was used for counting in food from locals or traders, or counting it out to troops. Whichever it is, it represents a regulated system.

The Vindolanda writing tablets are explicit in their references to many different commodities, all usually undetectable in the archaeological record, such as bread, wheat, wine, beer, fish-sauce, and pork-fat (*TV* ii.180, 190). Another provides an even fuller list, together with prices. Thus we learn that alongside a quantity of pepper for 2 *denarii*, a pair of axles cost 3½ *denarii* and a length of red curtain cost a phenomenal 54½ *denarii*, or around one-third of the annual pay of an auxiliary soldier (Bowman and Thomas 1996). That these needed to be sourced and ordered is plain from a letter which appears to be a shopping list sent to an employee or slave of someone called Verecundus, who was probably a merchant. It lists the required quantities — 20 chickens, 100 apples, and so on — and specifies requirements about quality and price (*TV* ii.302). Another, from Carlisle, implies an element of hit-and-miss in sourcing goods with the phrase *decem saga militaria si inveniam*, '. . . ten military cloaks, if I can find [them]' (Tomlin 1998, 66).

That the Roman authorities at Vindolanda, just one fort of many, were able to organize the collection, storage, packing, transport and distribution of the various goods mentioned in the writing tablets is the best evidence yet for the sheer 'fact' of the economic impact of the army, even if it leaves us all the more mystified by its operation. The analysis of animal bones from Roman military sites has shown that, compared to civilian and native sites, Roman forts in Britain tend to produce much larger proportions of cattle bones compared to pig and sheep or goat (the latter are almost indistinguishable as individual bones). Even within the military world a preference for, or greater availability of, pig at legionary sites compared to auxiliary forts where sheep and goat are commoner than pig can be noted. This seems to be a reflection of tastes found on military and civilian sites in Germany (King 1999, 138), but it must also reflect either the army's ability to influence its supply or its power to control supply. Even where more general supplies of food were concerned it was possible for a governor to detach troops to accompany officials seeking sources of foodstuffs, though whether this was for security en route or to act as muscle if faced by reluctant suppliers is unknown. During his governorship of Bithynia and Pontus under Trajan, Pliny the Younger was presented with the imperial freedman and procurator Maximus who had arrived to secure corn from 'Paphlagonia', probably for Rome. Pliny had assigned ten *beneficiarii* to accompany Maximus, who promptly asked for six more. He got two (*Letters* x.27, 28).

During the last 50 years in Western Europe the proliferation of manufactured goods has caused a colossal decline in the real cost involved in purchasing them. A basic television set now costs in pounds roughly the same as it cost nearly 30 years ago. This is a function of supply and demand, and is a well-known economic phenomenon. It must have been the case that the Roman army's buying power completely altered the Romano-British civilian market, though we cannot measure it. Prior to 43 imported wines and other quality products were available only to the élite, something obvious from the level and nature of distribution of the evidence. Economies of scale must have driven down prices, though we have no idea by how much, perhaps with devastating consequences for aspects of economic control formerly wielded by tribal ruling classes.

Artisans and craftsmen

The Roman army was also a concentrated source of skills. The most efficient source of much of what the army needed was the army itself. Vegetius said that, 'the legion should carry everything with it considered necessary for waging war, wherever it goes, in order that it creates a fortified city whenever it pitches camp' (*Military Science* ii.25). These included places where armourers could thrive, builders of fort structures and siege engines, as well as blacksmiths, potters, bone-carvers and tanners, all galvanised with a mood of expectation in the air. Some of these skills are mentioned in the writing tablets from Vindolanda, showing that auxiliary units were also equipped. One tablet cites *structures ad balneum*, 'builders of the baths', and *tectores*, 'plasterers', another a *veterinarium*, 'vet', but without specifying whether these were serving soldiers (*TV* ii.155, 310). Elsewhere we have a *fabriciensis*, 'armourer', and architect-engineers (**57**, **97**, and *RIB* 2096).

There are some examples of dies used by soldiers to stamp goods. One of several from Chester names Victor, a soldier of the century of Claudius Augustanus (*RIB* 2409.4). This lead die was probably used for stamping food — Victor may have been the century's baker. Marks of ownership by soldiers, or military units, are rather more common but they probably appear on goods produced by or specifically for the army. One piece of leather from York, thought to be part

57 Bath, Aquae Sulis. *Tombstone of Julius Vitalis*, fabricie(n)sis *(armourer) of* XX Valeria Victrix. *Aged only 29, he may have died here while visiting the spa, or because he was detached here on official policing duties. Interestingly, he was of Belgic origin which must mean that he either came from northern Gaul or southern Britain.* RIB 156

of a second-century military tent, carries the inscription >SOLLIIVLIANI, 'the century of Sollius Julianus' (*B* xviii, 373-4). *IXB* on a fragment from Vindolanda must stand for *(cohors) IX B(atavorum)*, known to have been part of the garrison there at the end of the first century (*RIB* 2445.2). The bronze *trulleus* from Caerleon, made by Maturus, also bears the stamped name of *ala I Thracum* and was clearly produced for the cavalry unit (Ziienkiewicz 1993, 106). Maturus himself is known from other examples and clearly derived work from military and civilian commissions.

These are just scattered instances but they represent the influx to Britain of a whole range of trades and professions. Some of course will have already existed, such as metalworkers and potters, but the quantity and concentration of military artisans not only generated a vast increase in manufacturing, building and surveying, but also resulted in these men entering the civilian community later in life. This will have been most obvious in the colonies, especially Colchester, which was instituted so early. The distribution of tombstones shows that veterans could settle further afield but apparently preferred to remain in colonies or near their former bases. It is impossible to tell but the manufacture of many Roman goods in Britain may have been undertaken by ex-soldiers, or the sons of soldiers who had learned their fathers' trades.

The economic infrastructure

The physical infrastructure of Roman Britain both made the wider economy possible, and was developed to enhance it. Roads were built to join up forts in the first instance, not provide convenient communications between British tribal settlements. A conquering military power had the freedom to use whichever routes offered the greatest flexibility and convenience. On the whole that meant the shortest point between two distances, while taking into account natural obstacles. The process was not straightforward, because of the continuous demands of maintenance; one road between Catterick and Vindolanda was bad enough to be complained about and another near Bitterne needed repair (*TV* ii.343, *RIB* 2228).

The system of roads was integrated into an Empire-wide series of route maps based on locations and distances between them, which must have originated in military planning and exploration of Britain (**Map 4**). We have no Romano-British evidence for this beyond Tacitus' statement about Agricola's strictures against corrupt tribute-collection practices (*Agr* 19.4). His proclamation was said to name specifically *divortia itinerum et longinquitas regionum*, 'side routes and distant areas', to make sure tribes delivered what they owed over as convenient and short a distance as possible. Obviously this would be meaningless without comprehensive records of roads and where they led. Milestones are not particularly helpful in this respect. The vast majority of surviving examples are late in date and belong to the third and early fourth century, usually naming little more than the emperor(s) of the day and occasionally the governor or (in the south) the local civic government — information of little practical use even to the most earnestly sycophantic traveller. The reason for this is probably cyclical replacement of milestones, produced en masse in quarries with local information about mileage being painted on at the position they were erected. Such flexibility is obvious common sense, but the paint would obviously not survive.

Only on the northern frontier, in areas which remained under Roman control for a short time, do we find specifically military milestones. One from near Ingliston, four miles from Cramond on the Antonine Wall, provides the titles for Antoninus Pius in the years 140-4 on a milestone erected by *cohors I Cugernorum*, and can be clearly attributed to the opening up of this area again during the building of the Antonine Wall (*RIB* 2313, see *RIB95*, p800).

However important roads were, waterborne freight will have been of vital importance. It can never be stressed enough just how laborious transporting goods by land in a non-mechanical civilization is. Work in the Cheshire, Merseyside and south Lancashire area has shown how the road system was tightly linked to waterways with evidence for early military activity at Wilderspool and it has been suggested that early forts are yet to be located at crucial crossings (Rogers 1996). The system would have been established during the early Flavian suppression of the Brigantes to make movement and supplies a great deal easier. The idea certainly makes sense, and indeed reflects Tacitus' description of the fleet's movements under Agricola and his simultaneous prosecution of the war on land and sea (*Agr* 25.1). The appearance of Lincolnshire Ancaster stone in London must be evidence for waterborne bulk freight along the east coast.

Waterpower was of vital importance in a developed world without steam or combustion engines. Several military watermills have been identified on the Hadrian's Wall system, usually integrated with bridge abutments as at Chesters and Willowford, though the interpretation is disputed by some. The harnessing of water-power here and at mines such as Dolaucothi in Wales, as well as countless other unidentified places, allowed the Romans to exploit the natural environment much more effectively. Here it is hard to specify this as a consequence of the military, other than the fact that most of the evidence is in the military zone. The concentration of trades required could only have been supplied by the army in the earliest stages, with architects, masons, carpenters, and hydraulic engineers all being needed to design and execute working mills or other water-powered installations such as drainage facilities for mines. In the fourth century the *Notitia* refers to the *procurator gynaecii*, 'procurator of the weaving mill', in Britain at *Venta*. Several towns are possible candidates for this installation, which was both official and intended for production of late military clothing. Spindlewhorls found in earlier military contexts, for example at Castleford, show that cloth production went on alongside metal and leatherworking.

The location of forts on rivers also required the development of shipping lanes and port facilities. At York after *c.*122 was one Marcus Minucius Audens, *gubernator* ('pilot') of *VI Victrix* (*RIB* 653). It is also the case that some of the river control facilities in northern Britain may have been considerably more sophisticated than hitherto thought, using dams and canals. This remains a controversial issue but the potential for more detailed surveying is fascinating (see Fitzpatrick and Scott 1999 and their bibliography).

The inevitable consequence was that the new Romanized economy gravitated to the military communications links. Just like the railway junctions of the nineteenth century, places previously passed by, or of little importance, could quickly become military bases and then develop as civilian towns or villages. York is perhaps the prime example, but there are many others such as Wall in Staffordshire, and Cirencester. Ancaster is known to have had a very early marching camp close to where the later town developed, and casual finds from the vicinity include a very high proportion of brooches associated with the mid-first century. Recent groundwork and reinterpretation of earlier finds at Alchester in Oxfordshire has raised the possibility that this settlement was yet another which began life as a Roman fortress on a road junction (Sauer 1999). Finds of coins and brooches point to a very early date for the military installations, soon after the invasion. Barely a mile to the east is limited evidence for an Iron Age hillfort, perhaps the original reason for building a fort there at all. Whatever the initial motives the development of the Roman road system placed Alchester on the east-west route, Akeman Street, from Verulamium to Cirencester and the south-west, and also on a north-south route from Chichester and Silchester on up into the Midlands, North Wales and northern Britain. Ancaster's position on Ermine Street, the highway from London to Lincoln and York guaranteed perpetual through-traffic. The network of local roads in the area is less well known than at Alchester, but the large number of minor settlements and villas in the area point to a more complex pattern than current road information suggests.

Even if the military period of the place, like Cirencester, had been comparatively brief, the economic impact was permanent and has frequently remained so until our own time. This was quite unlike other parts of the Roman Empire where the Roman economy developed in and around existing civilian communities, for example in north Africa, and in Asia Minor, where cities like Dougga and Ephesus respectively were already significant local centres of trade and commerce. In these places the Roman army made no conspicuous difference to the basic framework of the economy, not least because the army itself was scarcely involved in the provinces' assimilation.

The same principle applies to the development of Britain's resources (**Maps 1, 2 & 3**). We know from Strabo that alongside cattle and other agricultural goods, metals were already being extracted and exported long before the Roman invasion (iv.5.2). During the governorship of Ostorius Scapula (47-51), Roman extraction of lead under military supervision may have been underway. A long lost lead pig or plaque found 5 miles from the lead-mining settlement at Charterhouse-on-Mendip in Somerset was recorded as having the titles of Claudius for the year 49 (*RIB* 2404.1). The evidence for *II Augusta*'s involvement in the work on another pig is distinctly unconvincing though it seems to bear a highly abbreviated consular date for 49 (*RIB* 2404.2). Two other lead pigs do seem to confirm its role. One found in France is dated to the reign of Nero (54-68) and has the abbreviation L.II, while another found at Caerwent carries [L]EGIIAVG but no date (*RIB* 2404.24, 25) (**58**).

Silver is a by-product of lead extraction and was probably the main purpose of these lead pigs. With so little evidence for the work it would be difficult to argue that this was a primary reason for invading Britain, even if it was a convenient consequence, not least because the rate of silver content was low. Evidence from other pigs dated to the year 60 and later generally attributes their origin to private organizations working on behalf of the emperor, so it seems unlikely that the army had much sustained involvement, particularly as at the time they had other fish to fry, unless the lead mines were in territory they supervised and which had failed to attract private companies. A number of lead dies from Brough-under-Stainmore mention LEGII together with the word *exp(edivit)*, thus 'the Second Legion despatched this'. The clue to their activity comes from more sealings from the same place stamped CIINE META, for *cohors II Nerviorum* and *meta(lla)* (*RIB* 2411.123-7). The presence of lead mines in the vicinity makes it more than likely that this was what they were doing. Monumental inscriptions by *cohors II Nerviorum* show that they, or individuals, were intermittently present at several different northern forts but several from Whitley Castle, nearly 30 miles (50km) away by road, indicate that to have been their long-term base (*RIB* 1202-3).

The evidence for the fleet's involvement in iron extraction in the Weald of Kent is more certain, though all we know for certain is that fleet tiles were used at a variety of

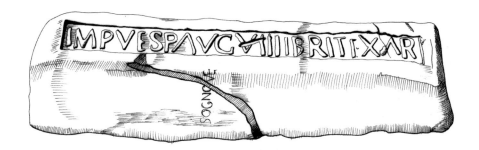

58 *Lead pig from Syde, Gloucestershire. It bears the titles of Vespasian for the year 79, and states that it is* Brit(annicum) ex ar(gentariis), *'British [lead] from the silver mines'.* RIB *2404.13*

installations associated with iron-smelting in the area, for example Beauport Park and Cranbrook (East Sussex) (**Map 1**, **colour plate 14**). This may only mean that the fleet was responsible for removing finished iron pigs, rather than having any duties in the smelting process, probably handed over to private lessees. But in truth it is even possible that the fleet did no more than supply hardware for installations. The fleet after all had built on Hadrian's Wall but there is no evidence that it was ever stationed there.

Metals prey on the archaeological mind because the products usually survive in some form or other. Timber is much less likely to survive though it is evidence from the physical remains of the forts, houses and public buildings of the first century that timber clearance must have been undertaken on a grand scale. Each turf and timber fort will have required the clearance of vast quantities of timber, a task so arduous it helped provoke a mutiny in the year 14 amongst the forces in Germany (Hanson 1978, and Tacitus, *Annals*, i.35). The consumption of timber for fuel cannot even possibly be estimated. The army required colossal amounts not just for day-to-day heating, cooking and ironmongery but the extraction of iron ore in the Weald, for example, required huge quantities for smelting. This kind of timber usage meant long-term timber management — the constant rotation of areas of woodland, making usable timber available at a reasonable distance rather than operating on slash-and-burn which was fine for conquest but hopeless for permanent garrisons.

It has been calculated that the legionary fortress of Caerleon will have required 150ha (380 acres) of woodland, and more for maintenance. The site is an appropriate one to mention, as a unique wooden writing tablet from a context dated to *c.*75-85 seems to mention the collection of *materia*, 'building timber' (*B* xxvii, 450-2). An inscription from the Rhineland, dated to 211-17, or 218-22, records a vexillation of *XXII Primigenia*, charged with the gathering of *abiegnas pilas*, literally 'fir pillars', and thus presumably tree trunks or planks (*CIL* xiii.11781). However, an estimate is based on so many imponderables and unknowns that it is extremely difficult to do more than conclude that the requirements must have been 'massive'. Only when we come to the practical realities of operating replica bathhouses do we start to hit on the epic scale of potential demand. Estimates based on the small bathhouse at Welwyn involve a 23ha (58 acre) area of managed woodland to provide the fuel (Rook 1978). The same process leads, as a

59 *Lanchester,* Longovicium. *Another stylish dedication slab by* cohors I Lingonum *in the reign of Gordian III (238-44), recording the erection of a bath with basilica under the governorship of Egnatius Lucilianus. See also* **43**. RIB *1091*

minimum, to the epic quantity of 5500 managed hectares (14000 acres) to service the legionary baths at Caerleon (Reece 1997). It is, incidentally, quite interesting to see how many military bathhouses are recorded as having been restored after periods of dereliction. Sometimes this was caused by fire, as at Brougham (*RIB* 791), but one might speculate that a possible reason was that bathhouses were occasionally given up on as far too much trouble to maintain unless coal was available as well — which is known to have been used at Wallsend (**59**).

A highly-detailed assessment of Inchtuthil, a useful one-period timber legionary fortress tightly dated to *c*.82-7, produced an estimate of 16,100m^3 of timber for the whole fortress, together with the suggestion that a single timber barrack block could have been built in 23 days by 40 men and that the whole fortress with outworks, tiles and other features could have been produced by 1000 men over the course of a little under a year (Shirley 1996). Rather curiously, a beam from the Roman quay at Regis House in London seems to bear the branded impression of the name of a unit of Thracians with the epithet *Augusta* (B 1996, 449). None of the possible candidates is otherwise known in Britain but this is not a serious objection as the beam is dated by dendrochronology to the year 63. Almost no dated evidence for auxiliaries for the first century in Britain is known and, given the rapid movements of military units such as *XIIII Gemina* in 68-9, there is no reason to doubt that a cohort or ala of Thracians might have passed through. This is not to say they built the quay in London but if they formed a part of a London garrison they may have contributed to it (as it would have been useful to the army), or they may have constructed buildings which left military timber available for reuse later (**60**).

The consequences of demands on timber will have been quite significant. Not only did the work result in opening previously uncleared areas of forest, and eventually exposing it to agricultural development, but may also have resulted in surplus stocks of timber becoming available when the forts were either consolidated in stone or abandoned (unless of course the timber was routinely destroyed. However, it would be wrong to exaggerate the effects. Pollen evidence suggests that deforestation was already advanced by the end of the prehistoric period, even if during Roman times it was continued and increased particularly in the Hadrian's Wall area (Dark 1999, 254-5, 260).

In the longer-term, the timber forts and fortresses were either given up or replaced with stone versions. Stone of course is infinitely reusable, unless it has been shattered by heat and flame, and therefore the physical remains of many forts have been severely destroyed or robbed out. Of course, like timber and metal, the exploitation of stone was scarcely a financial activity to the extent that it was obviously free and most of the military resources were being paid anyway. But they do illustrate the considerable effects of military logistics, the identification of resources and the infrastructure to move the resources to where they were needed. Exeter's mid-first-century legionary bathhouse made use of Purbeck marble, as well as a variety of other types of stone sourced from around the fortress area (Bidwell 1980, 41). There is no better example of the level of resources needed than Hadrian's Wall. Much of the stone was quarried from sources along or near the Wall, and needed around 3.7 million tonnes including core clay (Kendal 1996,

60 *London,* Londinium. *Massive timbers of the Roman wharf exposed in Lower Thames Street*

Table 2). Even a single building like the bathhouse at Chesters shows how work had gone into acquiring and dressing stone. The forts of the Saxon Shore seem to have been built from stone brought from further afield thanks to the reduced availability of stone in the south and east, but this only goes to show what the military command was capable of organizing (**colour plate 20**). Brancaster on the north Norfolk coast, for example, was built of sandstone sourced along the south coast and in the Midlands, as well as local stone (Allen and Fulford 1999, 165-6).

Greater variety appears in inscribed and decorative stonework, the artistic aspects of whch we will look at in chapter 6. But the sources of stone show that from an early date Britain had access to exotic pieces, albeit in very small quantities. The successive 'palaces' at Fishbourne are the earliest known examples. The stone at Fishbourne included marbles from Skyros and Turkey, and may have been brought in as part of the military development of the province, depending on who was responsible for the building (see chapter 7). The exceptional early monumental marble inscription of Trajan, naming *II Augusta*, from Caerleon (*RIB* 330), is thought to be made of marble from Tuscany. The text has been updated by an inferior second hand, altering Trajan's titles to those of 99-100, from 98. This makes it possible that the slab, together with carving, was prefabricated on the continent and despatched to Caerleon where it was amended. The tombstone of the procurator Classicianus, which cannot date much beyond the 70s, was made of large slabs of British limestone shipped into London (*RIB* 12). Its early date, and official nature, does not guarantee a military association in supply but it is possible and even likely.

Individual examples of stone, unlike ingots, coins and pottery, cannot usually be dated except by context. So, the scattered traces of exotic stone found in the temple precinct at Canterbury and widely in London, are just as likely to be evidence for a growth in the civilian trade as well. Fragments of Pyrenean marble found in the so-called Flavian governor's palace at London are slightly more convincing, especially given the possible connection in function with Fishbourne.

Coal has been an occasional find on many Roman sites though we tend to consider it only in an Industrial Revolution context. Analysis of coal recovered from a variety of Roman sites in Britain has now shown that coal was being widely exploited in the Roman period, though there is little evidence for it having been so before the conquest (A.H.V. Smith 1997). Coalfields in County Durham, for example, were being used to supply forts on Hadrian's Wall. There is also plenty of evidence for coal use in civilian settlements, for example Warwickshire coal which found its across the Midlands to East Anglia and Oxfordshire. This makes it difficult to see whether coal usage was organized by the army in the first instance or whether it was all part of a general exploitation of the province (Dearne and Branigan 1995).

Roman coinage

Goods of course cannot be moved about unless acquired first by force, manufactured, or by being paid for. Before the arrival of the Romans, coinage was well established in certain tribal areas of Roman Britain. Thanks to the adoption of Roman models, Roman script and Latin words, many are identifiable and attributable to known tribes and rulers. To numismatists these issues are known as 'Celtic coinage' and knowledge of them has moved on apace since the emergence of metal detectors. Although coinage was circulating before Caesar's invasions of 55 and 54 BC, it became much more widespread, and 'Roman', in appearance in the century leading up to the Claudian conquest.

The fundamental differences though are that the majority of British coins were gold and silver and, judging by finds, they existed overall in tiny quantities compared to coins of the Roman period. One reason could be that the Romans demonetised the British coins and called them in for melting down. That would reduce the available site finds, but it ought not to affect the proportion of metals other than to make gold and silver even less well-represented for the obvious reason that gold and silver are much more desirable. In any 'normal' coin series, precious-metal types are always rare, and much rarer as site finds than they were in circulation. So, if gold and silver types predominate, then that must have been the case in pre-Roman Britain. From this we may deduce that the tribal coinage did not serve as a means of day-to-day exchange, other than the limited bronze types issued by, amongst others, the Catuvellauni.

Tribal coinage falls into two categories: dynastic, and the rest. The dynastic coins generally name the ruler, perhaps his lineage, and the settlement of origin. Thus the coins of Cunobelinus (*c*.5-40) often name his father(?) Tasciovanus, or the settlement at *Camulodunum* in the form CAMV. Coins issued by less well-known tribes also provide exotic names of leaders who are otherwise entirely unknown, such as Volisios Dumnovellaunos of the Corieltauvi. Although a very small proportion of these types, and some of the uninscribed others, feature symbols which can be linked to Roman coin types there is no useful pattern of portraiture or themes that can be used to show a series of denominations, or even policy. The coins of the Iceni are decorated with a variety of crescents, rampant horses and the occasional face. Whatever the original significance of each type, it is very largely lost to us. The general impression we have is that these coins were primarily for the storage of wealth by the upper classes in certain tribes. The rarity of casual finds shows that they featured little in ordinary commerce, though they are found in significant quantities on Roman temple sites which turn out to have pre-Roman origins, for example at Wanborough in Surrey, and Canterbury. Their parochial use is clear from the distribution of types, showing that they largely circulated in their tribal area of origin, and other tribes, such as the Brigantes, did not issue them at all.

To say that this changed after 43 would be an understatement. It comes as a surprise to many people that Roman coinage is still so common that examples may be purchased for paltry sums of modern money. Field-walking a Roman occupation site is liable to yield significant quantities, while the metal-detector user is likely to be inconvenienced by the numbers of poorly-preserved, low-quality, Roman coins which he or she recovers, though almost all of these belong to the late third, and the fourth century. Long-term excavations can recover tens of thousands of such coins. Unfortunately, we cannot translate these finds into knowing precisely how coinage was utilised in a liquid economy.

Gold and silver Roman coins remain scarce. Gold almost never turns up as a casual find and around half the silver coins recovered by any means, except for those found in hoards, turn out to be ancient forgeries made of silver-plated copper (known as 'plated *denarii*'). All the rest are brass, copper, and bronze low-denominations, with the majority belonging to periods in the late third century and the fourth century. Even these were

61 *Roman coinage (dates are for the coins). Clockwise from left: brass* sestertius *of Domitian, 90-2; bronze* as *of Marcus Aurelius as Caesar, 154; silver* denarius *of Hadrian, 128-38; gold* aureus *of Hadrian, 119-38; silver* antoninianus *of Gordian III, 238-44*

subject to faking, both for supplementing shortage of supplies and also from downright dishonesty. But the finds from almost any date not only vastly out-weigh the coins from before the Roman period but almost every period afterwards as well, right up to the eighteenth and nineteenth centuries. In other words, base-metal coinage existed at times in the Roman period in astronomical quantities. Unfortunately, it does not tell us who was paid it, and how it was used.

Roman coinage did not stay the same. The system of the first and second centuries rotated around the silver *denarius*, about the size of a modern five-pence piece (**61**). Twenty-five of these were equivalent (nominally) to a gold aureus, though the latter existed almost entirely in hoards and in the payment of taxes. Silver was similarly liable but it also played a part in day-to-day transactions. Below these came the base metal issues: the brass sestertius, at four to the *denarius*; the brass *dupondius*, at two to the *sestertius*; and the copper *as*, at two to the *dupondius*. There were also the *semis* and the *quadrans*, worth a half and a quarter of an *as* respectively, but they were issued only occasionally and were swiftly seen off as inflation rendered them as useless as the old halfpenny and farthing. As site finds in Britain they are almost non-existent.

The system depended on intrinsic value; that is, the coins were made of materials equivalent to their value, which is why plated *denarii* were never hoarded. Always preferred for spending, plated *denarii* were more easily lost or discarded when an outraged recipient discarded it. When the true silver coins were gradually debased, a process which accelerated in the third century thanks to emperors like Septimius Severus seeking to fund army pay, the effect was to reduce the buying power of each coin. The gradual process of debasement and inflation led to silver coins which were little more than silver-washed bronze, and with an intrinsic value far lower than the old brass *sestertii* theoretically only worth a fraction. During the third century the old base-metal coins disappeared altogether, with the entire coinage system apparently dependent on what we call a radiate. The radiate, sometimes known now as an *antoninianus*, was introduced under Caracalla as a means of spreading silver further. It was probably a double *denarius* but had less than twice the silver. By the late third century it was no more than bronze with a silver coating. No one really knows how coinage was functioning by this date. A series of reforms had not really altered the virtual destruction of the silver coins, and gold was now only erratically issued.

The psychological importance of precious-metal coinage can be seen from Carausius' attempt to reform it during his usurpation in Britain between 286-93. The single most prominent feature of this reign in the record is his coinage. Carausian radiates were conventional bronze types, albeit of varying size and weight, but the old silver *denarius*, or a coin very like it, was revived at a standard of purity not seen since the reign of Nero (54-68) and was surely aimed at his supporters — by definition, the army. The Carausian silver reform did not outlast the reign, and even his successor Allectus (293-6) discontinued it.

The fourth century saw a succession of attempts to reform the coinage, but the nature of the denominations and their various relationships is largely unknown to us. In practice, silver was issued at a range of standards, but gold, now issued as the *solidus* ($\frac{1}{72}$ lb), was generally reliable and plentiful. Day-to-day coinage was made up of an array of bronze modules.

Within these systems there are several recurrent themes. Firstly, the Roman coinage system was always designed to return the gold and silver to the state, while acquisition of bullion was a prime factor behind conquest. Gold and silver were synonymous with credibility. Secondly, the emperor who could pay his servants, mainly the army, in bullion tended to remain in power. The man who offered more, and who could deliver, might usurp the incumbent. Thirdly, the cessation of conquest under Hadrian contributed to a long-term crisis in supply, which was met by debasement, and worsened by increasingly reckless promises of donatives and pay rises to greedy troops by would-be emperors.

The intrinsic worth of bullion coins made it vital that they were available for payments, particularly to soldiers, but their high value made them inconvenient for daily commerce. Gold and silver could be exchanged for bronze coins, and likewise gold and silver could be handed in to pay taxes. But wherever possible gold and silver would be hoarded in an attempt to hang on to it as long as possible. In the absence of a formal banking system this was the only means of saving. The need to provide gold and silver in the face of increasing demand from soldiers presented the imperial government with a perpetual problem. Ultimately resolvable only by having an unlimited supply of silver and gold, the dilemma was dealt with by debasing coins. That led to the collapse of silver in the third century, and the short-lived Carausian revival.

Another problem was the rate of striking. The Roman state did not issue coins regularly. While bullion supply will have affected the production of gold and silver, this cannot have applied to brass, copper and bronze. Yet it is apparent from the finds of coins

62 *Claudius (41-54), countermarked brass sestertius. Behind the emperor's head is the stamp NCAPR, possibly for* Nero Caesar Augustus PRobavit, *'Nero Caesar Augustus approves'. The idea was to help make good the lack of new coin struck during the reigns of Claudius, and Nero up to 64, playing a vital part in paying the army*

that not only were different types issued in hugely varying quantities, but that there were whole reigns when coin-striking of some or all denominations was minimal. The same finds also show that at certain times some provinces were well catered for, while others received far less (**62**).

This generated two results. In times of shortage older, worn, coins circulated for longer, and unofficial base metal coins were struck to make good the shortfall, almost always as copies of official current or slightly obsolete issues, or as copies of the copies. In Britain this is most evident in the mid-first century, the late third century and sporadically in the fourth. The only exception is the cessation of coin supply in the late fourth and early fifth century, which was not followed by a spate of unofficial coin-striking. That production of local copies was necessary at all points to a demand for coinage, and by extension the failure to produce copies in the fifth century suggests that demand had all but disappeared. But there were still people in Britain. The only conspicuous difference was the termination of Roman state employment of officials and soldiers.

Military pay and coinage

Unpaid, an army is no more or less than a gang of armed dangerous looters, and providing cash for them was more important than any other part of the government payroll, making the army a vital conduit through which cash entered provincial economies. In the year 14, on the German frontier, Germanicus faced a dangerous mutiny when the army of the Rhine rose up in protest at conditions, punishments, and pay. Two legions, *V* and *XXI*, declined to accept the settlement until Germanicus and his colleagues paid up from their own resources (Tacitus, *Annals* i.37). On 7 November 83, at Carlisle, one Quintus Cassius Secundus, of *XX*, recorded his personal debt of a hundred *denarii* to his fellow Gaius Geminius Mansuetus (Tomlin 1992). Not only had the latter apparently a hundred spare silver (or four gold) coins to lend, but his fellow was in a position to service a debt, which fell little short of half his annual pay. An inscribed tile from Holt, the works depot of the *XX* legion, lists *sum(p)tu[aria]*, 'expenses', paid in *denarii* to various recipients perhaps as the publishers suggest to cover food costs while away from base (*B* 1995, 387).

The coins themselves tell us little about to whom they were paid. Occasionally we can guess that certain issues were targeted at troops, but the most explicit examples were produced by usurpers, needing to buy instant power. During the civil war of 68-9, Lucius Clodius Macer, governor in North Africa, refused to accept the new emperor, Galba. Calling himself *propraetor Africae* for uncertain reasons, he struck silver *denarii* including some legionary types. One commemorates *III Augusta*, the legion stationed in Africa, and another *I Macriana*, which Macer founded himself. In Britain, the legionary radiates of Carausius are probably the best example. They name a number of legions, including several not under his immediate power, and it seems they must have been produced as loyalty-buying handouts. Official issues are generally less explicit. Hadrian issued a series of *sestertii* with references to provincial garrisons, such as those with the legend *Exerc[itus] Britannicus*, 'The British Army', but the coins are so rare it seems unlikely they amounted to more than a short striking perhaps handed out as souvenirs at parades Hadrian personally addressed.

Base-metal coins tended to circulate within the provinces they had been supplied to, but gold and silver were far more mobile. A number of base-metal issues have now been recognized as being more or less exclusive to Britain, identifiable thanks to the prolific range of reverse types and minor details of legends denoting imperial titles and epithets. Coins issued by Antoninus Pius in 154, depicting Britannia, circulated almost exclusively in Britain and might, given their supposedly pejoratively triumphant tone, be seen as special military army issues (**colour plate 16**). They appeared in unusually large numbers in the sacred spring dedicated to Coventina at Carrawburgh on Hadrian's Wall (Allason-Jones and McKay, 74). This rather suggests that soldiers in the vicinity were well supplied with them. But alongside the 154 Britannia issue an innocuous issue of Marcus Aurelius as heir apparent for the same year circulated, so it is not usually possible to draw any sort of conclusion about directed types (**61**). Of course ultimately it makes little difference, since once the coins were into the system they were available to anyone who could earn them.

The Roman legionary was paid about 225 silver *denarii* in the year 43, making a theoretical wage bill for legionaries alone of about 28 million *denarii*, some 3.5 million of which would be nominally required to pay the British legionaries. Another estimate for the whole army including auxiliaries at this time in Britain is 6.5 million *denarii* (Millett 1990, 58). Making a precise estimate is impossible because various conditions, posts and duties carried pay increases for individuals of 50 per cent, double or triple ordinary pay, as well as allowances to cover, for example, footwear (Le Bohec, 212-13). Around 20,000 legionaries at least were operational in Britain by the year 60. The number in the 17 preceding years may occasionally have been much greater.

Soldiers were generally only paid a proportion of their wages in silver, the remainder being withheld for savings, food and board, equipment and so on. We do not really know how this operated, apart from being aware that the system was prone to failure, hence the mutiny faced by Germanicus. Little coinage was struck between about 37 and 64, for example. Military pay during this time will have relied on using old silver or substitutes in kind. The wooden tablet from Caerleon already cited includes part of a phrase, which may refer to the estimated requirements of cash sent to the provincial military high command, and then returned under escort to the unit for payment. This probably happened three times a year. A second-century papyrus from Egypt is a rare instance of detail. Apion, a recruit to the imperial fleet at Misenum in Italy, has written home to let his family know he is safe and well. On arrival at Misenum he was paid *krysous treis*, 'three gold coins' (presumably *aurei*), to cover his travelling expenses (*SP* 112). The sum, equivalent to 75 *denarii*, or 300 *sestertii*, was substantial and equal to as much as half his annual salary. Here we have a specific instance of a cash payment in bullion. Apion may have chosen to hoard the gold, or perhaps convert some of it at a moneychanger for day-to-day bronze and copper coins. Either way here is high-value coinage passing to an ordinary member of the armed forces. Apion's experience was repeated on countless occasions throughout the Roman world.

Let us assume our first-century legionary had about 110 silver *denarii* per annum in his pouch — that is, if the pay arrived on time and in the right amount. Some of this he will have hoarded quietly, effectively removing it from circulation. The rest he will have spent, or changed into base metal coin for casual transactions. If our soldier converted just half that into ready cash, he had some 8-900 copper coins which across the whole legionary establishment means some 35-40 million coins circulating in Britain just from the legionaries. The auxiliaries will have theoretically had access to around half or a third of that number. On discharge a soldier collected his savings as well as a cash gratuity amounting 3000 *denarii* (elevated to 8250 in 212). But it needs to be remembered that there were other sources of cash injections. Dio states that Seneca had 40 million *sestertii* out on loan prior to the Boudican Revolt and he was not alone (lxii.2.1).

Thanks to the failure in official supply, the army seems to have been given the green light to strike its own copies. This proves the need to make cash available, though it is quite possible that supplies were still short of what was actually needed. The evidence is circumstantial but studies of finds and distribution suggest that at least one of the production centres was actually in the fortress at Colchester, though much may have come from Gaul. To this day the copies are found in large numbers on early military sites. Much of this coinage will have been recycled through the normal process of trade, but it is evident from finds that few found their way out of Britain. Under Nero until 64, the continuing shortage was partly made good by over-striking coins of Claudius which were considered to be still of good enough weight to be serviceable (**62**). The new coins of Nero in 64, and prolific coin production under the Flavians, together with a reopening of the mint intermittently at Lyons until *c*.82-3 to service the western provinces, eventually caused the copies to drop out of circulation, and they are not normally found on military sites post-dating the reign of Nero (**6, colour plate 4**). The finds from the sacred spring at Bath are interesting here, not only because they show the sort of proportion of copies available, but also that they were discarded as votive gifts in preference, presumably, to new and better coin. Of 38 Claudian coins found here, 34 were copies (Walker 1988, 285).

Roman silver and gold coins are rare site finds, and if one only counted gold and silver then the difference between tribal, Roman and medieval Britain in terms of coin finds would not be so conspicuous. What marks the Roman period out, from the invasion onwards, is the prolific quantities of small change in base-metal issues. They must have served a purpose, and that is likely to have been for day-to-day transactions. Coins are liable to a long life, and in Britain extremely worn late first-century coins were still circulating in the late third century. Official use of older silver for military pay meant that Republican silver coins, and issues of Augustus and Tiberius were entering Britain's money system a century or more after they were struck. Finds from short-term military sites, identifying issues specific to Britain, and also those from the Lyons mint, show that coinage was available in Britain in large numbers from an early date. This was undoubtedly primarily due to the army. What is very difficult to estimate is how quickly those coins moved into the civilian world, though their ubiquitous presence on sites of all classes shows that they did.

The best evidence for how some of the Roman army paid for its goods as a body comes from Egypt. Supplies were obtained on an almost piecemeal, ad-hoc, basis by units and their officers as required (Alston 1995, 110-11). Here, there is no evidence that there was some sort of provincial Central Office of Army Contracts. Cash itself was only occasionally handed over in exchange for goods. Instead, suppliers were handed receipts, which functioned almost as banknotes do today — intrinsically valueless, but which could be used against some sort of other liability like tax. Thus, discussions of prices and money in the Vindolanda tablets might be referring to values, rather than the usage of coin. However, in one of these letters Octavius writes to Candidus to ask for money to pay a debt. The published translation supplies the word 'cash' where the original Latin simply provides a sum. Thus Octavius needs 'at least five hundred (of something, presumably *denarii*) to pay for his five thousand *m(odii)* of grain' (*TV* ii.343). Later in the same letter, the specific term *pecuniam* appears for cash. Here at least cash was actively circulating as the lubricant of exchange though at the same time it is equally clear that purchases were arranged on deposits and promises in the first instance.

The abundant finds of bronze coins of the Gallic Empire, and copies, as well as those of phases in the fourth century might point to a high level of usage but they also point to a high level of disposability, which at the very least suggests a low unit value for each coin. But the colossal rate of copying demonstrates that supplies were inadequate and that there was a demand for them. The same phenomenon occurred in the seventeenth and eighteenth centuries in Britain when erratic production of copper coinage led to the widespread production of the so-called token by factories, businesses, and institutions across the United Kingdom to make good the shortage. They too were discarded once official supplies were restored.

In Roman Britain by the early fifth century supplies of official coinage had ceased, and mysteriously copying had ceased too. Exceedingly scarce finds of Roman gold and silver coins of fifth-century date, like those of the Patching hoard (W. Sussex) with a *terminus post quem* of 465, show that some people held on to their wealth in coin form. But day-to-day coinage had gone and this must lie in the severance of Britain from the cycle of taxation and the official payroll, at the heart of which was the military wage bill. It will also have brought to an end the military need to have cash to pay for goods and supplies. Just as the coming of the army in 43 led to the gradual emergence of a cash-based economy, so its disappearance led to the virtual cessation of coin use which implies that either coinage itself never truly entered the psyche of the greater population or that the political and social conditions of the 400s prevented its local production.

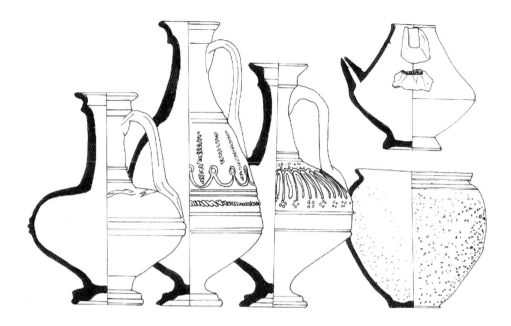

63 *Colchester,* Camulodunum. *Group of imported mid-first-century fine wares, including three lead-glazed Central Gaulish flagons, and probably from the grave of a veteran's family member, perhaps a child (note the feeding vessel). (After Greene)*

Pottery and glass

Pottery of Roman origin was entering Britain long before the conquest, but in restricted amounts and only in a few places. Some was decorative, such as Arretine red-slip ware, or functional like amphorae, but was restricted to major southern settlements like *Camulodunum*, ports of entry, or rich graves. Local Iron-Age industries existed in southern Britain, making a range of sophisticated wheel-thrown wares but mostly for limited local markets. In much of the north and west pottery was almost unknown, and such communities must have used wood, leather or skin vessels. Conversely, excavation of almost any site of Roman date will generate epic, and bewildering, quantities of Roman pottery. They include types imported from around the Empire, but predominantly Gaul, Germany, Spain and Italy, and types manufactured in Britain. Generally speaking, pottery is not recorded in any useful way in the historical or epigraphic record.

The economic impact of the army is patently obvious first in the small quantities of imported pottery brought in for them, and secondly in the local potteries which sprang up to service them. The effect on Britain as a whole was not, hardly surprisingly, immediate, as studies of very early pottery assemblages has shown (for example, Pollard 1988). Where a legionary connection is probable, as at Lincoln, assemblages of Neronian date show a much higher incidence of Roman pottery as opposed to local wares. For example, the Lincoln East Bight group had over 60 percent Roman material whereas groups from Leicester were below 14 percent (Willis 1996, 197). At Colchester a single grave yielded a

1 *The tombstone of the centurion M. Favonius Facilis of XX (see also* **9***). Found outside Colchester, the stone is mid-first-century in style and of unusually high quality for Britain. It must date from shortly after the invasion up to around the time of the Boudican Revolt. Although the colony was founded in 47, detachments of soldiers, or individuals serving as police and official escorts, will have been stationed here thereafter.* RIB *200*

2 *Maiden Castle, Dorset. These vast banks, which represented the climax of Iron Age military architecture might have been effective against sporadic assault by tribal rivals. Against the invading Roman force they provided little more than a concentrated opportunity to bombard defenders*

3 *Replica legionary equipment, as displayed in Leicester City Museum, and based on excavated components, typical of the second century*

4 *Nero (54-68) on a brass* dupondius *of 64-8, struck at Lyons. This issue diverts from the convention of using the radiate crown on* dupondii *(see* 6*). Nero's base-metal coins of 64-8 were the first significant small change issued for decades and flooded into Britain to supply the army*

5 *Tombstone of Longinus,* duplicarius *of* ala I Thracum, *found at Colchester. Mid-first century. For the text see* **11**. RIB *201*

6 *Chesters,* Cilurnum. *Inscribed slab of* cohors I Dalmatarum, *found reused as a step down to the headquarters building strongroom. The unit probably formed part of the garrison of the fort during the late second century, along with* ala II Asturum

7 *Decorative fittings from auxiliary cavalry horse trappings found at Newstead*, Trimontium, *in southern Scotland. This was a late first-century foundation temporarily reactivated under Septimius Severus. (J. Curle)*

8 *Replica auxiliary infantry equipment of the early third century based on excavated finds from around the Empire, here posed in the sacellum of the replica headquarters of* cohors IIII Lingonum *at Wallsend,* Segedunum, *on Hadrian's Wall, by Jamie MacLean of the re-enactment group* cohors V Gallorum. *(See also **colour plate 9**)*

9 *Replica auxiliary shield (see* **colour plate 8**) *made of painted wood with a central bronze boss. Modelled on excavated examples from Dura-Europos in Syria (see Connolly 1981, 259)*

10 *Housesteads fort,* Vercovicium, *the north gate looking out from the fort to the north-east. The difficult access by road to the north gate meant that it fell rapidly into disuse and was later replaced with a gate through the Wall in the valley below (see* **colour plate 12**, *also* **122**)

11 *Samian ware, Central Gaul c.100-25. This lurid red-slip ware flooded into Britain from the mid-first century until the early third with the army as the most important market. Scenes such as this matched pair of gladiators played a significant role in disseminating Roman imagery in Britain*

12 *Hadrian's Wall at the Knag Burn, close to Housesteads fort. A small gateway here allowed trans-Wall traffic to pass, but it was not installed until the fourth century, showing that use and practice at military installations changed, and thus the purpose or function of the works was not fixed*

13 *The Museum at Chesters,* Cilurnum, *is a vast repository of the inscribed stones found at Chesters, and several other forts in the vicinity gathered by collectors, antiquarians and archaeologists over the last couple of centuries. Much was collected by John Clayton (1792-1890), who lived here. The collection symbolizes the vast contribution made by the army to the record of Roman occupation in Britain*

14 *Roof tile from the bath house at Beauport Park, East Sussex, in the middle of a Roman iron-working settlement, stamped CL.BR for the* classis Britannica. *Most of the tiles of this structure bear similar stamps, found elsewhere at a number of military and iron-working sites in south-east England. It seems likely that the fleet was charged with supervising iron ore extraction and smelting*

15 Sestertius *of Antoninus Pius for the year 143, depicting the figure of Britannia*

16 *Bronze* as *of Antoninus Pius for the year 154 depicting Britannia. This issue, unlike all others of Britannia, is not rare though distribution is largely confined to Britain and is distinctive for the generally poor style. It has been suggested that they were manufactured as handouts for troops in Britain — one of the largest groups was found in the spring of Coventina at Carrawburgh*

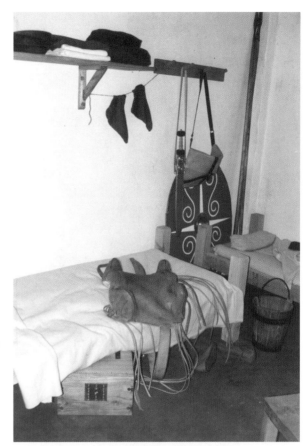

17 *Reconstructed auxiliary barrack at Wallsend*, Segedunum. *Note the leather saddle. Photographed by courtesy of Tyne and Wear Museums Service*

18 *Modern reproduction of an 'Imperial Gallic' helmet, typical of the second- and early third-century legionary*

19 *Carausius (286-93), from a bronze radiate. His usurpation exploited his own military success in controlling the seas around Britain, and led the province into a short-lived breakaway Empire. The vigorous and dynamic personality of the man is evident, even in a coin portrait. Painting: author*

20 *On the south side of Pevensey, the Saxon Shore fort of* Anderida, *a lone fragment of accomplished and decorative Roman wall still projects from the soil. The walls on the north, east and west sides, are far better preserved*

21 *The fort at Risingham,* Habitancum, *looking west. Although no buildings are visible, the fort platform is still a prominent feature and illustrates the commanding locations chosen for strongholds on the principal Roman route into Caledonia. The fort seems to have been abandoned by the late fourth century and apart from farm buildings in the vicinity has returned to nature*

22 *Foundations of the granaries at Birdoswald,* Banna, *on Hadrian's Wall. By the fifth century the semi-derelict remains of these buildings had been adapted into a timber hall. The occupants are unknown, but may have been descendants of the fort community*

23 *Reconstructed model of a fort timber gate of the type used in first-century forts, for example Great Casterton and Longthorpe. Functional and efficient, they were ideal for forts unlikely to be in use for more than 10-20 years*

24 *The baths at Hardknott, Mediobogdum. Although of second-century, or later, date, the remains illustrate the way in which this fire-prone structure was usually built in stone, and at some distance from the fort*

25 *Model of Wallsend,* Segedunum, an auxiliary fort on Hadrian's Wall. *Compare with* **99**.
Photographed by courtesy of Tyne and Wear Museums Service

26 *Housesteads,* Vercovicium, *the latrines. A view of the south-east corner of this well-known fort. Here the latrine building, and adjacent water-tank, lie at the lowest point in the ridge-hugging stronghold, enabling full use to be made of rainwater falling on the fort and providing even a remote establishment like this with full facilities*

27 *Wallsend, Segedunum. A modern replica of the fort baths built on a former industrial site next to the fort platform, and based on the extant remains at Chesters*

28 *York, Eboracum. Inscription recording the erection of a temple to Serapis by Claudius Hieronymianus, legate of* VI Victrix. *Late second century, or very early third.* RIB *658*

29 *The Multangular Tower at York, forming part of the early fourth-century rebuilding of the western river front defences of the legionary fortress by Constantius I. The upper part of the work is medieval*

30 *The* vicus *at Vindolanda. The main street through the* vicus *runs from lower left up to the fort's west gate (centre). The only* vicus *still visible to any significant extent in Britain, it was typical of the straggling settlements which developed around almost every fort. However, the coin list suggests it had fallen into decline by the early fourth century, some 50 years or more before the fort*

31 *The so-called bridge abutment at Piercebridge, Morbium(?), just east of the fort. The massive scale of the masonry here is not in question but it has remained a matter of doubt whether this is part of a bridge, or possibly a dam. Either way, the site bears witness to the Roman army's ability to control the landscape*

32 *York. A 6.7m-tall (22ft) Roman column stands re-erected outside the York Minster, under which it was found amongst the ruins of the legionary* principia *cross-hall. It remained standing until at least the ninth century, showing that reminders of the Roman army's presence endured for generations after the Roman period*

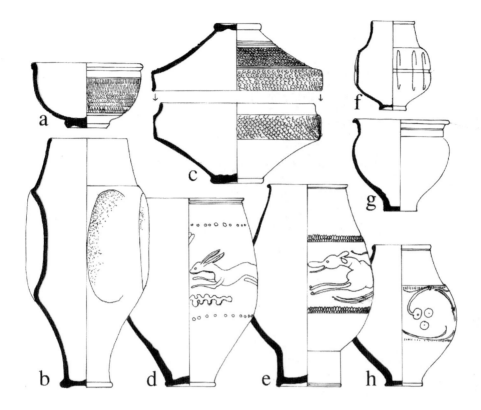

64 *Nene Valley, colour-coat wares (except **g**). Scale about 1:5. **a**. bowl with rouletted decoration emulating samian Form 37, c.270-350. **b**. indented beaker. **c**. 'Castor box' (bowl and lid). **d**. 'Hunt cup', c.170-230. **e**. 'Hunt cup' with a base resembling Central Gaulish products, c.200-30. **f**. 'slit-folded' beaker, fourth century? **g**. wide-mouthed grey-ware jar, third century. **h**. barbotine-decorated beaker, c.170-200. Dates very approximate. (After various sources, including Howe, Mackreth, Perrin and Swan)*

remarkable collection of imported pottery (**63**). The early legionary fortresses at Usk and Kingsholm have both produced large quantities of imported fine wares, as well as examples of imitations produced in the vicinity.

Pottery manufacture began in the Nene Valley with the establishment of the mid-first-century legionary vexillation fortress at Longthorpe. By the second century the concentration of raw materials, including clay and water, together with a prime location on the trunk route north — itself a direct consequence of the military control of the new province — had guaranteed Nene Valley potters with a market across much of the province but particularly in the south-east, the east and the north. It benefited enormously from the end of samian manufacture in the first half of the third century (**64**).

So, pottery from very early military sites might not have a recognizably Roman profile. Conversely, there is a marked bias to Roman wares at the major military sites, usually legionary fortresses. However, the establishment of a military pottery production industry

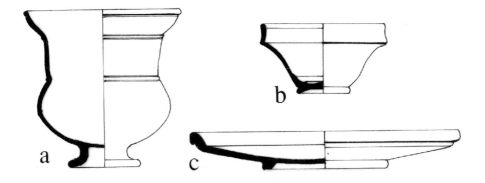

65 *Gallo-Belgic wares. Scale about 1:5.* ***a***. *Gallo-Belgic butt-beaker, mid- to late first century.* ***b***. *Gallo-Belgic cup emulating an Arretine type, mid- to late first century.* ***c***. *Gallo-Belgic platter emulating samian Forms 15 and 17, mid- to late first century. (After Hawkes and Hull, and Rigby)*

might introduce potting to a new area, with consequences lasting long after the army had moved away. This shows the pragmatic economic approach by the army, using local wares when it was expedient to do so, and introducing its own products or imports more rapidly where it was not. In the north this was a greater requirement because of the reduced availability of local wares.

Military sites have a greater range of samian forms, a virtual monopoly on Lyon ware, and a preference for olive-oil-bearing amphorae, whereas civilian sites have limited types of samian, use Gallo-Belgic ware, and prefer oil-carrying amphorae (**65**). Usk is the classic example in the mid-first century, where Lyon ware predominates to the virtual exclusion of other sources of colour-coat ware despite not being the closest (Greene 1979, 139). This has been explained by *Lugdunum* (Lyons) having already developed a major ceramic industry to supply the Roman military Rhine frontier from the late first century BC, operated by professional specialist traders, *negotiatores*. An urban fire in 65, and disruption during the civil war of 69 conspired to damage the city's commercial interests, and the military trade moved elsewhere, with Gaulish samian being the prime beneficiary.

What this illustrates is the vast commercial interests involved in servicing the army's needs, and how the army's requirements influenced the market. This army-led pattern of trade has been found elsewhere in the north-western Roman Empire. It cannot be coincidence that the minimal evidence for pottery traders in Britain is connected with York, the principal northern military centre and comes from much later when the province had had time to develop its own mercantile tradition. By the third century York was capital of Britannia Inferior. An undated altar from near the mouth of the Scheldt at Domburg in Holland records one Marcus Secund(inius?) Silvanus (*ILS* 4751). He calls himself *negotiator cretarius Britannicianus*, normally interpreted as 'trader in bowls with Britain'. *Cretarius*, a rare word, may refer to a specific type of bowl, *crater*, used for mixing wine and water, or more generally to earthenware products made from light-coloured or whitish clay, *cretae*. The altar, together with many other dedications to the goddess

Nehallenia found there, probably marks a gift after a successful voyage across the North Sea but whether he was shipping goods into, or out of, Britain, is unknown. Lucius Viducius Placidus was also a *negotiator*, though of what we do not know, and came from Gallia Lugdunensis. In York in 221 he dedicated an arch and gate to Neptune, the Genius of the Place, and the Spirits of the Emperors (*B* 1978, 430), but also made dedications to Nehalennia at her shrine in Holland. Placidus thus apparently plied his trade between York and the Scheldt, and Silvanus may have done the same.

Where pottery went, other, perishable, goods must have gone too, some of which are recorded in graffiti scratched or painted on pottery or other containers. It is rare for these to mention military units, but a wooden barrel bung from Carlisle was cut from a plank of wood previously branded LEG XX, though this might be a simple case of reuse (*RIB* 2442.11). A 'Rhodian' amphora from Caerleon, with an internal resin coating, has LEG.II.AVG painted on it (*B* 1994, 310-12). The resin is thought to suggest liquid contents, perhaps wine or honey. The type is associated with raisin wine shipped in from the Aegean area, and bought either for the legion or by an individual soldier.

Evidence from Pannonia is more unequivocal, where several amphorae have been identified with graffiti marking the contents. A barrel from *Aquincum* contained *immune*, 'duty-free', goods for the use of *II Adiutrix*, a legion formerly in Britain (Bezeczky 1996). Back in Britain inscribed labels made of bone, or more usually lead, testify to the storage of goods destined for, and held by, divisions of the military unit. Thus one from Chester states it to have identified the 'property of Lucius Vanius of the ninth cohort for Setinus, by pack animal' (*RIB* 2410.8).

The movement of mortaria was for the product's sake — it was a specifically Roman form, required for Roman cooking. It had scarcely been used in Britain before, and it disappeared after the Roman period. Initially sourced from Gaulish potters, mortaria were soon being supplied by immigrants and Romano-British potters who apparently moved their premises further into Britain to service the dispersing army. It took some time though for the demand to be satisfied. The evidence from pre-Flavian Longthorpe is that mortaria 'were in short supply' where the small assemblage of almost identical mortaria had had to be manufactured on site (Dannell and Wild 1987, 67, and K.F. Hartley in *ibid*, 128).

Gaius Attius Marinus can be tracked from his name stamps and fabrics. He was producing mortaria at the end of the first century at Brockley Hill (95-105) and Colchester (90-100). Within ten years he seems to have moved north to Radlett in Hertfordshire (100-10), and then Hartshill-Mancetter in Warwickshire (110-30). His Hartshill-Mancetter base was probably part of a movement of mortaria potters away from the south-east, chasing the military market. Pottery production in this area was on a major scale from *c.*100, a time by which legionary fortresses had been established at Chester and York, and a northern border of sorts was being structured around the Stanegate forts. More than three-quarters of the second-century mortaria from the civilian settlement by the fort at Greta Bridge (N. Yorks) were from this source.

Legionary fortresses had their own works depots. Chester's was at Holt, where pottery and tiles were produced on a huge scale. Stamped legionary tiles were also produced at Tarbock on Merseyside, where one is handily dated to 167 (Swan and Philpott 2000).

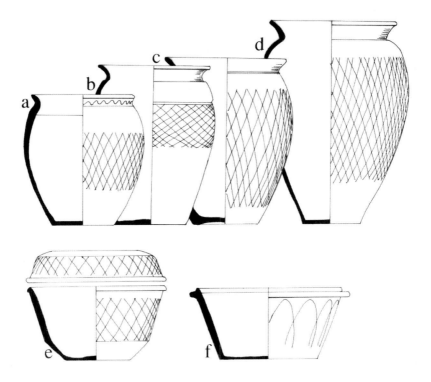

66 *Black-Burnished wares. Scale about 1:5. **a**. BB1 jar, early second century. **b**. BB1 jar, late third century. **c**. BB2 jar, second century. **d**. BB2 jar, third century. **e**. BB1 flat-rimmed bowl with lid, mid-second century. The angled base gradually disappears through the period. Similar products were manufactured by the BB2 industries. **f**. BB1 flanged bowl, late third to early fourth century. (After Gillam)*

Scattered timber buildings about 250m to the east of the early fortress at Exeter have been interpreted as a possible works depot. At York, an area immediately east of the fortress was occupied in part by potters also for producing tile and pottery.

It is difficult to believe that kitchenware was worth shipping large distances. But the fact remains that what we call Black-Burnished, made in Dorset (BB1) and around the Thames Estuary (BB2) in similar but hand-made and wheel-thrown versions respectively, was dependent on the army trade (**66**). This is based on distribution, showing large gaps between the sources and the northern frontier where they are prolific finds. Other goods were shipped in them, about which we know nothing. But it makes no difference to the evidence the pots provide for trade across the province to serve the army of the north from the early second century until late in the fourth.

The overall extended population involved in producing South-East Dorset Black Burnished 1 pottery has been estimated at up to 3750-10,000, based on a variety of factors and also acknowledging a fluctuation due to seasonal requirements (Allen and Fulford 1996). Even if only very approximately true it means a community of a size comparable to a legion or more could be supported largely by army contracts. Some enterprising Dorset BB1 potters seem to have moved themselves north to Rossington Bridge in Yorkshire to service the northern military market. Their goods turn up at various forts, but particularly along the Antonine Wall. The question here must be how far we can take this kind of association between a military force and a pottery industry. One study would have it that *II Augusta*'s movements are trackable in 'bulges' in the frequency of BB1 wares up into Wales (Fulford 1996), but this ignores incidences of bulges prior to the legion being testified in the area and is one of those examples of archaeological optimism that believes history can be reconstructed from artefacts. It may perhaps be possible to link pottery industries with the army, but generally attaching them to specific units is taking things beyond the limits of archaeological evidence.

Even so, a number of pottery producers supplied more to the army than anyone else, particularly up to the end of the third century. Gaulish samian is the prime example, but it is just as applicable to Dorset BB1. Samian was widely used in the Western Empire during the first two centuries AD, but whether its massive growth was a consequence of military sales, or a cause, is unknown. Other fine wares, for example beakers from the Rhineland and Nene Valley goods, seem to be more concentrated in the major military bases than anywhere else, reflecting their roles as regional commercial centres. Corbridge began life as a fort under Agricola. A complicated series of developments on a nearby site about half a mile to the east began with a second-century fort which eventually ended up as a town. One of the buildings is the so-called 'unfinished store building' which, it has been pointed out, resembles the Piazza of the Corporations at Ostia, the port of Rome. It was perhaps intended as a frontline trading centre where the commercial world of the Roman Empire mingled with the frontier troops of northern Britain.

So the Roman army was fundamental to the circulation of particular wares not only in the first instance but continuing to do so for many years. Other, local, wares remained local when they were not brought into the military market and continued to service local demand. It would be interesting to know whether the military effect on pottery (and by extension other industries) was due to contracts, long-term or short-term. None survives, so there is no means of telling but it is improbable that the definitive bias noted in ceramic deposits was due to piecemeal sales. Formal long-term arrangements of a sort must have existed.

Large numbers of troops were withdrawn from Britain by the governor, Clodius Albinus, to support his unsuccessful bid for power in the civil war of 193-7. The appearance at the end of the second century of North-African-type kitchenware forms (mainly casseroles) in York, but made locally, has been attributed to the arrival of reinforcements from North Africa for *VI Victrix* after 197 (Swan 1992). This is an interesting conclusion to draw, as the reason might equally be local fashion or a fad but it does not affect the point that the military settlement seems to have been the centre and stimulus of the trend. The pottery forms here make the connection easier to draw, but it may very well be that much of the ceramic market was similarly directed by military tastes.

Another overall effect of this military ceramic market was not just to make Roman types and wares widespread, including areas where pottery was a novelty, but also to create universal products. A soldier in Britain, and a local person, will have been presented with a similar range of products in almost every part of the province. The well-known hemispherical decorated samian bowls of the Antonine potter Cinnamus (140-80), and many others, turn up frequently in sites across Britain. The same applies to Nene Valley beakers, and even the widely distributed BB1 kitchenware forms. Roman pottery was therefore both widespread and often broadly consistent in forms, but styles also evolved locally, drawing influences from regional markets and traditions.

The archaeological basis for many of these conclusions is thanks to the easily identifiable products of named potters, and well-known sources. By the early second century, military pottery production had almost ceased as local industries, together with imports, were not only able to supply the army but also the burgeoning civilian market in the developing towns. In the late third and fourth centuries the position is very different. Imports dwindled as pottery production, along with much else in the Roman economy, became more regionalized. Secondly, the Romano-British products which were created to fill the gaps are much more difficult to date owing to the virtual disappearance of samian, the cessation of name-stamping by mortaria potters, and the absence of idiosyncratic and personalized decorative styles. The fine wares of the Oxfordshire region, and the Nene Valley, for example, are almost completely anonymous, and along with almost all other late wares, dating relies on typology. Typological dates depend on finding varieties in tightly dated deposits. Whereas this is comparatively easy for the first and second centuries, thanks to the sound historical framework for events like the Boudican Revolt and the building of Hadrian's Wall we have no such well-dated events, associated with identifiable deposits, in the later period. So, it is commonplace to see vessels attributed to a period of up to 150 years.

The overall consequence is that in late Roman Britain, unless a pottery industry was physically close to a military area its products were normally unlikely to find their way into the forts other than in small quantities. There was no imported equivalent of samian, which saturated the market in the same way, and few testified events, which would fix deposits in the chronology. The third- and fourth-century fine wares produced in the south, for example Oxfordshire and the Nene Valley, have distribution patterns heavily biased to the south, supplemented there by other, even more regional sources, such as Portchester ware — named for the Saxon Shore fort where it was identified — which appears only in south-east England.

Dorset BB1 continued to buck the trend and remained important in the north, showing that whatever drove the military market was still functioning. The Crambeck industry, sited on hills to the south of the Vale of York, started operating in the late third century. It remained modest until about 350 by when it had become one of the biggest single sources of pottery at a number of places in northern Britain. By then it had added fine wares to its repertoire of grey wares. Crambeck grey ware was distributed prolifically to the north of its production source in the forts and civilian settlements, supplanting even BB1 by 370-400. Perhaps caused by restrictions following the late division of Britain into four provinces, it is scarcely known further south. In southern England the Alice Holt/Farnham grey ware industry monopolised the civilian and military grey ware market.

Glass is less well known than pottery, partly because less survives and is much harder to attribute to a production source. Glass manufacture in York, at Coppergate in the late second and early third century, might have been by *VI Victrix* (Cool et al 1999). At Caerleon, the legionary museum site produced 134 irregular small cubes of blue glass of a type recognized elsewhere in the fortress and civilian settlement (Zienkiewicz 1993, 105-6). They are believed to have been for use in the production of beads, or possibly enamel. Enamelling was widely used as a decorative inlay for metal objects, typically brooches and other decorative items, but even so this at first sight seems to be a remarkable luxury even for a legion. In fact it only goes to reflect the complexity of the Roman army, and Vegetius' description of its camps as small towns.

Metalworking and leatherworking

Metalworking meant in the first instance, obtaining the metals. That the military had involvement in lead and iron extraction has already been mentioned, but it is not possible to track these and other metals into the forts in the way pottery fabrics can be linked to specific sources and even kilns. Only stamped ingots can help us and, naturally, their value means that they were rarely lost and by definition were made to be used. There are, for example, no ingots of copper stamped with anything demonstrating military connections yet Roman armour made great use of copper-alloy fittings.

Iron was the most widely used metal in the Roman army, not just for weapons but also for more mundane goods like nails and fittings. Iron nails were buried in their hundreds and thousands at Inchtuthil and Elginhaugh once both were abandoned in the mid-80s and demolished, to keep them out of enemy hands and save transport (Pitts and St Joseph 1985). The evidence for manufacturing though is normally confined to traces of slag, for

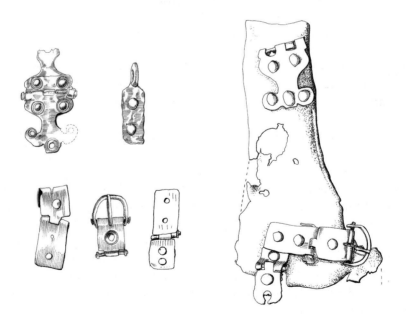

67 Lorica segmentata *parts. Clockwise from upper left: hinge unit, and tie-hook from Verulamium; neck plate and buckles from the Bank of England, London; buckle from Kingsholm, buckle from Richborough, and buckle from Verulamium. Compare with* **39** *and* **47**. *Note that several of these parts come from towns, not forts. (After various sources)*

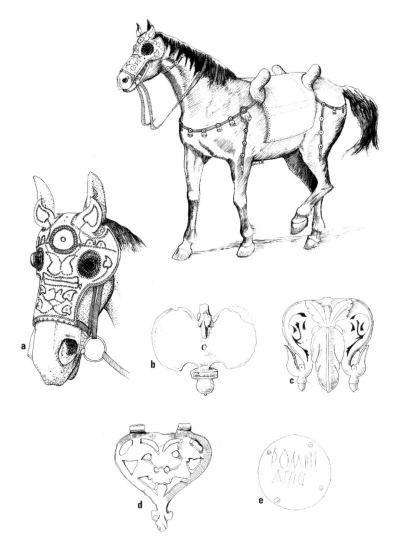

68 *Horse fittings.* **a**. *studded leather head-dress from Newstead.* **b**. *tinned bronze pendant from Kingsholm.* **c**. *tinned bronze pendant from Newstead.* **d**. *tinned bronze pendant from Vindolanda.* **e**. *tinned bronze pendant from Newstead, inscribed* Dometi Attici, *'property of Dometius Atticus'*

example in the works depot at Longthorpe where iron ore from a source a little over five miles (9km) away upriver was exploited (Dannell and Wild 1987, 65). Forts were thus equipped with a *fabrica*, literally a manufactory, where smiths could turn out the goods on demand, produce new components for repair, and stockpile reserves. Only a small part of the Exeter legionary *fabrica* was excavated, but amongst general rubbish and material gathered from troughs designed to collect lathe waste were components from a type of armour now known as *lorica segmentata* (**39**, **47** & **67**). The type is normally now associated with legionaries, but this is not completely certain and concluding the presence of legionaries on the basis of a few scraps of this armour is surely not tenable. Created out of

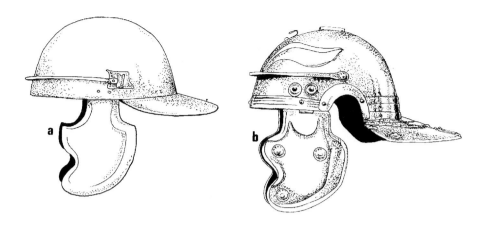

69 *Helmets.* ***a***. *'coolus' helmet of mid-first-century date.* ***b***. *'imperial Gallic helmet' from the late first century on*

a series of overlapping iron plates, the armour was held together with leather and a variety of buckles and will have 'required frequent repairs to its flimsy fittings' (Bidwell 1980, 35). Together with the fittings required for horse equipment, every military installation featured this kind of work as a continuous daily activity (**68**, **69**).

Evidence for associated leatherwork is considerably more dependent on waterlogged or anaerobic conditions, allowing its preservation. But leather was an integral part of the production of arms and equipment for the Roman army. Castleford, for example, has yielded traces of evidence for the production of leather saddles, and extensive evidence for repair and renovation of leather equipment. The exceptional conditions at Vindolanda have not only preserved a vast array of leather goods, but also evidence for the process of tanning. This primarily subsisted in the form of animal skulls and hoof bones, probably the remains of butchered carcasses sent to the tannery as a hide from which the main part of the body had been removed for meat. However, the organic preservation here meant that traces of urine and faeces remained — essential for the process of curing leather, however revolting that might sound to a modern ear, and is a reminder that the Roman fort and associated settlement was a place which stank.

That retention of equipment through storage and repair was managed is plain from the helmets bearing a series of names punched into the neck-guard. One from London, of mid-first-century date, carries the name of four different soldiers (*RIB* 2425.2). During the first two centuries AD at least, production of equipment seems to have been mainly on a fort self-sufficiency basis. Julius Vitalis, an armourer of *XX* who died at Bath, was buried at the expense of his colleagues in their *collegium fabricensium* (**57**). In the fourth century, as part of the centralisation of control, production was largely removed to the state manufacturing centres, recorded in the *Notitia Dignitatum*, which specifies location and the goods manufactured. The purpose may in part have been to compensate for military disruption and consequent difficulties in maintaining production within units (James 1988, 270). For example, the apparently permanent loss of a vexillation of *XX* through its possible transfer to Pannonia under Gallienus could have wrecked an organisation, which was earlier able to operate its works depot at Holt.

The most remarkable cache of military equipment from Britain was found in the remains of an ironbound wooden chest buried at Corbridge *c.*120-50 (Allason-Jones and Bishop 1988). The box contained parts from several *lorica segmentata* cuirasses, along with parts of tools such as a saw and a pulley wheel, spearheads, nails and various other items. As none of the cuirasses was complete and many of the parts were damaged or worn from use it was probably material collected as a general 'spares' box. Any engineer or mechanic today is likely to accumulate something like this on the 'it might come in handy one day' principle.

Metal goods are rarely marked in any way that would help us date or attribute them. The most important of all are the lead water pipes from the fortress at Chester naming Gnaeus Julius Agricola and give imperial titles for 79 (*see* **18**). At the very least these are evidence for lead extraction and use by military authorities, at the governor's behest, to introduce facilities of a type beyond comprehension to the Britons a few years before.

Decorative personal items like parade armour shield bosses, brooches and baldrics have an additional significance and are discussed in chapter 6, but their production too probably took place in or around military settlements. Castleford, for example, has produced evidence of copper-working, as well as an unfinished brooch (Cool 1998, 359). The Ribchester helmet (**93**) is a considerable technical achievement and illustrates the availability of highly skilled artists as well as artists amongst metalworkers servicing the army. Brooches in particular already existed in Britain but the coming of the army led to a proliferation of types and designs, which eventually generated a British range of forms representing a synthesis of continental and British traditions.

Summary

There is no means of compiling any valid economic breakdown of the Roman economy in Britain. All we can do is look at the artefactual record to build up some sort of picture. While the military impact was neither exclusive, nor ubiquitous, it does seem to have been very substantial. The army was a major factor in influencing a liquid economy, and its demands on resources, products and infrastructure, as well as its capacity to produce these where they were not otherwise available, were fundamental to building up Britain as a province. Artefactual evidence is one of the best reflections of Josephus' contemporary description of the Roman army as a mobile town. Most significant civilian settlements developed at locations which had earlier been forts, like Cirencester, or which lay on routes associated with the military advance, like Verulamium. In time, the impact became more diffuse, but part of the reason for this is that the evidence from later periods is simply less helpful for any kind of detailed, dated, typological analysis.

6

ART, RELIGION AND CULTURE

As a source of skills, finance, and stimulus through patronage in Britain, the Roman army was unparalleled and unprecedented. This led to a conflation of indigenous culture with Roman military provincial culture, itself a mixture of different traditions from across the Empire and beyond its boundaries (**70**). Throughout the first two centuries of Roman occupation the army was the most conspicuous, albeit brutal, face of the classical world. It also served as the most effective conduit through which indigenous British tribal culture has come down to us.

While it was never the exclusive force behind Roman culture the army was always significant and often the most important. This is illustrated by the fact that its impact depended on the level of its presence either in the form of stationed units or individuals serving on detachment, or whether places were associated with the communications network serving the frontier zones. The south-west peninsula beyond Exeter, despite being home to a small fort at Nanstallon and being a source of useful metals like tin (*see* **Map 2**), seems virtually to have escaped a Roman military presence and the evidence for Roman culture in almost every form is practically absent. No further from London than Hadrian's Wall, the only difference was the absence of the army, and the absence of much evidence for an associated infrastructure until the fourth century when milestones show that a road system existed there. The example serves to show that Romanization was an intensely variable phenomenon, reflecting almost certainly that it was a piecemeal and largely transient force which depended on a military momentum and was thereby almost incidental, rather than a deliberate and concerted policy.

The impact of the army began from the outset, bringing fundamental new ways of perceiving the world. These were not exclusive to the army, but the army was the main force bringing them. Many towns of consequence began life as a fort, however briefly, even if a tribal settlement had existed nearby before the invasion (**71**). The colonies were even more prominent installations of Roman society in a military form. Explicitly devised as models of civilised Mediterranean urban life, they were occupied very largely by ex-soldiers from Britain and elsewhere. They were supposed to serve as living examples of the benefits of Roman law, culture and society. However, colonies were usually inhabited by people whose experience and standards of life had been developed in the Roman military world, even where they were patently bad, corrupt and ruthless. This was in complete contrast to conquered territories around the Mediterranean and the East where sophisticated urban civilisations were already well established. Britain experienced urbanization in a brutal military form from the beginning.

In the surviving record Roman soldiers are always disproportionately prominent. Tombstones, statues, altars, dedications, building inscriptions — anything in which the

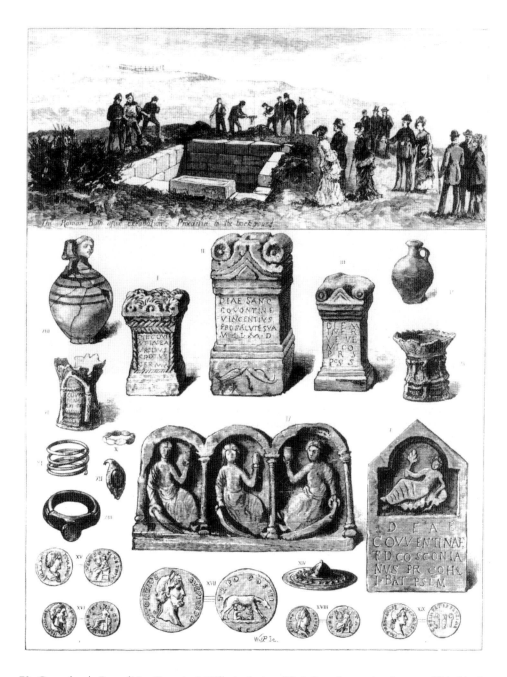

70 *Carrawburgh, Brocolitia, Coventina's Well. A selection of finds from the sacred spring, as published in the* Illustrated London News *of 15 November 1876. Altars, carved reliefs, jewellery, coins, and a curious pair of pottery pedestals (see **87**), were all found tumbled into the spring, resulting from the Roman military veneration of a local goddess. Visitors are shown clustering around the findspot — many finds were removed and lost as a result of popular interest*

71 *Leicester,* Ratae Corieltauvorum, *part of the baths' exercise hall, which owes its exceptional survival by being incorporated into a church, itself superseded by St Nicholas church, visible beyond. Evidence for a fort here survives in the form of military artefacts, a military-style ditch, and early timber buildings. The name* Ratae *may preserve a reference to the pre-Roman defensive ditches of a tribal settlement. By the end of the first century the site had been given up to the civitas capital of the Corieltauvi, with the baths being part of a major civic centre development of c.130-50, perhaps directed by military architects. This pattern was played out at many other towns*

identity of the person or persons responsible is known — were set up, commissioned or made more often by soldiers than any other identifiable group, and turn up at military sites more frequently than anywhere else (**110**). But at around one percent of the theoretical population it is surprising that soldiers dominate the tombstone record, even in 'civilian' settlements (**2, 24, 40**). This is partly due to the distribution of surviving monuments, but the same bias turns up in places like London and Bath, or where a brief but significant military period was followed by establishment of a colony or civitas capital, like Lincoln.

The dearth of tombstones at prominent towns such as Verulamium or Silchester may be because there never was a large-scale military presence there, rather than being due to post-Roman stone-robbing, in spite of a suggestion that Silchester's street grid may preserve an otherwise undetected legionary fortress (Crummy 1990). This helps confirm a suggestion already made that structural and artefact evidence points only to brief and peripheral military activity at these towns (Millett 1990, 77). That leads to the more radical suggestion that a far higher proportion of the detritus we interpret as evidence for the Romanization of Britain was restricted to the military population than ever thought, even in the settled civilian zone where Romanization has been traditionally considered to have been more successful through 'an alliance with Roman power' for the native élite (*ibid*, 101).

The demand for these symbols of Romanization amongst soldiers was in spite of the quality available. Most sculpture, for example, from the military zone is not only crude to our eyes but the average Roman soldier would have recognised that the products were often less accomplished than the work available to his colleagues on the German frontier. A tombstone from Chester and the Mithraic sculptures from London provide instances from opposite ends of the spectrum (**75**, **110**). The patrons in both cases were legionaries.

Coinage and the image of Britannia

Finer points of circulation aside (see chapter 5) in antiquity coins were vehicles for publicity and a means of disseminating Roman standards of weight and reliability as well as imagery. The image and name of the emperor were propelled into every corner of Britain. Those who could not read still became accustomed to the image of their ruler. Even for them the coin legends will have brought the Roman alphabet into everyday life on a routine basis. British coins were much more abstract in the images they portrayed and lettering was minimal, quite apart from circulating in far smaller numbers.

Roman coins distributed the classical idiom of realism, converting the apocryphal tales of emperors into vivid images, some of which have the power to shock or impress even today. The climax of Roman coin portraiture was roughly equivalent to the first century of Roman occupation in Britain, dispersing compelling portraits of Nero, Vespasian, Domitian and Hadrian amongst others, across the province (**6**, **61**, **colour plate 4**).

Events in Britain were generally absent from the coin types in the first century. Claudius' victory was commemorated on extremely rare silver and gold coins in a reign marked in any case by a general dearth of coin striking. Nero, not surprisingly, omitted any celebration of defeating Boudica but in any case exercised little personal control over his regime until 64. Equally, as he had murdered Claudius' son Britannicus (named for the invasion), any coin referring to Britannia might have encouraged the idea that he had assassinated the legitimate heir. Neither Vespasian nor Titus mentioned Agricola's activities, which is curious given Vespasian's personal experience in the province. Domitian had his own reasons for ignoring Agricola.

Instead, reverses presented a series of Roman concepts, formulae and styles (**72**). Typical was the radical (for Britain) idea that values, gods or places could be presented in human form. While the Roman army was not specifically responsible for this, as the main route through which coinage arrived it was fundamental to the proliferation of these concepts, and equally their disappearance when coinage no longer arrived to pay them. Not surprisingly then, the dominant coinage issues tended to promote virtues or topics of appeal to soldiers like Victory or Moneta, and a more general pride in Roman imperial qualities, such as Aequitas, Felicitas or Pax. In the fourth century this suggestiveness gave way to more explicit appeals, such as *Gloria Exercitus*, 'the Glorious Army', under Constantine, and *Gloria Romanorum*, 'Glory of the Romans', under Valentinian. It is almost impossible to know whether any attention was paid to these, but Coventina's Well at Carrawburgh and the sacred spring at Bath contained a disproportionately large number

72 *Many coin reverses carried figures which evoked Rome's martial and triumphant image, frequently reflected on sculptures found in Britain's military zone. Clockwise from left: 'Eternal Rome' on a brass sestertius of Antoninus Pius, 138-61; Victory on a denarius of Vitellius, 69; Minerva Victrix on a denarius of Domitian, 92-3; Victory on a denarius of Commodus, 185-6; Victory on a denarius of Septimius Severus, 202-11*

of female-type reverses, suggesting they had been specially chosen as gifts to female deities (in spite of the ambivalent identity of Sulis).

The image of Britannia was a product both of the presence of the army as well as the classical perception of concepts in human form. She found her widest expression in coinage. The oldest word known for Britain is *Albion*, but the Greeks called her *Pretannia*, eventually Latinized into *Britannia* by the mid-first century BC. Britain as an entity was a concept created by those beyond her shores who needed a name for the remote island. To the indigenous tribes it was a continent, their homelands their nations. It is much more likely that they saw themselves as Catuvellaunians, Trinovantians, Atrebates, and so on, rather than 'Britons'. Indeed, Tacitus perceived this endemic sense of tribal individuality as the secret of their failure to resist Roman conquest (*Agr* 12.2).

Britannia the personification appears first as a defeated female figure being beaten down by Claudius on a marble relief of the mid-50s found at Aphrodisias in Asia Minor. There is no doubt about the identification — an inscription on the base identifies both Claudius and Britannia (Erim 1982). This device was entirely recognized, and used, across the ancient world to represent cities, provinces and places. The most familiar of all was Roma (**72**).

Under Hadrian Britannia was presented more widely as a personification, and labelled as such, on the reverse of a copper as issued around the year 119 (*see* **1**). She reappeared on now exceptionally scarce *sestertii* of the reign in part of a general series recording all the provinces, and again under Antoninus Pius on coins, which were struck in larger numbers in 143 and 154 (**colour plates 15, 16**). Her portrayal as a martial female in the Roman idiom is hard to reconcile with the idea that this is displaying the province in defeated form.

Perhaps the image is subtler, and instead she represents Britannia as a military Roman province, rather than the defeated enemy who in any case by then existed physically and psychologically outside the Roman province. Necessarily this reflected Britain's position on the edge of Empire, her own mix of the barbaric and the classical, mirroring the nature of her garrison. The general rareness of these coins, and the disappearance of Britannia or even references to her after the reign of Severus (except under Carausius), makes it unlikely they had much effect, unless they were removed from circulation for their notoriety and interest — a phenomenon well known throughout the ages.

The human form

When the Roman army arrived in Britain the concept of realistic representation was still new. Apart from the tribal coins, some of which bore recognizable human forms, representations of beings were largely confined to imported goods such as the decoration on Roman silver, glass or fine red-slip ware, as well as Roman coinage. British coins bearing realistic human images were very derivative of Roman models. Naturalistic statues did not exist apart from imports, gods were rarely portrayed in human form, and individual portraits were not made, though there were figures and representations of humans exhibiting characteristics normally described as 'native'. This has always been a rather controversial point of view. 'Native' styles of human representation tend to have much in common with juvenile efforts, such as exaggerated eyes and a tendency to construct features from protuberances rather than imply them. Style, or lack of it, was certainly durable and lasted into and through the Roman period (**76**). The forum at Wroxeter has produced parts of a column capital decorated with curly-haired male busts and their distinct protuberant lozenge-shaped eyes (White & Barker, 97). Examples which retained these features continued to be produced in the Roman and medieval period.

There is an important distinction to be made here. Animals were well established in the canon of art in Britain before 43, with particular interest in beasts symbolic of power and strength, such as boars and stags. This preference can be seen on tribal coinage, which featured an extensive array of abstract animal images, gradually developing into more realistic representations in the decades just before the invasion.

Generally speaking, maturity of skill tends to involve more subtle treatment of features. So, whether native art represents a different technique, a lack of technique, or even a deliberate sleight on classical styles, is an interesting subject to debate. Perhaps a useful comparison is the tradition of portraiture in the seventeenth to nineteenth centuries. The work of painters like Thomas Gainsborough and Sir Joshua Reynolds, whose paintings of the great and rich are regarded as amongst the pinnacle of portrait art of their age, was emulated with increasing crudity by provincial artists, not only in Britain but also in the colonies, and later states, of America. The customers of the lesser artists wanted to buy into an artistic trend but had neither the funds to purchase the labour of first-rate artists nor even, perhaps, the critical faculties to appreciate the difference. The results are simply poor by comparison, and there is really no need to see works like the High Rochester Venus (**77**) as anything other than the product of a Romano-British country town would-be Reynolds.

It is impossible to measure the rate, and distribution, of classical sculptural models into Britain. Titus was popular in Britain and Germany and was said to have been the subject of numerous statues in both provinces (Suetonius, *Titus* iv.1). None survives so either the information is wrong, or the statues were all destroyed, with some perhaps yet to be found. A small number of portrait busts from southern Britain have survived but dating them more than very generally is impossible. The fragment of a child's bust from Fishbourne is dated to 'the late first century AD' and the identity a mystery. Even the well-preserved marble portrait busts from the villa at Lullingstone can only be attributed to the mid- to late second century and remain generic examples of well-known types rather than identifiable individuals. But the exceptional circumstances of recovery at both sites just goes to show that we will never know how and where classical imagery entered Britain in this form.

On the evidence of other parts of the Empire, the major buildings and precincts within towns and forts will have been decorated with sculpture on a variety of martial and imperial themes, and of classical

73 *Housesteads,* Vercovicium. *Relief of Victory found lying in ground south of the fort (compare with **72**). Probably once displayed on a gate, or perhaps the headquarters. Height 1.39m. CP 100*

form. An eagle's torso, carved from marble and found in a pit in a mid-first-century barrack block at Exeter, is probably all that survives of a group depicting an emperor, presumably Claudius or Nero, as Jupiter (Bidwell 1980, 38, fig. 22). Larger pieces of lesser quality pieces survive from the gates and major buildings in the forts of Hadrian's Wall (**73**). Bronze statues are extremely rare, for fairly obvious reasons, but they were once prominent features of cities and fortresses as scattered fragments demonstrate, like the severed bronze finger from a life-sized statue once erected in the fort at Carvoran (*CP* no. 364). Most major settlements have produced traces, but larger examples like the bust of Claudius from Suffolk and that of Hadrian from London are exceptional. Both survived only through being hacked from the main figure and dumped in rivers (*see* **4**).

This classicism extended to small, private, figures as well but in a more provincial form. The Fossdike Mars (**74**), a bronze figurine hurled into the dyke as a votive offering, and the Plaxtol Minerva, are both essentially classical in proportion and posture. Neither is specifically associated with the military though the Mars was found only a few miles from the legionary fortress and colony at Lincoln. The Minerva was found in a villa in Kent in the nineteenth century and probably once sat in the household shrine. Having

145

74 *Fossdike. Bronze figure of Mars, dedicated to Mars and the Spirits of the Emperors by the Colasuni brothers, Bruccius and Caratius, who had paid 100 sestertii for it. Made by Celatus the coppersmith who contributed three-denarii worth of bronze. Height 270mm. RIB 274*

said that, by far and away the majority of surviving dedications to both these martial deities comes from the military zone.

The Fossdike Mars was made for the Colasuni brothers, Bruccius and Caratius, recorded on the plinth (*RIB* 274). Their family name was manufactured from a 'Celtic' form, and the statuette itself was made by someone with a name which is certainly not obviously Roman. There is no indication that the maker, or the purchasers, were soldiers but the dedication to Mars and the Spirit(s) of the Emperor(s) is far more typical both of the military zone and soldiers in general. Mars here is also represented in military garb — his hands are now empty but they probably once held a spear and shield.

Roman army personnel, regardless of their own provincial origins, brought to Britain all their expectations of appearance, form and taste. They were already integrated into the world of Roman products, and were accompanied by traders and contractors who existed purely to service these requirements, though some of the skills will have been available amongst the troops themselves. Primus for instance, *custos armorum* (custodian of arms) in an unknown unit, carved his own altar to Hercules and Silvanus found at Haile in Cumbria (*RIB* 796). At Carvoran, Sabinus, who does not specify his position, 'made' an altar dedicated to Hammia (*RIB* 1780).

In civilian areas sculpture with military associations forms an important part of the record. The best-known are probably the Mithraic sculptures from London, all found in or around the Walbrook mithraeum. Mithraism was particularly popular in military and port areas so it is not very surprising to find a mithraeum in Britain's premier Roman town. The cache of sculpture from the site remains the most

75 *Walbrook, London. Marble Mithraic relief found in 1889 close to where the Mithraeum was found in 1954. It shows Mithras slaying the bull, surrounded by the zodiac, and is inscribed: 'Ulpius Silvanus, veteran of* II Augusta, *paid his vow'. The phrase* Factus Arausione *may mean he enlisted at Orange, or, more likely, that that stone was made there. Diameter 558mm.* RIB 3

significant found in London. One of the reliefs, a piece of unusually high quality for Britain, identifies its commissioner as Ulpius Silvanus, a veteran of *II Augusta* (**75**). Other known British mithraea are all in the military zone, at Housesteads, Carrawburgh, Rudchester and Caernarvon, while Mithraic sculpture from Chester must mean there was a mithraeum there too.

London's importance means that the numbers of sculpture and inscriptions from it are high for south-eastern Britain. The major port meant suitable stone could be shipped in for official purposes, as well as the local military market like the Mithraic patrons. The rest of the region has produced minute quantities and even less that is identifiable. Almost the sole instance from the southern part of Kent is an altar, this time dedicated to Neptune by Lucius Aufidius Pantera, prefect of the fleet in the early second century (*see* **111**). Further west, Winchester's sole legible epigraphic product is an altar to various mother goddesses by Antonius Lucretianus, *beneficiarius consularis*, and thus a soldier detached to the governor's staff (*RIB* 88).

The Roman figure of Victory was a familiar theme from Roman coinage and military fort sculpture, for example from the headquarters building at Housesteads (**72 & 73**). The casual discovery of a small relief of Victory placing a wreath on an altar in a gabled niche at Bolton, 12 miles (17km) east of York, was made in a rural area where Roman sculpture is scarce, is hard to explain (Halkon 1998). However, the find-spot is only four miles from two locations with military origins, though a temple site is also known less than three miles away at Millington. One possibility which has been suggested is that it was erected on land owned by a veteran from the colony at York, though of course it might also be a small rural shrine. Although the style is crude, the present writer's own experiments suggest that the results are similar to those achievable by any reasonably handy person trying sculpture for the first time. As Halkon himself notes, such figures are almost all known from military sites, together with the general lack of anthropomorphic sculpture in the area, which makes it almost inevitable that the altar was made for, or by, a soldier.

One of the most conspicuous collections of carved stonework in Britain is the series of commemorative slabs set up by the legions on the Antonine Wall. These are distinctive for their indulgent use of elaborate decorative features, compared to which the inscribed slabs from Hadrian's Wall seem bland and perfunctory. In some cases, the indulgence went no further than complex borders, wreaths and scrolls, occasionally embellished by animal heads or animal symbols of the legion (for example *RIB* 2173, 2196, and 2198).

There is a marked crudity in much of the sculpture found throughout the northern military zone. The intention and desire to execute sculpture is there, but apparently little real skill, amply exhibited by a representation of Sol from Corbridge (**76**). A similar lack of finesse appears on the Adamklissi monument, erected to commemorate Trajan's campaign in Dacia. Both seem to have been a product of the will to erect monumental sculpture modelled on classical stereotypes, but without the skilled manpower available to execute something of the first or second rank. Although there is a difference in style, the Corbridge slab and Adamklissi figures share clumsy representation of the eyes, and a complete lack of fluidity and dynamic in the figures. Amongst educated Romans an accurate use of proportion was considered fundamental to a successful result (Pliny the Younger, *Letters*, i.20.5).

A figure of Victory from Castlesteads bearing a wreath is well proportioned but with little sense of depth or fluidity and a total lack of refinement in detail (*RIB* 1995, *CA* 103). In fact it so resembles the Victory coins issued by Antoninus Pius in 143 that it may very well have been copied from one. An even less well-executed example is a building stone from South Shields, recording the erection of 102ft of wall(?) by a century of *VI Victrix* (*B* 1987, 368, no. 8). The text is carved within a wreath borne by two figures of a type which might very well be described as 'Celtic' or 'native' had the context been a Cotswold rural shrine. But that does not alter the point that they were executed, and that the sculptors' superiors condoned or commissioned them. Here it is the desire that matters, and it was a desire borne out of a community that found its models in the classical world and this was what they brought to Britain's northern frontier. Had they been able to do better, or commission more competent work, they would have and this is what we can see in the Victor and Regina tombstones from South Shields (**84, 118**). The aspiration was towards

76 *Slab from Corbridge* Coriosopitum, *depicting the Sun-god, Sol. The carving either represents a fusion of Roman and 'Celtic' tradition in the depiction of a classical image with bulging eyes and protuberant mouth, or the failure of execution over intent produced by a sculptor who was unable to create competent work. Found reused in the east granary, but probably once from a nearby temple. Third century. P 56*

the classical; success or failure was dictated by the available skill. The relief of Venus washing from High Rochester is a good example of amateur art but in a sophisticated and educated idiom (**77 & 78**).

These themes were not confined to sculpture. A Gaulish samian bowl was not only a functional requirement brought in on trading systems driven by military demand, but carried on it familiar imagery which reflected, reinforced and promoted Romanized iconography. The range of samian forms available to the military market was much higher than it was for the civilian in Britain. In fact this mostly involved the plain types, but the hemispherical Form 37 bowl, found in huge numbers in military and civilian locations, was manufactured between *c.*75-230 and was invariably decorated with a variety of motifs (**79**). The standard leafs, tendrils, beaded borders, arches and columns, all generally recall aspects of Roman decoration and the love of gardens. Styles also include depictions of gods and goddesses, animals, hunting scenes, and gladiatorial bouts, which reflected activities and concerns soldiers were fond of, and transmitted them into more general Romano-British society (**colour plate 11**). Samian decoration also mirrored the rationalism and order of the classical world. Consistent in form, and produced in a variety of broadly regimented styles, each decorated bowl was characterised by repetition, just as coins repeated consistent imperial portraits. The tribal population of Britain had no idea what their leaders looked like unless they had seen them in person. For the same reason, we have no idea even of their names. But their descendants could recognize Vespasian, Domitian or Hadrian without hesitation, in a new concept of individual, naturalistic representation.

As new goods were produced in Britain so makers drew on that extensive panorama of Roman iconography, but also took their influences from local traditions. The results were often that special combination of barbarism and realism that was uniquely

77 *(above) Carved relief of Venus, bathing with her nymph hand-servants, from High Rochester, Bremenium. Classical in concept and layout, the work is entirely provincial in execution — reminiscent of a modern child's version of a classic Renaissance painting of a mythological subject, just as this was modelled on classical prototypes dating back to third-century BC Greece. Diameter 1.07m. P 218*

78 *(left) Figure of the 'Genius of the century' dedicated by the century of Bassilius Crescens.* RIB *944*

79 *Samian. Part of a late first-century South Gaulish Form 37 bowl with characteristic upper row of 'ovolo' devices, above a series of rectangular panels containing stock figures. On the right is a Victory holding a wreath, lower centre a cupid, upper centre a dog attacks a man, and on the left a hand can be seen holding a crested helmet appropriate to Minerva Victrix. Bowls like this flooded into Britain's military and commercial centres from the 70s onward*

Roman-provincial and found individual expression in every part of the Empire. There are innumerable examples such as the pediment from the Temple of Sulis Minerva at Bath, or the enamelled trumpet brooches (**89**). The principal exceptions were wall-painting and mosaics, features which became typical of civilian Roman Britain, particularly in the fourth-century villas, but which seem to have been substantially absent from Romano-British military establishments at all times though identification and recovery may be part of the problem. Only the legionary fortresses seem to be significant, but limited, exceptions. The legionary baths at Exeter and Caerleon, both fortresses being attributed to *II Augusta*, are two of these. Perhaps this was thanks to *II Augusta* having a taste for mosaics, or mosaicists-in-residence, in the late first century — there is certainly a case to be made for an architectural connection between the two places. Other fragmentary later pavements, or reports of them, at Caerleon, and rather more at York, may be better attributed to civilian tastes and skills. Caerleon, after all, was close to the civitas capital at Caerwent, and not much further from the proliferating world of third- and fourth-century villas. York of course was as much a civilian colony as it was a fortress.

80 *Decorative cheek-piece from an auxiliary cavalryman's helmet, depicting Castor or Pollux. From South Shields*, Arbeia. *Height 200mm*

Within 50 years of the invasion, soldiers had carried their possessions and preferences into every part of Britain. As the military economy spread systematically or haphazardly across the lowlands of the south and on and up into Wales and northern Britain, so the iconography of samian, brooches, intaglios, coins and sculpture went with it. While the density of soldiers inevitably reduced as the army was further and further dispersed, the importance will still have lain in the sheer conspicuousness of consumption and the supply trains which straggled across Britain. Soldiers, as individuals or in units, and their support systems will have been a continuous feature of all trunk routes and settlements along them. The samian, mortaria, and whetstones which tumbled into the gutter during the catastrophic mid-second-century forum fire at Wroxeter had been shipped that way up routes established to feed the forts of North Wales, including the fortress at Chester, and perhaps the forts of the north-west. This was an area which prior to the invasion had made no use either of coinage or pottery.

The very appearance of the army in its own right created through patronage and demand the most forceful, and unified, image of the Roman world. This extended from the underlying functional and aesthetic concepts inherent in the design of armour, helmets, spears, and shields, to the decorative details exhibited on helmets, shield bosses, scabbards, and hilts (**80, colour plates 3**, **8**, **9**, **17 & 18**). This sense of regularity and reliability was mirrored in the military camp which can be defined by its order and symmetry, being borne as it was out of a society which had grown powerful out of order.

A foot soldier is equipped with breastplate, helmet and a blade on either side of his body. The one on the left is much the longest, and the other is only nine inches [22cm] long. The CO's bodyguard of picked infantry carry a lance and small round shield. The other centuries a javelin and long shield, saw, basket, axe, pick, and also a strap, crop-harvesting hook, chain, and enough food for three days. The infantry soldier resembles a baggage mule!

Josephus, *The Jewish War*, iii.3-6

The army was not quite as regimented as the account implies, but the imagery was as potent then as it is now. The army even contributed to the definition and identity of the province.

Tombstones

If the coins bearing Britannia reflected the province's identity, it was an accurate one at least as far as the tombstone record is concerned. Tombstones form a limited, but the most significant, relic of the Romano-British population. A small proportion are amongst the most important evidence we have for naturalistic human representation, though few bear comparison with the quality of sculpture available in the rest of the Empire and there is great variation in quality and competence of execution. In Britain there is a distinct bias to the military at all times and in all places, but fewer survive than in other provinces and even fewer have complete inscriptions. The vicissitudes of time are partly to blame, with many examples only having survived thanks to being reused in medieval walls or churches.

Regardless of the level of competence, most Romano-British tombstones conform to stereotypes already well known from the rest of the Roman world, reflecting how the idea was imported. On the whole, they are very scarce in Britain and virtually absent from large areas, especially in the southern, civilian, zone. Part of a tombstone found in the 1980s at Wool, Dorset, was only drawn to the present author's attention in 2000 as a result of a television programme (*B* 2000, 433, no. 2). Recovered from a part of the country where inscriptions are virtually unknown, it had gone unrecognised as a Roman tombstone by local museums and goes to show how unreliable the extant record may be.

Even so, the likelihood is that tombstones were not widely used in Roman Britain though of course wooden examples may have been much more common than we can ever possibly assess. Ancaster in Lincolnshire was a small Roman town where finds of carved stonework are well known. No tombstones have been recovered, in spite of excavations of cemetery areas, making it improbable local inhabitants made much use of them. But Ancaster stone was certainly used for tombstones, and was exported around the province. Even when they do turn up, dating civilian tombstones is usually extremely difficult. Only when the names contain elements drawn from imperial names, such as Ulpius (from Trajan, 98-117), is it possible to suggest a *terminus post quem*. The only specifically early civilian tombstone we have is that of the procurator Classicianus (*c.*62-75, *RIB* 12). Conversely, at the fort of Brecon y Gaer in Wales, to take just one military site, three tombstones are recorded. Two at least of these record soldiers, while the third, of a man and erected by his wife, was probably also a soldier (*RIB* 403, 405, and 404).

This bias in the extant record reflects how Romano-British civilians apparently had little taste for monumental inscribed stones of any kind. Assuming that all examples were equally susceptible to reuse, destruction or removal, then the high proportion of military tombstones, even at civilian settlements, must be because the military had a marked preference for them. The tombstone is an emphatic assertion of status, with the auxiliary cavalrymen an especially interesting category. They exhibit a desire to promulgate amongst the descendants' peers their ancestor's *Romanitas* and rank, while in some cases proudly commemorating his own personal origins. Perhaps this was something the more general Romano-British felt no common desire to emulate, and which they never developed.

On the continent, military tombstones are commoner than they are at the principal legionary bases in Britain, even though many of the units operating in Britain had earlier been based on the Rhine frontier. Chester, for example, has one of Britain's largest groups at around 90 but at Mainz alone 300 are known (*see* **110**, Hope 1997, 247, n. 19). But numbers recording soldiers are still disproportionately higher across Britain. Of the remainder at most places, women and children — all potential military dependants — outnumber civilian men, raising the possibility that most of those women were actually military wives or daughters (*ibid*, 247 and n.17).

At Lincoln for example, only briefly a legionary fortress in the mid- to late first century, 12 tombstones record soldiers, but only nine commemorate civilians. Of the military tombstones, one of a *VI Victrix* veteran must be Hadrianic or later (*RIB* 252) (*see* **113**), but those recording soldiers of *II Adiutrix* (*see* **17**), and *VIIII Hispana*, as well as a veteran of *XIIII*, are all first century. In other words, just over half belong to at most *c*.71-100 and in fact they probably belong to little more than 10-15 years. Of the nine civilian tombstones, three cannot be assigned to either sex, four are female and two are male. That these might represent the next 300 years of Lincoln's time as a colony is a remarkable imbalance in any case, but the four female stones might very well also belong to the military phase.

The presence, or absence, of tombstones at all might then play a part in concluding whether there had ever been a fort on the site of a town. A military trade in tombstones might suggest, and make available, the practice to local civilians. But Sacer, who lived in Lincoln with his family, commemorated on a slab now built into a church (*see* **120**) was an Umbrian immigrant. Undatable, the stone might be contemporary with the military phase, or afterwards. Sacer's origin though makes it not improbable that he had been a soldier at some time. Verulamium is a large town where a military period is an hypothesis based on a few finds of military equipment. There is no epigraphic record to speak of. Had there been a fort at all, a handful of military tombstones might be expected on the example of other towns where a fort is testified from its physical remains. Silchester, another place without a military period, has produced more than 20 inscriptions but only one tombstone. Even the 20 inscriptions are more to do with the fact that the whole site was excavated in the nineteenth century. Had Lincoln, or any other city with a military phase, been treated thus we would probably have more than a hundred.

The bias is widespread. At Colchester, only a fortress in the 40s, three of the most important surviving tombstones are military and all are attributable to that short time or the years immediately following (*RIB* 200-1, 203). Fragments of around seven or eight others are known, but only one or two can be assigned to civilians and another is military (*RIB* 205). At Wroxeter, five out of six identifiable tombstones are military, and all demonstrably belong to a couple of decades in the first century. The other is of a woman, and a teenage boy, both of whom could have had a soldier for husband or father.

Gloucester, a legionary fortress established as a colony by the end of the first century, has yielded very few tombstones. *RIB* records two soldiers, and a third man who died too young to have had any significant military service at all. Both the military stones were found at some distance from the colony, probably from an earlier period military cemetery rather than one belonging to the town. A more recent discovery from a Roman cemetery site at Kingsholm by Gloucester adds another soldier, this time Lucius Valerius Aurelius, veteran of *XX Valeria Victrix*, but in 1995 one recording a civilian male was found (*B* 1984, 333, no.1, and 1998, 434-5). The latter is dated to the first century on style, but name and style attribute Valerius Aurelius to the late second century at the earliest and possibly the third. That the man depicted is elderly suggests an approximation of a portrait, but the clumsy distribution of the funerary text implies it may well have been bought from stock.

Caerleon remained a legionary fortress from the 70s until *c*.300 at least. Of 25 usable tombstones recorded in *RIB*, 12 are of soldiers including veterans, which is hardly surprising. Of the rest, eight are of adult women and three of teenagers or children, leaving two men of unspecified origin. None of the adult female stones name the husband as a soldier, though six of the soldier's tombstones credit the wife with having had the stone set up. It is unlikely the women were all wives to civilian men, given the context. It must be that soldiers and their wives were more likely to be commemorated this way.

Chester is similar. Here *RIB* records the tombstones of some 68 certain legionaries (mostly found reused in the city wall), one freedman, three slaves, and seven women (**110**). This is an exceptional cache, but perhaps more intriguing is the generally poor standard of production, reflecting the fortress's comparatively remote location.

Bath and London were two of Britain's premier settlements, but for completely different reasons. At neither place can the military tombstones be easily attributed to even short substantially military periods. Bath spent most of its time as a recreational religious health centre, and London was the provincial capital with a long-term but limited military presence. Bath, with its monumental shrine complex of temple, spring, and baths, sat on the Fosse Way, one of the great trans-Britannia routes of the Roman period. It was widely visited by pilgrims, those bent on revenge, idlers, pleasure-seekers, hypochondriacs and malingerers from across Britain and elsewhere in the north-western Roman Empire. If it ever had been a fort the time was brief and while it lay close to the military zone, it was also close to the largest concentration of great villas of the third and fourth centuries. Of the 11 identifiable tombstones from the site recorded in *RIB*, five are of soldiers (*see* **57**), one is a priest, one a decurion from Gloucester, and the remaining four are females. The same is true amongst the smaller group of Bath tombstones where no inscription survives. Of the four recorded, two are of soldiers, one is unidentifiable, and the fourth is an adult male of uncertain status (*CF* 45-8). The bias was not confined to tombstones. Eleven altars are recorded on which the dedicant can be identified (*see* **117**). Of those, six are by soldiers, three of whom served with *VI Victrix*, based the furthest away in York.

Bath might have been developed in the first instance as a military bathing establishment. Copies of Claudian coins, associated with early military sites, are well represented in the sacred spring though their post-64 obsolescence might have made them handy gifts from anyone at any time, and perhaps kept for the purpose. Bath's first-century origins make the spa difficult to attribute either to indigenous skills or inclinations, and in the mid-first century it is hard to see who else would have had the ability or tastes to develop it. On the Continent the army is linked to the establishment of several spa centres (Sauer 1999 (i)). However, any such conclusion in Bath's case rests almost entirely on the disproportionate number of military inscriptions erected by individuals. There is no evidence at Bath for the presence of units as a body, and no evidence of building by or for the army as a body. Others are happy to attribute Bath's development to romanized tribal leaders (Henig 1999). The case for either in this instance is not resolvable. But as we have seen, the military epigraphic bias is evident at every site where the army had a presence either as an institution, or as individuals. In this sense it is not necessarily any different from, say, Lincoln, which had a period as a fort and thereafter as a settlement to which veterans retired or through which soldiers passed.

Tombstones from London record members of several of the British-based legions. Of 14 legible funerary monuments recorded in *RIB*, seven are of soldiers (**24**, **40**), a baby and four females accounting for five of the latter. More recent discoveries include a *beneficiarius consularis* detached from a legion (and the shattered remnants of one recording a female child called Marciana (*JRS* 1962, 191; *B* 1982, 396). The standard of lettering on the latter is high and includes part of her father's name, Aurelius […]. Although not enough survives to give any indication of his career the name and the stone would be compatible with a soldier. Unlike, say, Lincoln or Colchester, London's military tombstones could belong to the longer-term. Not only were soldiers more likely to leave tombstones behind at places occupied by them for short periods, but they were more likely to be commemorated by them wherever and whenever they died. As L. Valerius Aurelius' stone at Gloucester suggests, this happened until the later third century and thereafter when epigraphy in Britain wholly ceased apart from milestones.

The practice, and the art and iconography, of the Roman tombstone in Britain thus was biased to the military, with probable implications for the availability of the skills to, and dissemination of the concept amongst, the civilian population. The recovery of what seems to be a blank funerary panel from the commandant's house at Housesteads suggests that sculptors built up stockpiles to produce a range, thereby contributing to the distinct genres which are so evident amongst funerary monuments (Crow 1995, 79). Their use as marks of status and identity, especially as symbols of entering mainstream Roman social structures, may have been a value structure not generally picked up by the wider Romano-British, unless they lived in and amongst current or former military communities and even then the evidence is thin. While the demand for conventional military tombstones evidently existed in the garrison of Britain it seems that getting hold of quality labour to produce them was difficult. A consistent characteristic is conformity to models found elsewhere, particularly in Germany, but to a standard almost always inferior. This implies importation of a demand, but a shortfall in the labour to satisfy it.

Having a tombstone was important to a soldier. It represented arrangements and investment. They were marks of distinction setting the Roman soldier and his family apart in death from indigenous communities. In time, fashions changed, perhaps linked to the gradual move to inhumation, though it is hard to explain why soldiers or anyone else should have become less inclined to commission a visible memorial, other than observing the decline in the epigraphic habit in Britain as a whole from the mid-third century on. Perhaps, as communities merged the need to mark distinction in death faded. But this in itself is a mark of the diminishment of Romanization once the army's distinctive identity and foreignness became diffused.

Even so, military tombstones do not represent the whole army: legionaries and auxiliary cavalrymen always dominate, while auxiliary infantrymen are much more scarce. This helps explain the variability in distribution. Military tombstones broadly fall into three categories. The auxiliary cavalry tombstone typically shows a dynamic profile image of a mounted trooper crushing a victim. The other tombstones, usually legionary, are either static face-on full figure portraits, or simple texts. The cavalry tombstones conform to a stereotype well known in Germany and elsewhere. Almost all belong to the first century AD. The stones of Longinus and Sextus Valerius Genialis have been discussed elsewhere (chapter 8, **2**, **11**, **colour plate 5**). The theme was repeated at Cirencester, where a similar stone records Dannicus, trooper of *ala Indiana* (*RIB* 108). A member of the German Raurici tribe, Dannicus was also commemorated in the stock mounted pose, crushing his foe. The carving is less accomplished, and the overall imagery a good deal less sophisticated, but the pose is the same. The unit was out of Britain by 135 but by then Cirencester was well established as a town. The stone must date to around 50-60 years earlier.

None of the British stones matches the standard of some of the continental examples. Titus Flavius Bassus was a trooper with *ala Noricum* and was buried at Cologne (*ILS* 2512). He is shown trampling a barbarian in a pose resembling that of Lucius Vitellius Tancinus of *ala Vettonum* found at Bath (*RIB* 159; *MF* 44). The Cologne example is fluid and dynamic, as well as depicting the details of armour, equipment and horse trappings. The Bath stone is astonishingly crude by comparison, possibly carved by someone unfamiliar with the pose, or even the proportion of horses. Here perhaps a hapless local sculptor, or even a soldier of the unit with a modicum of ability, had been shown a sketch to follow.

The genre was repeated with varying degrees of success wherever the cavalry units were stationed long enough for someone to die. At Wroxeter, a crude version survives as a fragment to record another trooper from a mounted cohort of Thracians and is probably of late first-century date (*RIB* 291). Further north, the same theme appears again on the contemporary tombstone of Flavinus of *ala Petriana* on a tombstone probably from Corbridge (**81**). A series of similar stones are known from Chester but, having damaged inscriptions, cannot be accurately attributed (for example *RIB* 550). The motif is not entirely exclusive to cavalry tombstones, and appears for example on the Antonine Bridgeness slab of *II Augusta* and another from Summerston Farm, Lanarkshire (*KA* 68, 137).

It is impossible to guess what the hapless Trinovantes outside Colchester thought of Longinus in his swaggering pose, especially as all such images were probably painted in lurid colours to enhance the realism. It is easy to forget that representing a human being in this way was a new idea in Britain. The Trinovantes were provoked to revolt by the colonists, and this sort of image was unlikely to improve matters. But the detached face, its removal long attributed to Boudican rebels, has now been found and had been broken off by an archaeologist's spade in 1928.

Tombstones of legionaries from this date are well known but are far less flamboyant than auxiliary cavalry memorials and usually consist of no more than simple inscribed panels. That of Gaius Saufeius of *VIIII Hispana* from Lincoln must date to somewhere between *c.*71-95 but it carries no more than a bald statement of his career and age on a slab with a simple triangular top and three rosettes (*RIB* 255). The tombstone of T. Valerius Pudens of *II Adiutrix*, also from Lincoln and roughly contemporary, has more curious

81 *Tombstone of Flavinus, trooper with ala Petriana. Built into the medieval abbey at Hexham but presumably taken from a cemetery near Corbridge,* Coriosopitum. *By 98 this unit had been made Roman citizens, so it probably predates that. Height 2.6m.* RIB 1172/ P 68

decoration (*see* **17**). On the top a pair of dolphins flank a trident, and beneath the panel is a hammer. The marine symbols could be references to some of *II Adiutrix*'s legionaries coming from the fleet, the hammer perhaps a reference to this man's trade. However, at Caerleon, the tombstone of Julia Veneria also bears one of what was probably a pair of dolphins too and there is no indication here that she, or her husband and son, had a maritime connection (*RIB* 375). Either way, the trident and dolphins add to the imported exotic new iconography of the age.

The tombstone of Vivius Marcianus at London, a centurion of *II Augusta*, is another complete, but undatable, full-length portrait. He was probably serving in the garrison at the capital's fort during the second century (*RIB* 17) (*see* **24**). A fragment of another can be dated by the II legion's temporary title *Antoniniana* to the early third century (*RIB* 19) (*see* **40**), while a third, found in Camomile Street, has much of the portrait surviving but little else beyond a flanking pilaster with ornate capital (**52, 82**). Here then we have three military tombstones with portraits from the provincial capital, and no comparable civilian examples.

The better-known tombstone of Marcus Favonius Facilis from Colchester, found near that of Longinus, is much more explicit — perhaps even a personal portrait, though the erratic layout of the text suggests it might have been bought off the shelf like those of the cavalrymen. Facilis is depicted face-on with all the trappings of a legionary centurion but minus helmet to denote death (**9, colour plate 1**). Unlike the cavalrymen, the form is much more classical in its tranquillity and realism. The sense of domination is implicit rather than blunderingly overt. The quality matches examples from the continent, even that of Firmus, an auxiliary soldier with a *cohors Raetorum* at Andernach (*CIL* xiii.7684, illustrated in Johnson 1983, 24). In general, though, Romano-British examples conform to the stereotypes but are almost invariably of lesser quality. At York, a cruder version of the same survives in the tombstone of the *signifer* L. Duccius Rufinus (**83**). Also facing the viewer, Rufinus wears a cloak, carries his standard, and another object, which may represent written records. It compares with Genialis, *imaginifer* (bearer of the imperial portrait standard) of *cohors VII Raetorum* from Mainz, but the latter is more detailed and better proportioned, and the lettering more finely executed (*ILS* 9167).

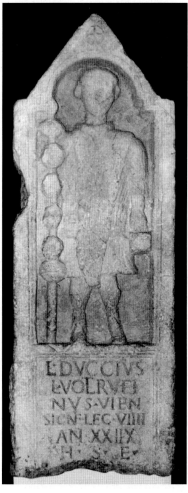

82 *(above left) Fragments of a centurion's tombstone found in the Camomile Street bastion at London (see* **52***). No inscription survives, but the style is good and of first-century date, and adds to the wealth of evidence for a substantial military population in the capital of Britannia*

83 *(above right) Tombstone from York, depicting a* signifer *of* VIIII Hispana, *Lucius Duccius Rufinus, with his standards, in a relatively crude version of a stereotypical military memorial. From Vienna, he died at the age of 28.* RIB *673.*

84 *Tombstone of Regina, Catuvellaunian freedwoman and wife of Barates the Syrian, from South Shields,* Arbeia. *The sculpture is one of the most celebrated from Roman Britain and Regina has become almost the 'archetypal' Romano-British woman whose enslavement was followed by legal and social integration into the exotic complexity that was the Roman Empire. The architectural style is unequivocally Eastern Empire, though Regina's posture is reflected in tombstones of women across Britain and the Roman world. Height 1.26m.* RIB 1065/ P 247

Given this, it is not very surprising that, like epigraphy, so much other sculpture from Roman Britain seems to have its origins in the military zone. Even where we have civilian tombstones with portraits they tend to turn up in places that, unlike London, either began life as major forts or fortresses or remained that way and often have non-British connections. The prime examples are the celebrated tombstones of Regina, wife to a Syrian, and Victor the Moor from South Shields, though a number are known from the colonies of York and Lincoln (**84, 118**). The style of carving on the South Shields slabs links them to the third century, and to the Eastern Empire, but they nevertheless retained the iconography of portraying the deceased in a semi-realistic form. While neither is signed, they bear every indication of coming from the same workshop and probably the same hand. The stonemason must have been attracted by the possibility of the military trade, unless he was drawn from amongst their ranks.

Regina faces the onlooker in a chair and is matched by a stone from the cemetery at Murrell Hill at Carlisle, close to the Hadrian's Wall frontier, with its depiction of an unknown woman, this time with a fan, her child, and a pet bird while above her the sphinx and lions reappear (*CP* 497). There are many other examples, such as Curatia Dionysia from Chester, or Julia Velva from York, but it is easy to overlook in their importance to us how clearly they were created out of stock types and images. Julia Velva's stone has an inscription far too short for the available space and includes two additional figures who go unmentioned (*RIB* 688). Curatia Dionysia's stone is similar to Victor's but much cruder though they share the image of the deceased dining on a couch — a theme well-known from elsewhere in the Empire (*RIB* 562). Stock these might all be, their appearance in the military zone shows it was the army, which also brought Roman civilian tombstone imagery into the province. It is also tempting to see the suppliers of stock military tombstones being utilised by the civilian market in military areas with the concept of portrait tombstones gradually becoming a characteristic of the whole community in the north and west.

Dedications

Tombstones, altars, and building dedications form part of the 2500-odd monumental inscriptions recorded from Roman Britain. No recorded written form of the indigenous British languages or dialects existed or exists. When lettering was used on British tribal coins before 43 the Latin alphabet was used. Roman monumental inscriptions were the most conspicuous and enduring evidence of a state based on literacy. It is impossible to know how the Britons reacted to something they could not have initially understood, especially something which was very largely restricted to forts and major settlements. The only possible way of measuring the spread of literacy is through graffiti on pottery (**85**). Unfortunately, kitchenware was paid relatively little attention until 30-40 years ago, meaning that a great deal went unnoticed or unrecorded on large-scale excavations at sites on the northern frontier. Samian ware has almost always been recorded and is probably more reliable as a datable product, but was only really available during the first two centuries. In general, apart from London, military sites produced the largest recorded numbers but the figures are obviously the result of where was excavated. Consequently, Caerleon and Corbridge have produced large numbers while places like Carrawburgh, scarcely touched by the trowel, have produced less than a handful. However, it is striking that Corbridge's 66 far outweighs the 24 from Silchester, a civilian settlement subjected to very large-scale excavation. Perhaps in the end in civilian areas it was a case of 'away with him! He speaks Latin' as Cade announces in *Henry VI Part 2*. Names of 'Celtic' origin are not unknown as graffiti on pottery, for example Belicianus on a piece of kitchenware from Housesteads (*RIB* 2503.206).

Belicianus, however, apparently lived at a fort and does not contradict the samian evidence which suggests that literacy levels amongst soldiers and their associates, perhaps even extending to use of Latin in a spoken form at all, may have been much higher than it was amongst civilians (see also Haynes 1999), and even higher amongst soldiers of senior rank. Five individuals are recorded on graffiti from the fort at Castleford; two of these are centurions, and a third a woman (Cool 1998, 356). The observation has been

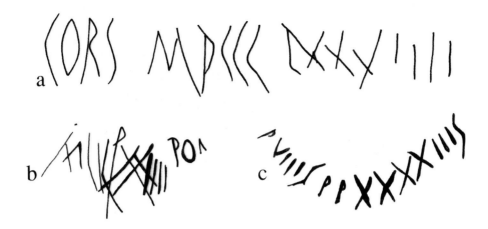

85 *Graffiti.* ***a.*** *from a Vindolanda storage jar, stating* cor(iandri) s(emina) MDCCCLXXXIIII, *for (?)* *'1884 coriander seeds'.* ***b.*** *from a Southwark storage jar marked* mel p(ondo) XXIIII pon(do), *'honey, by weight 24 . . . in poundage'.* ***c.*** *from a Vindolanda jug,* [v(acuus)] p(ondo) (librae) viii s(emis) p(lena) p(ondo) xxxxiii s(emis), *'8.5 pounds [empty?], 43.5 pounds full'. (After Frere and Tomlin)*

made in a study of the Egyptian village of Karanis that the numbers of extant papyri markedly increase at the same time as soldiers and veterans start to appear in significant numbers in the settlement (Alston 1995, 126). On inscriptions, there is tremendous variation in the degree of competence used both to form and lay out the letters with some units showing at particular times a very considerable degree of creativity. Few official inscriptions survive from before the period of the Walls. One of the most outstanding is the Trajanic slab of *II Augusta* from Caerleon. Made of Italian marble, and probably carved there, it was laid out with Trajan's titles for the year 99. It was subsequently modified, perhaps after arrival in Britain, by a lesser hand for the year 100 (*RIB* 330). The text is remarkable for its symmetry and balance. There is none of the splitting of words, haphazard compression and spread so often found on other slabs. An almost contemporary dedication from York for *VIIII Hispana*, of 107-8, is more complex thanks to Trajan's new Dacian war titles but shares the elegance of design (*RIB* 665).

Such high-grade epigraphy did not start in military contexts. The shattered fragments of the Agricolan inscription from Verulamium are a generation earlier and of high quality. In terms of style, both it and the Hadrianic Wroxeter inscription (*RIB* 288) are similar to the York slab. Chichester has yielded two major inscriptions of the first century, one of which records the dedication of a temple to Neptune and Minerva but explicitly in the name of the client king, Tiberius Claudius Togidubnus (see chapter 1). Both locations were probably part of the client kingdom and thus would never have been exposed to a significant military presence beyond the coastal installations detected near Chichester. Presumably they were produced as a direct result of the resources available to the client kingdom, but they seem to have had little general impact on the region in the long-term.

But over the longer-term it becomes obvious that military epigraphy overwhelms the extant record, albeit in a series of peaks and troughs. The largest peak of military epigraphy

86 *These small, crudely fashioned, altars and their modest dedications are typical of epigraphic religious material found throughout the northern military zone.* ***a****. Altar found within Housesteads,* Vercovicium, *dedicated 'To the God Hvitris. Aspuanis fulfilled this vow for himself and his family.' Height 305mm. RIB 1603* ***b****. Altar from Coventina's Well at Carrawburgh,* Brocolitia, *dedicated 'To the Goddess Minerva, Venico erected this at his own cost, for his welfare'. Height 330mm. RIB 1543*

in Britain was at the end of the second century and the first few decades of the third. Many of these were commemorations of building, or rebuilding, work to honour the incumbent ruling house, and are distinctive for their style and flair. They are discussed in more detail in chapter 4. At most military sites the majority of inscriptions are religious in tone. Many of these are crude and simple and were probably made by the dedicants for their own use (**86**). Of 61 inscribed stones from Birdoswald (including those found since *RIB* was compiled), 46 are religious dedications or tombstones. Of these, just four are tombstones and almost all the remainder are altars. It is plain that dedications in the name of the unit, or the commanding officer on behalf of the unit, are biased to deities from the classical pantheon. Of the 40 Birdoswald altars, 24 are dedicated to Jupiter Optimus Maximus alone usually by the resident garrison, *cohors I Aelia Dacorum*, in the name of the commanding officer. Maryport has produced a remarkable series of altars dedicated to Jupiter Optimus Maximus by the commanding officers of *cohors I Hispanorum*. Their fine condition makes it likely they were annually, or regularly, renewed, with the old altar being buried. The Birdoswald altars probably tell a similar story, which will have been played out at most forts.

Unlike Jupiter, Mars or Victory, the non-classical or 'Celtic' gods such as Cocidius and Garmangabis present a different problem. They tend to turn up in specific locations, and are much more likely to have been venerated by individuals: usually soldiers or people of unspecified profession in a military site. Brigantia, the personification of the tribe of northern Britain (**97**), turns up at several places on the northern frontier, but also at several places in close vicinity in Yorkshire: Adel, Castleford, and Greetland (*RIB* 630, 627-8). It is unknown whether she 'existed' as a deity beforehand, or whether she was manufactured in Roman consciousness out of the need to perceive location and identity in this form. These local finds were all close to or in rivers. Elsewhere she is known as Nympha Brigantia, and a further find of an altar to Nymphs at Castleford suggests that her origins lay as a water deity (*RIB* 2066, and *B* 1983, 337). Certainly the name, which means 'hilly' or 'high', is just baldly descriptive. In this sense she was Romanized into a more conventional guise as a regional personification.

Apart from Amandus the architect, her dedicants are fairly circumspect about their role in life except for Titus Aurelius Aurelianus, *magister sacrorum,* 'master of sacred ceremonies', at Greetland. That his dedication was combined with one to the Spirits of the Emperors shows she had been welcomed into the official pantheon so favoured by the army. Some local deities are only known from a single place. Coventina, the water nymph from Carrawburgh, is a good example and is a more explicit instance of the popularity of water-linked cults. Unknown elsewhere, her cult probably existed there before the Roman army arrived and was adopted by the garrison (**70**). In most of these cases, the location and the dedicants are military. Garmangabis is a name of Germanic origin and is likely to have been brought to Lanchester by the unit, a vexillation of Suebians, which commemorated her.

When Coventina's spring was dug out in the nineteenth century a vast quantity of goods poured out including a number of inscribed altars, and reliefs depicting the goddess, and nymphs. But crucially, had it not been for the capacity of Roman culture to absorb a cult like this, and the Roman military love of inscriptions, we would know nothing about Coventina at all (**87**). Evidence for votive goods might have been found from pre-Roman levels, had the site been properly excavated, but we would still have no idea of her name or how she was perceived. The Roman army neither created nor imposed this part of Romano-British culture. Instead it provided the medium through which a cult could be disseminated across space and time through the inscriptions and reliefs preserving it. This is not exclusive to the military zone but the numbers of deities known only from military zone inscriptions far outweighs those from the rest of the province.

Further east along the Wall at Benwell, Antenociticus would be lost to the ages, had soldiers of the garrison, or those passing by, not taken an interest in him. He had probably been venerated locally for centuries but not in any recognizable material form. The result of his recognition by the Roman military community was a small rectangular apsidal building, equipped with a cult statue and several altars, built outside the south-east corner of the fort. The soldiers who dedicated altars to him were of relatively high rank. Two were legionary centurions, and two were prefects, one of cavalry and the other probably also (*RIB* 1327-30). The fad may have been a passing one. Destroyed by unknown hands during the early third century, the temple was never rebuilt. In spite of his respect for this obscure deity, Tineius Longus, prefect of cavalry, seems to have had some trouble with adapting the name to a Latin form. On his altar, dated to *c.*177-84 by its reference to the governor Ulpius Marcellus, the god's name was truncated to 'Anociticus' in the process of transcribing a name out of an oral tradition. Coventina also appears as Covetina, while 'Veter' or the 'Veteres', widely venerated on the northern frontier, are recorded in a bewildering range of phonetic variants.

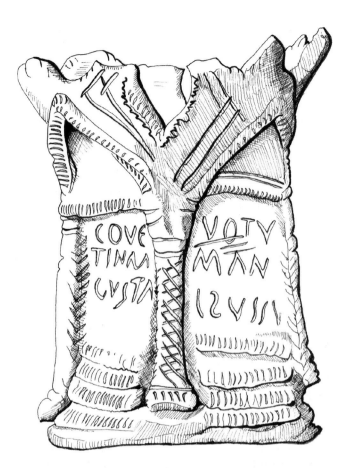

87 *Coventina. Clay vessel formed as a hollow pedestal, supporting an open dish, from Coventina's Well, Carrawburgh. The vessel is inscribed* Covetina (sic) Augusta Votu(m) Manibus Suis Saturninus fecit Gabinius, *'Saturnines Gabinius made this for Cove(n)tina Augusta with his own hands'. (After Finch.)* RIB *2457.2*

In other cases, the deity concerned may be known elsewhere but in Britain only appears for certain in verbal form through a military record, or in the military zone. Epona, normally described as a 'Celtic horse-goddess', is best known in Gaul. Although a figurine representing her is known from Wiltshire and a carving from Colchester, she is only named for us on an altar from Auchendavy by Marcus Cocceius Firmus (*RIB* 2177), a man responsible for several other religious dedications from the same fort, and by an individual whose name is lost on an altar from the fort at Carvoran (*RIB* 1777). The only other apparent reference to her is a scratched graffito on a jar found in a Roman pit of unknown nature from Alcester in Warwickshire (*RIB* 2503.123).

Some of the dedications seem almost frivolous. The Vindolanda letters include references to hunting as a leisure pursuit amongst the officers commanding auxiliary units. Another of their number, Gaius Tetius Veturius Micianus, prefect of the *ala Sebosiana*, left a dedication to Silvanus at Stanhope in Weardale, county Durham. The unusually lengthy text records the officer's gratitude at 'bagging a boar of enormous size which many of his predecessors had failed to kill'. Curiously, he seems to have had someone's earlier dedication to the Spirits of the Emperors erased for the purpose, suggesting his text was spontaneously carved on the spot, utilising an altar discovered by chance on the expedition (**88**).

Most of these dedications are not dated. However, by definition dedications from the Wall area probably do not pre-date the year 122. The vast majority of datable inscriptions belong to the second and early third century, so the undated ones are likely to belong to somewhere in the same period, and this is supported by stylistic analogies. What they show us that Roman soldiers were more likely to produce stone inscriptions than any other class of person in Roman Britain and that by far and away the majority of those stones from forts were likely to be religious in tone. The epigraphic bias to religion in Romano-British culture is observable elsewhere in the province, even in the towns. More inscriptions record temples or shrines than any other single class of building but, as usual, even these are dominated by the record from the military zone.

There are also the centurial stones from Hadrian's Wall, which only name the unit responsible for stretches of the curtain. Despite their perfunctory nature they reflect the integral part written records and commemorations played in military life. Nothing like them is known from civilian settlements, apart from centurial stones recording working parties sent from civitas capitals to work on the Wall.

Inscriptions recording gods and goddesses have the huge advantage often of being attributable if complete or restorable. Without a written record, only context or type makes attribution even guessable. Many artefacts defy this sort of classification. The votive gifts from the sacred spring at Bath show how difficult it can be. Few are in any way definitively military, though a bronze washer has been identified as a component from a catapult (Cunliffe 1988, ii, 8-9, no. 6). Many items are inscribed but usually just to the god rather than identifying the dedicant. None of the curse tablets can be identified as having been prepared for a soldier, either as dedicant or victim. If the proportion of inscribed stone dedications by soldiers reflects

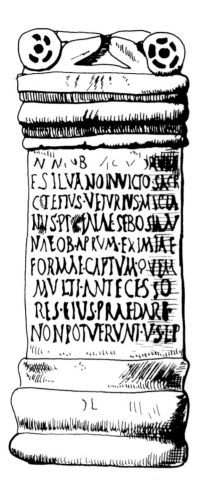

88 *Bollihope Common, Durham. Altar originally dedicated to the Spirits of the Emperors, and overlaid with a fresh inscription to Silvanus by Gaius Tetius Veturius Micianus, prefect of ala Sebosiana, in memory of the occasion when he bagged a boar who had escaped his predecessors. The unit is known to have spent time at Binchester and Lancaster, but it is quite possible it was on active duty in the vicinity at the time. RIB 1041*

their proportion as visitors then we might infer that around half the gifts in the spring were from visiting soldiers. Alternatively, soldiers might have preferred the inscribed stone (and the evidence from the rest of the province suggests this is a possibility) to other gifts. This does not affect the point that troops dominated the visible literary record in the form of altars and other dedicatory slabs, *despite* the fact that the sacred site was some way from their various respective bases and must have been far more accessible to civilians.

Evidence for Christianity in any community in Britain is distinctly thin. Apart from occasional examples of artefacts bearing the Chi-Rho, only the Water Newton treasure, and the late fourth-century wall-paintings at Lullingstone, have provided any reasonable basis for identifying active Christian communities. Soldiers were more easily drawn to the related promise of redemption in the form of Mithras, whose cult held physical endurance in great esteem and which was exclusive to men. The appearance of mithraea at a number of forts in Britain reflects this (see chapter 7). In any case Christianity's pacifist inclinations were not always compatible with military service and elsewhere in the Empire this led to recorded martyrdoms of third-century conscripts who refused to serve (Alston 1995, 149). Only the story of the martyr Alban preserves a folk record of Christianity amongst the soldiery of Britain. Alongside Alban was killed a soldier who had refused to execute him, while at 'the City of the Legions' (perhaps Caerleon), a pair of men described as citizens, called Aaron and Julius, were executed for being Christians (Bede, *Hist. Eccl.* i.7). The event is normally associated with the early third century when Geta was placed in charge of the administration of Britain.

The fourth century saw the legitimisation of Christianity but also saw the termination of the monumental epigraphic habit in Britain, thus depriving us even of the chance to identify Christian tombstones. We can take it that Christian soldiers must have been in service, but it is impossible to know how conspicuous they were, in spite of the Chi-Rho triumphantly brandished on a number of fourth-century coinage issues. The destruction of the depiction of Mithras slaying the sacred bull in the *reredos* at Carrawburgh has often been taken as evidence of Christian iconoclasts, but attributing such destruction to any specific group is ultimately untenable in the context of the evidence available. However, the subsequent appearance of a number of seventh-century Saxon churches in the Saxon Shore forts is interesting. Bradwell-on-Sea, Reculver and Richborough were certainly used this way. The appeal might have been the prospect of a semi-fortified coastal compound where the ingress of Christianity in its Saxon revival could be protected, as well as the availability of building materials.

The identification of a late-Roman font within the walls of the fort at Richborough has been taken to mean that an earlier small chapel, of Roman date, went unrecognised during excavations there. Considering that this is supposed to be where *II Augusta* was based in the 300s, a tenuous and insubstantial connection might be drawn with the tradition of the martyrdom of Aaron and Julius. What was true of Richborough may have been true of other forts, though the trouble with Christianity in Britain is invariably its invisibility. But perhaps some of the late army garrison communities of the coastal forts included Christian places of worship, official or otherwise, which subsisted as a tradition long enough for Christianity to be revived there. If so, even Christianity owed more to the army for maintenance of a tradition than anything else.

Place names

The preservation of the names of British deities through a Latinized medium extends also to the names of places. The name *Isca*, which forms part of the ancient names for Exeter, Usk and Caerleon amongst others, has a complex series of origins linked to the British words for water, *isca*, and fish, *esca*. The etymological arguments for which source led to what places being called *Isca* are arcane and inconclusive. None affect the point that the process of turning these unwritten names into recorded and transcribed labels for places was a Roman process, both acknowledging the past and adapting it. The nature of the Roman world was such that many soldiers, especially in auxiliary units, may have preferred to use their own indigenous languages on a day-to-day basis. For those recruited in northern Europe and Britain the existing names may have come naturally to them. Even so, the names need not have been long established. The name for Housesteads, *Vercovicium*, seems to come from *vercovices*, meaning 'effective fighters'. Presumably, but not demonstrably, the name was one applied by locals to the appearance of the Roman garrison, then adopted by the fort residents and Latinized.

Other names seem to preserve much older labels for the local terrain, though in truth there is much guesswork involved and very little fact despite the confidence expressed in the published catalogue (Rivet and Smith). *Vindobala*, for Rudchester, is thought to mean 'white peak', perhaps an allusion to the appearance of the landscape there in winter. *Eboracum*, for York, may refer to a local landowner of consequence or it may mean 'a place of abundant yew trees'. Of course, this was not an exclusive process. *Castra Exploratorum*, for Netherby, is a perfunctory Latin label, meaning 'camp of the scouts', and clearly belongs to the Roman period in its entirety. But it is exceptional. Benwell, on the other hand, was called *Condercum* in antiquity and is thought to be derived from British words essentially meaning a 'place with excellent views all round'. While this may have been what the local people called the hilltop, it is also perfectly possible that the garrison of the fort used either their own linguistic traditions or local words to create a new name for the place. The same might apply to *Briga*, a fort referred to in the Vindolanda documents but which remains unlocated. The word simply means 'hill' or 'high', and is well known in the 'Celtic' west.

This capacity to adapt local names reflects the Roman process of cultural synthesis but it also perhaps symbolizes a lack of a formal policy to Romanize either the place names of the frontier or even the civilian zone. If there had been one, then we might expect a much larger number of places with names like *Castra Exploratorum*. On the contrary, the transmission to our own time of place names ending in *-ceister*, *-cester* and so on, seems almost entirely due to an Anglo-Saxon labelling of any place they recognized to be Roman as a '*castra*' (fort), regardless of whether it actually had been a fort or a town. Oddly then, Anglo-Saxon names for Roman settlements frequently have more Latin in them than those of Roman date, and as a tradition have more in common with the label 'Roman Camp' which appeared in many old maps in connection with almost any earthworks.

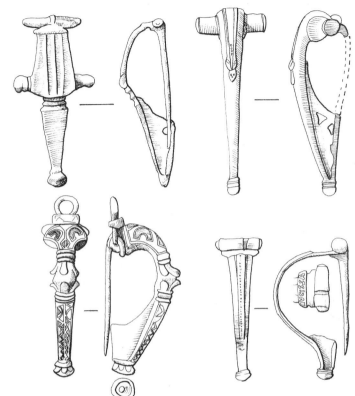

89 *Brooches. Clockwise from upper left: 'Hod Hill' brooch, from Richborough; Polden Hill bow brooch from Richborough; 'Aucissa' brooch, from Richborough (Bushe-Fox, 1949 and Cunliffe 1968); enamelled 'trumpet' brooch, from Verulamium (Frere 1984)*

Jewellery and other decorative metalwork

Like the Bath spring finds, decorative metalwork of almost any kind is extremely difficult to associate with the Roman army unless it is only found on military sites, or is explicitly military in function (such as a parade helmet). Equally, they are difficult to attribute to civilians, and in most cases even to either sex. Being portable, durable, and recyclable, items like brooches or rings are prone to be used and lost almost anywhere and at any time by anyone. Even so, there is some evidence that the Roman army was instrumental in introducing new types of decoration and goods into Britain.

The bewildering range of types of brooch manufactured in, or imported to, Roman Britain belies their very simple function as a decorative pin. Prior to the conquest, the one-piece bow brooch dominated the market, and resembled the safety-pin. It consisted of a single piece of metal, usually bronze, hammered and worked into a bow with catchplate. At the top of the bow the metal was wound into a spring, and then continued as the pin.

There was nothing new about the one-piece brooch, but by the beginning of the first century AD the range of types available in the Roman world had become much greater and included the appearance of two-piece brooches, where the pin was made as a separate component (**89**). Brooches in Britain were not a Roman innovation but the transition to two-piece brooches was. The separate pin made it possible to decorate the bow more elaborately. It is almost impossible to say who was responsible for manufacturing them. Excavations at Baldock (Herts), a site active in the late Iron Age and conquest period, have produced evidence for first-century work-in-progress, but not who was responsible. Differences in detail, and the range of types, found on early military sites in Britain show that each unit had access to slightly different suppliers. The varieties and designs even differ from those known on military sites on the Rhine. This makes it likely that either brooches were manufactured by the army units, or by individual traders and artisans who followed them around.

The army was responsible for bringing many new brooch types into Britain. These include the so-called AVCISSA-type. In profile the brooch resembles a large letter P, with a long thin arched bow, marked at the top with the maker's name, Aucissa. The type was widely copied, and it has been noticed that although Britain's total is relatively small its recorded numbers stamped Aucissa are much greater than parts of the continent (Hattatt 1987, 71 — since when *RIB* has recorded even more in Britain). Considering the early date a military contract for supply is possible explanation. They are widely distributed in Britain but were no longer being manufactured by the late first century. The find-spots are inconclusive, though *RIB* records several at Wroxeter, including one stamped instead by Atgivios (2421.3, and 2421.27, 28, 29, 37).

Hod Hill brooches are named for the Claudian fort where they were first classified, which tends to reinforce their military associations. Much flatter than the Aucissa type, Hod Hill brooches had a bow with two zones. The upper is a wider panel with side lugs, and the lower part tapers to an ankle and foot. Occasionally engraved with mottos, they do not bear a maker's name in common with other brooches, and are often tinned to create a silver effect. It has been suggested that the tinning made such brooches suitable for use alongside other military equipment (Johns 1996, 157).

Even if the Hod Hill or Aucissa types were introduced by the Roman army in Britain, they disappear from the record by the beginning of the second century and were replaced by other types, many variants of which are regional in distribution. A class of second-century enamelled brooch now called the 'Wirral' type has been identified from a number of sites in north-west Britain, including Scotland (Philpott 1999). The source has not been located, but similarities amongst the brooches make it probable that they came from one place. Distribution is primarily local to the Wirral but it is interesting that another scatter has turned up at a variety of forts in the northern frontier area. While that might reflect the interest shown in the frontier forts by archaeologists, it is also possible that the military market supported a trickle of the goods via tinkers or traders to the fort *vici*.

The new brooch types, such as the 'trumpet' or the 'Aesica' (see below), are widely distributed and it is not really possible to show that they had anything particularly to do with the army beyond noting that army supply routes may have encouraged their dispersal and the taste to wear them, and perhaps some of the metallurgical skills needed to make them. The use of enamelling, engraving and curvilinear decorative features shows that manufacturers were particularly drawn to styles which are non-Roman in nature, and are now usually described as 'Celtic', perhaps because indigenous metal-workers had started to produce them in individual variants.

90 *Left: the Aesica brooch. Found at Greatchesters,* Aesica, *in 1894 in a hoard. Made of gilt bronze and inlaid with enamel the piece is a highly elaborate variant of an ordinary fantail brooch. Height 11.5cm. Right: silver trumpet brooch from the same hoard. Height 18.5cm*

In some interesting cases military preferences may have encouraged particular designs within a general form. The lurid colours produced by enamelling, not something favoured much elsewhere in the Empire, seems to have appealed to military tastes and began to appear on cavalry horse-trappings and other items like belt fittings. The Aesica brooches are named for a particularly bizarre (to our eyes) example found in a hoard at *Aesica* (Greatchesters) in 1894 (**90**). More than 11cm in length, made of gilded bronze and decorated with ornamental symmetrical curvilinear features, it is dated on style to the late first century, though the possibility that it was made later to an older tradition should not be ignored, especially as the hoard included rings of third-century date, as well as an even more extreme brooch in the form of an 18.5cm tall silver trumpet brooch.

The Aesica hoard reminds us of the difficulty of dating and attributing items like these but the find-spot makes it likely that they belonged to a frontier soldier who was particularly fond of display, something which is a characteristic of other military metalwork. The overall style, combining elements of the Roman and Celtic world, is typical of how Romanization functioned in a provincial context with a fusing of multiple traditions.

Much more overtly Roman, and often military in tone, was the practice of wearing rings set with engraved gemstones, intaglios, which were used to impress seals on letters

91 Gem-stone, intaglio, depicting Victory, from Caerleon, Isca. One of 88 found in the drains of the fortress baths. Height 15.4mm

and documents and in a different way impress the recipient. They were Roman marks of wealth and status. Gemstones were easily loosened from rings, especially those made from iron, and once dropped easily lost, which explains why they are not rare. The drains of the fortress baths at Caerleon yielded 88. They were also deliberately extracted from old rings and reused by jewellers, making dating and attribution difficult (**91**).

One from Verulamium, thought to be mid-first-century in date, shows a Roman warship carrying a legionary trophy, standard and eagle (Henig 1978, no. 533, and also illustrated in Henig 1995, 33). Unlike brooches the style and decoration of the gemstone owes far more conceptually to the attitude of mind that created sculpture, tombstones, and figured samian ware. Although small, gemstone subjects were exclusively drawn from the same vast array of Roman symbols, fantastic beasts, gods and goddesses (including exotic Eastern deities), and military equipment. It has been noted that this 'uncompromisingly Classical' range of subjects was matched by the choice of subject matter on Romano-British mosaics (Johns 1996, 82). Either this was because British deities were excluded from the genre, or they were only silently perceived in the form of their Roman equivalents. It makes no difference to the monopolisation of iconography. Perhaps some modern interpretations of these images, and their powers, are a little exaggerated. But it is easy to see why heroes from the Trojan War, or gods such as Mars and Hercules, should have appealed to a soldier. Such gemstones are characteristic finds from forts.

Even the clasped-hand motif could have military connotations, frequently appearing also on coinage with the legend *Fides Exercituum*, 'the faithful army'. But where gemstones, or even plain rings, bear inscriptions of any sort they are usually statements of ownership, declarations of loyalty or love, or exhortations for a long life. Most gemstones, though, depict more general themes drawn from broader Roman imagery. Thus an example from Strageath, a remote fort originally founded by Agricola and reoccupied as an outpost fort for the Antonine Wall, shows a goatherd and a goat with a small tree (Henig 1999, fig 6). Drawn from the Roman love of idealised bucolic scenes, similar imagery can be found on oil lamps manufactured in Italy and North Africa. Other personifications were similar to those found on Roman coinage. Although little is known about where and when jewellery was actually made, the settlement outside the fort at Malton (*Derventio*) has produced a scrappy inscription set in an ansate panel (itself a characteristically military form) recording a goldsmith's workshop (*RIB* 712).

Gemstones had potentially exceedingly long lives, surviving into many settings as the Snettisham jeweller's hoard and the Thetford Treasure show to ample effect. They will have been handed down through generations, or sold and lost. The appearance of a Roman deity or mythological figure on a gemstone may have been the first time that the image had appeared in Britain. This need not have been during or after the Conquest. One gemstone from Eastcheap, London, depicts Pegasus (Henig 1995, 33). A coin issued by Cunobelinus of the Catuvellauni depicts a similar image, but in reverse (Mack 1975, no. 249). Interestingly, had the coin die been copied from a similar gemstone, then the coins produced would indeed show the figure reversed.

The introduction of the pottery mortarium has already been mentioned (chapter 5). As samian ware has significance in the iconography of its decorated forms, so the mortaria symbolise a change in cooking practices. There is no doubt that this was led by army requirements and practice, and gradually became integrated into Romano-British society. By the third and fourth centuries, the Oxfordshire and New Forest industries, for example, produced mortaria as a basic part of their range, and they turn up in all southern civilian areas including villas. Another utensil which became more common after the Conquest was the skillet, also known as the *patera*, or *trulla*, though as it is a metal item, examples are obviously far less numerous. The skillet resembles a small saucepan crossed with a military mess-tin. Its utilitarian nature, as well as being durable and portable, made it ideal for the soldier.

Often stamped with makers' names many skillets can be identified as imports, for example from the Capuan workshops of P. Cipius Polybius (*c*.65-85), while others may have been made in Britain to service the new market created by the army. Some bear owner's names but it is rarely possible to say who they were. One example, from Lincolnshire, belonged to CL SENIORIS/ANNI, 'Annius, from the century of Claudius Senior' (*RIB* 2415.51). Another, from York, bears two graffiti referring to two separate centuries in, presumably, *VIIII Hispana* or *VI Victrix*, while a bowl from a few miles north of the Hadrian's Wall fort at Benwell has two similar marks (*RIB* 2415.58, 63). These examples were thoroughly workaday, but the find-spots of more decorative examples, like the silver skillets from the Backworth and Capheaton (both Northumberland) treasures, belong to the military zone. The former included a skillet made by one Fabius Dubitatus and dedicated to the Matres, while the latter consisted of several vessels, which had decorative themes drawn from military imagery as well as religious activities.

The Rudge cup and Amiens skillet are two small bronze vessels manufactured in the same tradition as mainstream skillets (**92**). Both are made of bronze, and are decorated with a running depiction of what looks like a crenellated wall, decorated with enamel. This is reinforced by the addition of the names of Wall forts around the top (*RIB* 2415.53). Apparently souvenirs of the Wall, perhaps they were made in the Wall zone by an enterprising bronzesmith. But a skillet from the sacred spring at Bath is almost exactly the same apart from lacking the names making it more likely they belong to a wider tradition, occasionally adapted to order (Cunliffe 1988, 154, no. 23).

92 *The Rudge Cup. The small bronze vessel features the names of several Hadrian's Wall forts. The decoration appears to represent the Wall but is little more than a variation of decoration found on other vessels with no lettering (see text). Width 50mm*

Some metalwork is definitively military. A series of openwork military baldric attachments found at forts, and civilian settlements, bear the image of an eagle, and the words *Optime Maxime con(serva)* (for example *RIB* 2429.1 from High Rochester), and completed with other elements *numerum omnium militantium*, makes 'Best and Greatest, preserve all soldiers'. There is some evidence from casting features that a very few workshops, perhaps only one, were responsible for their production. The workshop need not have been in Britain, examples having been found in Germany as well as Nineveh, so it could have been standard military equipment (Reade 1999). But this does not affect the point that a military demand for a particular good was being met by targeted, or commissioned, production, and which depicted a Roman religious exhortation to Jupiter and a Roman eagle. It was worn widely enough in Britain not only to turn up in the far north at High Rochester, but also at Silchester, and the shrine of Mercury at Uley in Gloucestershire. The latter emphasise the presence of soldiers in the civilian zone.

Explicitly military personal metalwork with decoration tends to be more obviously classical in nature. A rare instance is the shield boss found in the Tyne naming *VIII Augusta*, and a soldier called Junius Dubitatus in the century of Julius Magnus (*RIB* 2426.1). The tombstone of T. Pontius Sabinus, *primus pilus* of *III Augusta*, from Ferentinum states him to have been in command after 117 of detachments of three legions in Britain including *VIII Augusta* (*ILS* 2726B). We can guess that this was when Dubitatus lost his shield, though vexillations may have been sent at other unrecorded times. The decoration on the boss, with its central eagle, surrounding panels depicting standards and the Seasons, Mars and a bull, is probably generic but its exact form is probably a one-off, done to order. There is also something reminiscent of mosaic panels in its layout and thus we have here a small piece of private military art which played its own part in disseminating basic canons of Roman design, genre and imagery. While Dubitatus himself may only have been passing through Britain, his boss will have been matched by thousands of other, lost, examples.

A bronze cheek-piece found in the Tyne near South Shields, and probably made *c.*150-250 carries punched decoration depicting Castor or Pollux with a horse in an accomplished and well-proportioned form, together with a dolphin (*see* **80**). Clearly drawn from broader classical traditions, this has to be seen alongside the other classical-style imagery brought by the army. The piece is probably from an auxiliary cavalry helmet, a reminder of the Thracian tombstones, which a century before had already been responsible for introducing the potent image of the mounted Roman soldier crushing barbarians. A similar subject appears on a cheek-piece from Brough in Nottinghamshire (Webster and Dudley 1965, 119). Another, from Bath Lane, Leicester, is decorated with a relief image of Cupid holding grapes, together with an exotic bird (Clay and Mellor 1985, 64, no. 2).

The Ribchester helmet is the most complete and impressive example of a parade helmet known from Britain. Decorated with reliefs of fabulous beasts and soldiers fighting, it served as a complete head and face covering, unlike the helmets from which the separate cheek-pieces came (**93**). It concealed any sense of individuality beneath an idealised and blemish-free image of the Roman warrior. Several were found also in a pit of Flavian date sealed by an Antonine bathhouse at Newstead. Another of this early group illustrates a chariot race, perhaps an activity still generally unknown in Britain at the time (*KA* nos. 54-6).

Other examples are known from elsewhere in the Empire, such as Vize in Bulgaria. They formed just part of complete suits of parade armour. A leg greave from Straubing in Bavaria

93 *Auxiliary parade 'sports' helmet with visor-mask from Ribchester,* Bremetennacum. *Featuring various embossed battle scenes, this helmet will have been worn on mock battle displays and at ceremonies*

depicts a heavily embossed relief figure of Mars in full military equipment, together with a separate knee-joint cover showing what seems to be a gorgon-type face. The horses were also decorated. A leather chamfron from Newstead though is rather low-key compared to the Straubing collection, which included a bronze example, but the site produced many other examples of decorative trappings (**colour plate 7**). A plate depicting a god sat on the horse's brow with a pair of hinged eyepieces depicting Castor and Pollux as pronounced, three-dimensional, busts. The altars from Maryport are a prime example of one military unit's constantly reinforced relationship with the Roman religious and secular hierarchies. Parades and displays of prowess and skill were as much a part of consolidating that as the unit dedications to Jupiter and myriad private dedications to Mars and his various associates. Of course, performances of military skill were unlikely to be convincing without a suitable enemy. Some pieces of parade equipment are distinctly non-Roman and may have been used by soldiers posing as mythical or historical enemies. One of the Newstead helmets has been identified as depicting an Amazon — a popular variety of 'enemy' in mock combat tournaments. If correct it becomes easier to track the dissemination of Rome's mystical self-perception as the predestined product of divine legend into Romano-British culture, leading ultimately to the imagery of myth on the mosaic floors of the third- and fourth-century villas.

If that sounds all rather too profound for the mundane world of the Roman fort, then one need only consider the military aviation displays which are now a constant feature of the British summer. However presented, each display invariably resorts to some sort of re-enacted scene from the Second World War, fast itself becoming part of our own modern myth. Heavily restored and highly polished Spitfires now do mock battle with cod Messerschmitts (in fact normally adapted from post-war Spanish-built versions), flown by colleagues of those in the Spitfires. The year 2000, as the 60th anniversary of the Battle of Britain, saw a climax of these displays and one show at Biggin Hill included a full-scale cod raid and 'scramble'.

The examples of Roman parade armour are all extremely rare, for obvious reasons, but we can take it for granted that all the auxiliary units in Britain, particularly the mounted wings, would have put on displays and parades using this kind of equipment (**94**). While they are overtly martial, and barbaric in their graphic intensity, the iconography and subject matter are all drawn from the Roman world. A passage from Arrian shows that they were a routine part of performances.

> Troopers who are officers or first-rate horsemen sport gilded helmets made of bronze or iron to attract attention from the crowd. These helmets do not just cover the head and cheeks, in the manner of helmets used on campaign, but are made so that they cover the whole face of the rider, with slits for the eyes . . . Horses have chamfrons made carefully to fit, along with side-armour.

> *Tactica* xxxiv

Arrian does not specify who went to make up the crowd. At the very least it will have concluded the people who lived locally to the fort. But a display might have attracted sightseers from further afield.

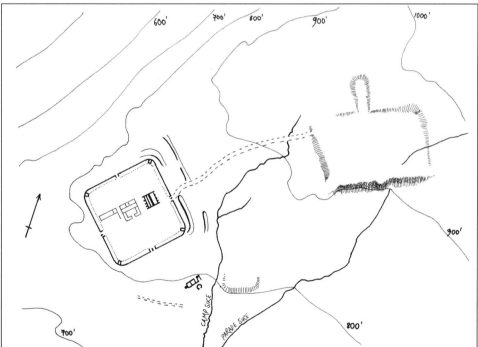

94 *Hardknott, Mediobogdum, fort parade ground looking south-east, and plan. The plan shows the fort in relation to an area interpreted as its parade ground where displays, parades and inspections will have been held. All forts will have had such areas but they are scarcely ever recognisable*

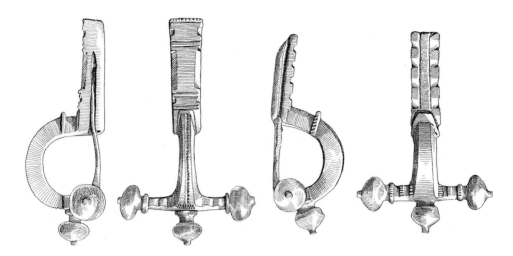

95 *Bronze crossbow brooches from the fourth-century temple and bath shrine complex to the god Nodens at Lydney Park, Gloucestershire. The brooches are likely either to have been gifts by visitors, or perhaps had been for sale. Shown 'upside down' in the manner actually worn. Fourth century. (After Wheeler)*

Much of the parade armour seems to belong to the third century, also the time from which many of the most explicit and detailed military inscriptions date. There must be a connection. This was also a time when the Empire was changing in major ways, with a steady fragmentation of imperial authority. A strictly hierarchical and centralized society mutated into something close to medieval feudalism by the fourth century. Decorative metalwork began to be worn in a more overt way as marks of status. There is no better instance than the so-called crossbow brooches of the fourth century.

Unlike earlier brooches, crossbows are specifically associated with men, and more particularly men in positions of power. Unlike other brooch types the crossbow had evolved as a trans-Empire symbol of status, which in Roman terms usually means a military association (**95**). They are never decorated with enamelling, a practice which was commonplace in Romano-British versions of other brooches, raising the suggestion that they were either imported or made to a quasi-official pattern (though in fact there are many differences in decoration and construction). Precious-metal examples are rare but examples are known. An exceptional instance of an early, and dated, example is the gold crossbow found at Erickstanbrae in Dumfries and Galloway. It bears an openwork inscription on the bow — IOVI AVG VOT XX, '(Gift) of Jupiter Augustus. (For) twenty (years) of vows' — together with what was probably a scratched-in name, Fortu(natus?) (*RIB* 2421.43). Here Jupiter is Diocletian — he and Maximianus were associated with Jupiter and Hercules respectively in imperial panegyrics of the day (de la Bédoyère 1998, 83). The twentieth anniversary of Diocletian's accession was in November 303 and this brooch would have been given to someone of high rank, probably a senior military officer. The handing-out of gold and silver plate as imperial donatives to loyal servants is a familiar feature of the age, and a number of treasures from the period have been interpreted as these gifts. Crossbow brooches probably formed part of this practice with the more widely known bronze versions serving as economy versions for men of less-important rank. Even so, many of these may once have been gold-plated.

Cultural integration

The fact that we only know about gods like Antenociticus through a Roman idiom shows how much of a one-way street our experience of Roman Britain, or even pre-Roman Britain, is. Likewise, after 43, Roman coins moved into general usage and tribal coins disappeared from circulation. The adoption of a local cult shows how Romans acquired aspects of indigenous culture. It is a good deal less easy to see influences the other way. Continuity of pre-invasion practices or beliefs is generally invisible. If visible or datable at all it is normally in a Roman form. If a Briton bought into Roman culture he was likely to do so through a military career and adopting a Roman name. When we do known about a Briton, the most likely means is through an altar or dedication in Latin. In other words, he may well be difficult to distinguish from a 'Roman' in the context of the record we have. Aurelius Tasulus made a dedication to Belatucadrus at Old Carlisle, calling himself (conveniently) a *veteranus* (*RIB* 887). The prefix Tas- on the cognomen Tasulus is distinctly 'Celtic', recalling British names like Tasciovanus. But the unit most frequently testified in the fort is the *ala Augusta ob virtutem appellata*, not one to which any sort of ethnic origin can be attributed. We therefore know nothing else about this man but the location and his name supplies us with the possibility that he was British by origin, joined the unit, served, and retired to become a senior member of the civilian community that clustered round the fort. In these senses he, or someone like him, could represent different strands of continuity that conflated British social and Roman military status.

With so much evidence for a military presence, road and water routes, and the settlements along the way, the province might have resembled the railway stations of Britain in the Second World War, with a constant traffic of military personnel. Most forts or military establishments normally developed a settlement outside its walls. If the location had advantages, the settlement might last if the fort was abandoned. These are usually interpreted as civilian villages, occupied by families of soldiers, veterans like Aurelius Tasulus, traders and hangers-on (see pp223-5). Hadrian's Wall was particularly attractive to settlement, drawn not only by the commercial potential but also the physical protection of the Wall zone (Biggins and Taylor 1999).

The distribution of sculpture, epigraphy and tombstones is in part due to the circumstances of survival. But the dominance of the epigraphic record by soldiers in particular, even in civilian settlements far away from the northern frontier, suggests that literacy was significantly higher amongst soldiers and has consequences for understanding the dissemination of broader Roman culture throughout Britain. This general picture is reflected amongst graffiti where there is a marked bias to inscribed potsherds from military sites. The earliest reference to Virgil's *Aeneid* in Britain comes from the late first-century documents found at Vindolanda, where a writing exercise records a single line (ix.473). And it is interesting that the most explicit subsequent references to his works in Britain comes 200 years later on the coinage of the rebel commander of the fleet, Carausius (de la Bédoyère 1998 (ii)). But this will still have been broadly an oral society, and it is therefore generally difficult to assess the impact of Roman literary culture on the

96 *Miniature ivory theatre mask from the amphitheatre at Caerleon, Isca. Perhaps a souvenir of theatrical performances, or a decorative motif once fixed to the wall. Height 108mm*

greater Romano-British population. The military love of display and pageantry, reflected in the ceremonial sports helmets and other equipment, played an important role in publicising aspects of Roman and classical myth. The arena at Caerleon may have been primarily for military ceremony but a miniature ivory theatre mask found on the site may be a souvenir of more mainstream Roman theatrical entertainments put on for military and civilian audiences (**96**). The London arena was clearly part of the fort complex, lying immediately outside its south-east corner but it was well within the city's walled area and must have also played a part in the capital's broader cultural experience.

7

ARCHITECTURE AND ENGINEERING

There are two sorts of Roman military building works. There are those which are recognizable in the material record, either by upstanding remains, excavation, or from aerial photography; and those only known to us from inscriptions recording their erection or repair, or passing mentions in literary sources. Very few are known from both sources, and in no case is the complete appearance of the original structure known. Even so, military building dominates the extant record of all architectural work in Roman Britain, with the forts of the northern frontier monopolizing even that.

Most significant Romano-British civilian settlements of the south have either been built on since antiquity or were subjected to massive bouts of stone robbing on and off throughout a period from the fifth century onwards until well into the nineteenth. Consequently, there are only a few instances where buildings are either partially extant, such as Lincoln's north gate, or wholly traceable in the archaeological record, like most of Silchester and parts of Verulamium. Urban inscriptions recording lost buildings are exceedingly few.

Military buildings are far better known from inscriptions and excavations. There are several reasons. There were more stone forts than large towns in Roman Britain. The forts are mainly distributed in places less prone to clearance and development, and lie where stone is more widely available. Even where forts, such as Portchester and Pevensey, lie in areas heavily developed since antiquity they were occasionally liable to be reused and incorporated into medieval castles, thereby guaranteeing their survival (**107**). Finally, there is the traditional interest shown by antiquarians and archaeologists in the activities of the Roman army.

In spite of the record we have, the extent to which military architects influenced building in Britain is a mystery because we know so little about architects themselves. The word *architectus* is best translated as 'engineer', meaning a practical expert in the construction process rather than someone sitting in an office making drawings. The Roman architect was much closer to the master-builders whose skills lay behind the erection of many of Britain's great houses and monuments of the seventeenth and eighteenth centuries. *Architectus* normally appears as a legionary post where it earned immunity from normal duties, but fleet architects are known and civilians are well known in continental contexts, such as Gaius Postumius Pollio at Terracina in central Italy (*ILS* 7734, 7731).

The only Roman architects known in Britain are those who recorded their profession on private religious dedications, rather than their buildings. All the inscriptions come from military contexts. Strictly speaking the individuals concerned do not state themselves to be soldiers, but the idea that they were not is simply implausible. Amandus and

97 *Carved relief of Brigantia dedicated by Amandus,* arc(h)itectus. *From Birrens*, Blatobulgium. RIB *2091*

Gamidiahus are recorded on separate altars at Birrens, and Quintus at Carrawburgh (*RIB* 2091, 2096, 1542) (**97**), and therefore probably date to somewhere between *c.*120-250. Their given names do not suggest that they were citizen legionaries, but it is unlikely that they were attached to auxiliary units (as Evans 1994, 146, suggests) for a variety of reasons. Birrens has produced several undated building stones by *VI* and *XX*, and vexillations of *VIII Augusta* and *XXII Primigenia* (*RIB* 2112-14, and **41**). At least one of the appearances by *XXII* in Britain is associated with the Severan period (see chapter 4), which ties in neatly with *RIB*'s suggestion that Amandus is the same man described on a building inscription of 209 from Iversheim of *I Minervia* as Val. Amandus *discens*, 'Val. . . Amandus, the learned one' (*ILS* 2459), subsequently elevated to the post of *architectus*. However, it is as likely that he had been allocated to *VI*, being dispatched to locations needing his services. Architectural work could also be undertaken by a *mensor* (surveyor) or a *librator* (responsible for levelling the ground). No Romano-British *librator* has been identified but Antonius Quintianus, *mensor*, is testified on an altar from Piercebridge (*RIB* 1024).

This leaves us none the wiser about the first 30-40 years of Roman military building in Britain, yet the archaeological evidence shows there was a continuous process of military building, mainly in turf and timber, from the invasion onwards. These range from marching camps, through a range of forts such as Hod Hill (*see* **8**) and Great Casterton, to early legionary fortresses like Longthorpe and Usk (**colour plate 23**). Characteristic building techniques were beam and slot construction, generally leaving only traces of trenches and post-holes, lattice-work and plastered walling, and turf timber-laced ramparts laid over pile foundations.

Each fort represents not only a colossal amount of physical labour, but also the exploitation of the surrounding area for the resources (see chapter 5). Stone was occasionally used where necessary, like bathhouses and ovens (**98**, **colour plate 27**). Essentially stereotypical in design and layout, the Roman fort was a fortified compound which contained a fairly standard range of buildings: headquarters, commandant's house,

98 *The fort baths at Chesters*, Cilurnum. *Built of stone to resist fire damage and rot, the baths were also located close to a supply of water and some distance from the main fort complex*

hospital, workshop, armoury, granaries, barracks, as well as facilities like lavatories, water-tanks, and ovens (**99**, **colour plates 25 & 26**). Contrary to popular imagination the range was liable to be adapted according to local requirements, with even the layout being modified where the terrain required a flexible approach. But the 'system' required in theory some or all of a standard suite of buildings to be produced in fairly short order for the fort to function. The utilization of a fortified annexe for associated structures was commonplace, and has been identified at many places. Typically, the annexe might contain baths, and industrial structures — all of vital use but not for defence, and sometimes wisely removed from the main complex because of the risk of fire.

Vitruvius tells us very little about military building works, restricting his account mainly to fortifications. This implies that he did not regard military architecture as a separate branch of the discipline, but it also reflected the contemporary mobility and early development of the imperial army. At the end of the first century BC the Roman army was an army of conquest, which campaigned in the summer and retired to barracks in the winter. It was also not long after the general disorder of the civil wars and therefore the imperial military establishment was still flux. There was no time, inclination or need, invariably to engage in substantial stone building works. Only once the German frontier started to become more settled in the 40s, incidentally, helping to make the forces available for the invasion of Britain, did more elaborate stone-built forts start to appear in frontier regions. Even so, the substantial masonry buildings of the legionary fortress at Vindonissa were contained within an irregular polygonal layout, a characteristic of most turf forts of the period (**100**).

This was a time when major civilian building works were underway in Rome and across provinces like Gaul and Spain. The headquarters building, and the baths, at

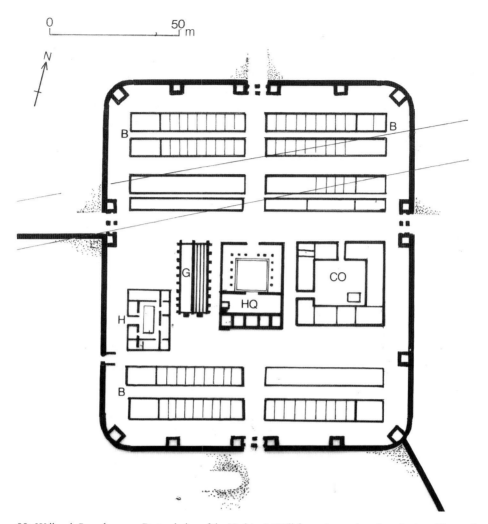

99 *Wallsend, Segedunum. Restored plan of the Hadrian's Wall fort as it may have been in the mid-second century. The fort is one of very few where almost the entire layout is now on public display. Most of the area is given over to barracks (B), while the centre featured a headquarters building (HQ), the commandant's house (CO), granaries (G), and a hospital (H). Compare with **colour plate 25***

Vindonissa are comparable in layout and scale to the public buildings, which started to appear in Britain towards the later first century. But general consolidation of military establishments in stone did not take place until after *c.*75, coinciding with the evidence for public building works in stone. Even earlier than that, Tacitus reports the existence of a theatre, senate house and Temple of Claudius in Colchester by 60 though tells us nothing about details of construction (*A* xiv.32) (*see* **10**). The context of Britain's earliest military colony makes it highly likely that soldiers or veterans must have both been involved in some of the Colchester structures, though it is impossible to demonstrate a connection.

By the mid-50s a legionary fortress at Exeter had been established. There is no epigraphic evidence for the garrison though *II Augusta* is the most likely candidate. The fortress did not remain in use after *c*.75, but it is set apart from earlier sites like Longthorpe by being operated long enough for significant 'permanent' building to take place. The monumental masonry legionary bathhouse is amongst the earliest major architectural works ever seen in Britain, and built on traditions already established elsewhere (**100**). As at Wroxeter, this feature seems to have played no direct part in the establishment of the later civitas capital. It continued in use for a while, though it was reduced in size. But by *c*.80 the building was demolished to make way for the new basilica and forum complex of the civitas capital. Part of the building was retained to form some of the basilica. The fact that the town had a major operational baths looks like a gift horse and it is hard to see what would be gained by demolishing them, quite apart from the difficulties of consolidating the site to make it suitable for new building work. One possibility is that the former baths were modified to act as a sort of basilica and forum — after all, it had large covered areas, as well as an outdoor palaestra. Wroxeter's legionary baths suffered a similar fate. In both cases, new public baths were eventually erected in adjacent blocks.

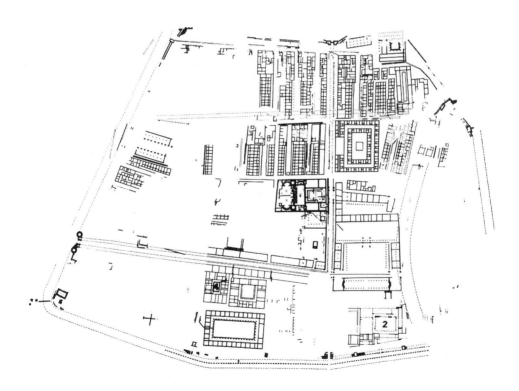

100 *The Claudian legionary fortress at* Vindonissa *(Windisch, near Basle). The layout lacks the regularity and symmetry of later fortresses, for example Inchtuthil (see **19**). The legionary baths are in the middle, close to the barracks in spite of the fire risk, while the headquarters lie at lower right centre*

At the very least, the demolition work suggests an administrative separation between the military and civilian periods, and probably therefore also a completely different design and building process, even if military architects were still involved. The introduction of the concept of large vaulted public buildings made of stone, concrete and brick, can only have had a dramatic impact on the local population and perhaps helped provoke the idea that this sort of work was the mark of status in the Roman idiom. One need only consider how modern civic worthies embark on building projects to equip their towns with what are presented as appropriate features — though it is often the case that business connections and lucrative contracts play a part too. The prospect of making money through new facilities, selling contracts, and even positions, could all have played a part.

One of the few datable building inscriptions from this period is the slab recording the Temple of Neptune and Minerva dedicated during the lifetime of Tiberius Claudius Togidubnus in Chichester some time between *c.*54-85 (see chapter 1). This is particularly interesting because it comes from an area where there is increasing evidence for a primary role in the invasion of Britain. Although this was a client kingdom area and thus semi-autonomous, a number of early military-type timber buildings have been discovered just to the west of Chichester at Fishbourne. The so-called palace, in both its Neronian and Flavian phases, built on the same site, remains a unique early example of sophisticated architectural design and embellishment in a Mediterranean idiom. Traditionally attributed to Togidubnus it remains possible that it was for at least a time the governor's residence. If so, that would tie it in to the military systems responsible for the influx of building skills and techniques.

Several of the principal urban settlements of the new province were being equipped with major public buildings by the reigns of Vespasian and Titus (69-81). Tacitus gives us good reason to see Agricola as a major factor in the initiative, either as the initiator or as the medium through which imperial policy was exercised (*Agricola* 21). Tacitus does specify that Agricola encouraged the Britons to build *templa fora domos*, 'temples, forums and houses', by encouraging individuals and actually helping communities. Given all that, we have to conclude that Agricola played an important role in promoting the active development of Romano-British towns, but whether he made use of military manpower is quite unknown.

The inscription from the forum at Verulamium recording Agricola is fragmentary. What remains does not mention the building, and the section referring to the local community can be restored in at least three different ways. But enough survives to show that it belongs to the year 79 or 81, and that it seems to include the name Agricola (**101**). Now, we do not know whether that inscription records the inception of the building, dedication prior to completion or at completion. As Agricola did not come into post until at least 77 the obvious conclusion would be, if it commemorates completion, that he was not responsible for initiating the structure but happily took the credit.

There is no inscription allowing us to pass the credit to any other first-century governor, or to contradict Tacitus' claim. In any case, there is no real reason to dispute the point other than natural historical scepticism or the desire to create an issue when one may not really exist.

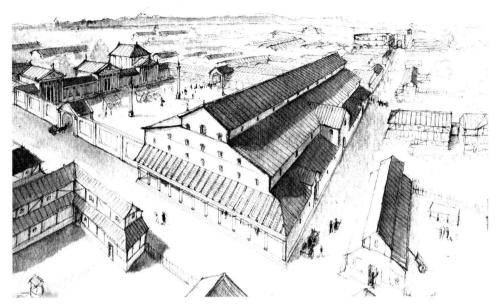

101 *The forum and basilica complex at Verulamium, as it might have appeared after its dedication in 79 or 81 under Agricola. The architect is unknown but a military connection is plausible*

As the governor, and an uncompromisingly military figure at that, it is easy to see how Agricola might have sought architectural talent from amongst his garrison, but Tacitus implies that the desire for Romanized living came as much from ambitious natives as it did from the provincial government. This has certainly been suggested for the Flavian development of the temple and spring complex at Bath (Henig 1999, 162 — who goes as far as suggesting that Togidubnus might have been responsible; *RIB* 172 in the name of Vespasian helps date the work).

This overlooks the army's enthusiasm for spa centres on the continent (see chapter 6) but baths are popularly regarded as being synonymous with a Roman lifestyle. Although every Roman fort seems to have been equipped with baths, that is not always the case with the towns and townhouses of Roman Britain. The epigraphic evidence from Bath makes it much easier to generate a case for a military background to its development. Verulamium, conversely, deficient in evidence for the Roman army and epigraphy in general, has yet to show that it had public baths and a characteristic of its townhouses is a lack of baths, reflected in varying degrees elsewhere. Lacklustre in its enthusiasm for the decadent comforts of Roman life, perhaps the local population at Verulamium had the forum-basilica foisted on them by the provincial authorities.

London, conversely, has not only produced evidence for more soldiers than any other town but has also yielded a large number of public baths. While the evidence is distinctly variable — Silchester for example had some public baths (but of an early date) — it may be that the presence of bath establishments in an urban context is more linked to the presence of military trade than we might have realized up to now. Wroxeter was a comparatively 'frontline' town, and had once been a legionary fortress. But it is difficult to tell — we cannot know who the customers were, but it is intriguing that the distribution of known urban bathing places is so patchy. Similar considerations might apply to amphitheatres — the military examples at Caerleon, Chester and London are all more sophisticated than civilian instances, like Cirencester, and again we may be looking at another Roman activity which never preyed much on the civilian mind. Similarly, classical-style theatres were limited in their urban distribution, though examples are known at Verulamium, Colchester and Canterbury, along with one or two other possibilities. But those known are linked closely to temples, diminishing perhaps their roles as showcases for Roman theatrical entertainments. It is impossible to know, but the Romano-British urban world seems to have had little interest in places where classical literature could be presented.

At London, Silchester, Canterbury and Cirencester the evidence for Flavian work remains purely archaeological. Canterbury's theatre was built around this time. Here the forum and basilica have yet to be explored in detail though it seems likely that they will have formed part of the same complex. Cirencester presents an interesting problem. Its new basilica was built partly over the ditches of the earlier fort and suffered partial subsidence as a consequence. That might mean a total separation of responsibilities, as one might expect a military engineer charged with erecting the new basilica to know about the possible problems. On the other, it would have been fairly obvious to whoever supervised the work what was being done. Many Romano-British buildings can be shown to have suffered subsidence of one sort or another, often because they were built over ditches, roads, and earlier buildings, or had unsatisfactory foundations. This was because, regardless of the background of an architect, much of the work was empirical and lacked any scientific or mathematical background, in spite of accurate measurements. Personal experience of these problems might have been very limited.

Unfortunately, unless a building is identified either as an unequivocally military form, or in a military context, then military responsibility cannot be proven without epigraphic or literary confirmation. But to reject the possibility is to sustain the view that military and civilian communities were somehow separate. Given the increasing evidence for the detachment of military staff into the greater community it is very unlikely that military architects and engineers were not made available for urban projects, at least in the earlier part of the period. Pliny's letters to Trajan from Bithynia and Pontus refer to instances where incompetence and rivalry had compromised unsupervised civic ventures. Under Hadrian the authorities at Bougie in Mauretania wanted an aqueduct but had nobody to design the project. Consequently, they asked the governor who passed them onto the legate of *III Augusta*. The latter produced Nonius Datus, a *librator*, who drew up a plan for approval in 137. Things did not proceed apace, and in 149 and 151-2 Datus had to turn up and supervise the work in person. The only reason we know all this is that Nonius Datus recorded everything on an inscription dated to *c.*153 (*ILS* 5795). Not only was he mugged along the way, but turned up to find that the tunnel component of the watercourse had been started on opposite sides of the mountain concerned, but gone off alignment.

This incident does not refer to the design and erection of a specific urban building, but it does tell us a lot about the problems facing a town determined to equip itself with a new facility. Firstly, they did not have the relevant skills. Secondly, the only convenient source of the skill in the province, which had been part of the Empire only a couple of years longer than Britain, was a retired legionary. Thirdly, even with a plan the townsfolk could not execute the work competently and had to summon the architect in person. Fourthly, the whole project had clearly taken more than 15 years, which makes it possible that dedication inscriptions might be much later than the inception of the work. It was not a unique event. The biography, admittedly not wholly reliable, of the emperor Probus (276-82) (*see* **45**), states that 'there are extant in many cities in Egypt his works, which he built through the use of soldiers' (*SHA Probus*, ix.3). Communications across any province were important to general administration and military interests. In the year 90 a bridge was built in Egypt at Koptos by *III Cyrenaica* and in 123 *III Augusta* paved a road from Carthage (*CIL* iii.13580, viii.10048).

In this context, when public building projects were mooted as a result of local initiative or state cash being made available, a Romano-British town government might seek the governor's assistance to provide the necessary skills. The governor need only then turn to one of the legions and instruct that a basic design for a forum-basilica be drawn up and presented to the townsfolk, and a legionary sent along to organize the work. This might be all the military involvement there was, leaving the influence scarcely apparent to us but fundamental nonetheless.

The military headquarters building, with basilican hall and open piazza with covered wings, resembles the civilian basilica-forum complex of the north-western provinces to such an extent that it seems obvious that there must be a link. But the form was basic, and applied in a number of different contexts. The basilica, for example, was utilized in major bath complexes as a covered exercise hall, and also adapted for use in Mithraic temples and churches. The design was suitable for any congregational gathering where a focus of attention and view was required, and allowed large or small volumes of space to be contained and roofed in a durable form. The vaulted public baths at Wroxeter resemble the legionary baths at Caerleon. While the baths at Wroxeter could have been by a military architect, imitation is just as plausible. Stamped tiles from public buildings in towns such as Cirencester, Gloucester, Silchester and London seem to exclude the possibility of any military involvement in the manufacture of building materials (though this is obviously a separate issue from design). At London the procurator's office was responsible, whereas at Gloucester tile production seems to have been in the control of the urban magistrates and at other places in the hands of private concerns except for Silchester where stamps name Nero.

Military influence could also have been more subtle and indirect. At the time of the invasion, regularity of proportion and form in the military fort was becoming more common. The timber fort at Valkenburg contrasts with Hofheim in its regular and coordinated layout, and closely resembles the forts along Hadrian's Wall built 80 years later. At the Claudian fort of Hod Hill this regularity is visible in a timber fort pragmatically built into the corner of an Iron Age hillfort. In Britain's terms the army was introducing concepts of regularity, order, and consistency. Fundamental to these were surveying skills, using equipment like the *groma*, and the *norma*, which made it possible to establish straight lines and right angles. There has been something of an enthusiasm for trying to find complex mathematical patterns in building plans and from this deducing elaborate evidence for arcs, circles and arcane systems of proportion (for example Evans 1994, and Zienkiewcz 1986). This does not sit easily with the fact that while military buildings conformed to stereotypes, no two are the same and there is colossal variation in the treatment, including inaccuracies and erratic measurements. It is also much easier to draw circles and grids across neatly ruled paper plans than it is to lay things out on the ground that way.

Vitruvius is vague about operating surveying equipment, instead assuming some familiarity amongst his readers. This may explain things rather better in terms of men who were involved in sporadic production of buildings, usually of timber, in less than ideal conditions. They will have used some theoretical knowledge with practical experience, while dealing with local features of drainage, soil, woodland clearance, all of which will have dictated size, orientation and accuracy of the building. There will also have been considerable variations in skills and opportunities. The irregularity of the headquarters at Hod Hill might be the consequence of incompetence or, when one looks at the plan, adapting to the slightly different orientation of the barracks on either side, itself a consequence of the site. Whatever the reason, the calibre of the designer of the baths at Exeter, and Caerleon, must have been greater — but then time, resources and conditions were on his side.

No plans of any Romano-British building exist, and no accounts of the work. In fact, it is not until the seventeenth century that extensive documentation of substance starts to survive. The paperwork reveals a much more ad-hoc arrangement than the executed great country houses of the period suggest. Belton House in Lincolnshire is a useful example in this context. The house remains substantially in its original 1680s form and is notable for its fine use of proportion. The normal process was to approach a master-builder and commission him to design and execute the work. Or the owner, Lord Brownlow, could, in the words of the architect Roger Pratt (1620-84), 'get some ingenious gentleman who has seen much of that kind abroad . . . to give you a design of it in paper, though but roughly drawn' (cited by Tinniswood 1992). Brownlow is thought to have commissioned William Winde (d. 1722) to come up with the basic design, and the master-builder William Stanton (1639-1705) to execute the project, introduce detail and modify it as required. If that seems complicated enough, the finished house was clearly based on the short-lived Clarendon House by Pratt himself, in Piccadilly.

This case obviously proves nothing about Roman Britain and military architecture, but it does show how the design of a complex and prestigious structure involved several different people and stages in haphazard form, as well as absorbing influence from an archetype by then only extant in engravings (Clarendon House was demolished in 1684) and adapting it to local circumstances. Significantly, as a coherent and essentially one-period structure, none of this process would be evident from an examination of the ground-plan showing that it is ultimately rather futile attempting such an analysis without the paperwork. Even if the designs 'were simply made up as the builders went along' (Evans 1994, 163), what does matter is that Roman Britain was being introduced to the general process of rational construction according to models. More importantly (and wholly lacking from modern studies of ground-plans), Britain was also being introduced to three-dimensional structures, which had simply not existed at all prior to 43. In this context the headquarters building at Hod Hill, for all its inaccuracies, was radical to an extent we can scarcely appreciate.

Consolidation

The Trajanic inscriptions at Caerleon and York show that *II Augusta* and *VIIII Hispana* were engaged in major stone-building projects at their respective fortresses by the first decade of the second century. There is some comparable evidence from Chester but archaeological evidence from all three points to this work having been underway for at least 15-20 years beforehand in some shape or form. Whether that means there was a concerted programme to rebuild *everything* is quite unknown. The fortress baths at Caerleon have been attributed to *c*.80 from excavation evidence, and were designed as a sophisticated vaulted structure built of stone and concrete in a tradition of substantial, but conventional, monumental baths of a type known 40 years earlier at Vindonissa as well as in the contemporary baths of Titus in Rome.

Lead pipes at Chester bearing Agricola's name and imperial titles of Vespasian and Titus for 79, and an inscription naming Domitian, show that sophisticated development work on facilities was also in progress on the fortress at there (*RIB* 463, 2434.1-2). One of these was found in the curious, and so far mysterious, so-called 'Elliptical Building' (Mason 2000) (**102**). Of unprecedented design, its central feature was an elliptical courtyard surrounded by a colonnade leading to radial chambers and entrances on the long axis. Whether it was of religious, ceremonial or practical use is entirely unknown, but it is one of the most convincing pieces of evidence for original military architecture in the new province. Unfortunately, it was abandoned early in the construction process, and remained incomplete and apparently buried until *c*.230. When a new version of the structure was begun above and this time completed, it can (on the face of it) only have been because some sort of manuscript record remained of the original project. This seems a lot to read into limited evidence gathered under arduous conditions more than 30 years ago. Some visible physical traces must have remained in antiquity.

The Elliptical Building is also interesting because its abandonment might be linked to the transfer of *II Adiutrix*, the resident garrison until *c*.86, out of Britain. Perhaps this legion enjoyed the services of a proficient and imaginative individual architect. While the headquarters was of conventional design it lay next to a much larger enclosed courtyard, also of unparalleled form. These additional structures meant that Chester occupied a significantly larger footprint than either York or Caerleon (*see* **22**).

That this enigmatic building was not finished in its first stage even by the successor garrison does raise the interesting possibility that legionary fortress works were sometimes beyond the legions to complete. The basilican cross-hall of the Caerleon headquarters seems never to have been completed though it was laid out, and other parts of the building were completed and put into operation. Perhaps this was because of garrison responsibilities and building duties in developing the civilian settlements. But it is far more likely that the need to work on other forts, such as Gellygaer where Trajanic building is testified on inscriptions (*RIB* 397-9), and then on the northern frontier,

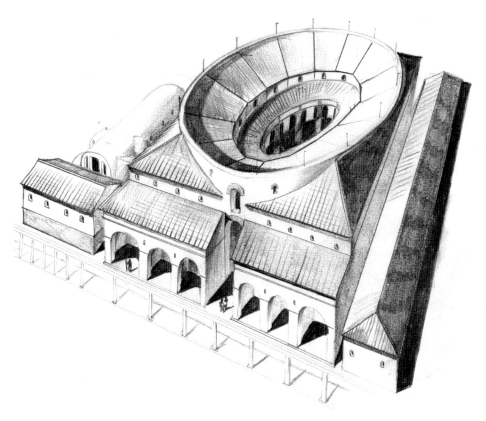

102 *Reconstruction drawing of the so-called 'Elliptical Building' at the legionary fortress of Chester in its late first-century form as it might have appeared if the work had been finished. The building was completed more than a century later on a similar plan*

stretched resources to breaking point. This may, for example, help explain why Caernarfon's conversion to stone might have had to wait until after *c*.140. Excavators at Chester believe they have identified various examples of delayed reconstruction work, vacant lots, and abandoned new work in the 120s (Strickland 1999, 107). The obvious context is the need to move resources to the Hadrianic frontier. But it is also apparent from the sources for the period that Hadrian was frustrated to find institutional and individual inertia amongst soldiers in Germany, and implicitly, in Britain. While completion might have been delayed by the new frontier it is also quite possible that work in the fortress had subsided through idleness and indifference for many years. It is impossible to say, though an interesting conclusion is that building work at Chester remained in a thoroughly inconclusive state for another 80 years or more. There is no need to avoid the obvious conclusion that the needs of the north not only deprived Chester of its manpower, but also removed the need for much of the facilities at all, perhaps begun on the whim of a governor like Agricola, and as quickly forgotten. Just as the evidence of units themselves is for constant dispersal and separation, so the evidence from the actual bases reflect this lack of cohesion in contrast to the traditional image of the Roman army in regimented garrisons.

Hadrian was not exclusively concerned with the army, and one suggestion is that Chester's disrupted plans might have been part of a plan to convert the part-built fortress to some sort of civilian role (*op. cit.* 107, 109). This is not testified. The nearest major public building to Chester confirmed by date is the forum and basilica complex at Wroxeter, dedicated in 129-30 (*RIB* 288). The date is significant because if we take it to represent completion of the works, then the project had probably begun around a decade earlier when Hadrian visited Britain. This entirely fits Dio's note that Hadrian's general policy was to encourage the provision of public works through making cash available (lxix.5.3). There is no suggestion of any military involvement in the largely complete text, and the dedication is exclusively in the community name of the *civitas Cornoviorum*, but as we have seen there is every possibility that a basic design could have been drawn up by a legionary architect summoned for the job, or even travelling with Hadrian, and left with the people of Wroxeter to execute or put out to contract (the latter is, for example, testified at Pompeii on *ILS* 5706). However, the geographer Ptolemy also associated Chester with the Cornovii which might mean there was more of a formal relationship between the canton and legion than our minimal epigraphic evidence suggests (*PNRB* 325).

The time that the Wroxeter forum-basilica was built is of course a time when all three legions, and the *classis Britannica*, were building Hadrian's Wall, and confirmed on numerous inscriptions mostly attributable to 122-6. Records of the cohorts involved makes it clear that only a part of each legion was deployed on the works, but this does not take into account the internal buildings of the forts. That the fleet had to help out at Benwell is revealing (*see* **26**). Overall, it seems unlikely that legionary muscle could have been provided to help in civic building projects but there would have been nothing to prevent design and supervision being dealt with by legionary architects, especially during the winter months.

Although excavations at Birdoswald and Chester have shown that forts were not necessarily completed at this time, military architects and engineers will have been substantially occupied on fort and frontier building from the early second century right on through to the time of the Antonine Wall and then back on Hadrian's Wall. Scattered inscriptions from the other forts, like South Shields (*VI*, *RIB* 1061), Bewcastle (*II* and *XX*, *RIB* 995), and Corbridge (*II*, *VI*, and *XX RIB* 1148, 1137, 1149), show that some part of each legion was engaged in major building work on and off throughout the second century. Although structures like the headquarters building at Housesteads conformed to generic forms and were competently executed, they pale in comparison to the major public building works further south both in terms of scale and decoration (see below).

Each fort on the northern frontier alone was a miniature version of the legionary fortresses further south, requiring a supply chain of raw materials, as well as the skill to execute the project efficiently and in a durable form (**103**, **colour plate 25**). The most productive consequence of the work carried out at South Shields in recent years to reconstruct the west gate of *Arbeia* according to elements of collapsed superstructure found on the site, and partially extant examples like Bu Njem in Libya, has been to demonstrate how potentially awe-inspiring each of these forts might once have been and how much effort had to be expended to complete them (**104**).

Together with the curtain Wall and its installations of milecastles and turrets, the frontier system is a remarkable example of the architectural power of the Roman army. It

103 *Vindolanda, the headquarters building*

includes the most substantial evidence for masonry bridge building, at Chesters and Willowford, together with the controversial and little-understood site at Piercebridge. Chesters, for example, went through at least two phases: a Hadrianic footway, later supplanted by the much larger Severan structure which carried a roadway as well as the frontier itself. The evidence of the centurial and other building stones here, and on the Antonine Wall, shows that all of the legions were involved but the physical remains show that each legion built to slightly different models. So, while there was a coordinated basis for the project, the exact design and execution seems to have been the individual responsibility of the units, recalling the idiosyncratic projects at Chester (**102**). Hadrian is often credited with the basic concept of the frontier, but whoever was responsible cannot have done more than draw up a basic design. The milecastle gateways and plans alone make this clear. *II Augusta* is associated epigraphically with milecastles featuring monumental arched gateways, characteristically constructed from much large blocks than the rest of the milecastle, and a plan where the north-south axis is shorter than the east-west, for example milecastle 37 (Housesteads West). Some of the other milecastles have reversed proportions and much less imposing gateways, for example milecastle 39 ('Castle Nick') (*see* **27**).

This flexibility may have helped stimulate the building work by allowing units to compete for the prestige of swift completion. But it could also have been part of the Wall's construction problems. Despite being produced with a technique that was effective and quick, the use of a rubble core was liable to cause internal collapse and the Wall to disintegrate as Vitruvius warned (ii.8.7-8). This undoubtedly happened, causing cyclical rebuilding throughout the Wall's history. Such haste might be behind the Wall being started as a 10-Roman-foot wide curtain, and then rapidly narrowed to 8ft (**105**). Further changes led to the demolition of some turrets and installation of the forts around every 7-8 Roman miles. These details are discussed widely elsewhere (for example Breeze and Dobson 1987, de la Bédoyère 1998). Here the important point is the clear evidence for alterations 'in the field'. Despite being a unique project, it enshrined a lack of total regimentation in Roman military building.

Later building

Another major phase of military building began in the late second century and lasted into the early third. This forms an important part of the historical evidence for that period and is discussed in detail in chapter 4. Unfortunately, the evidence is almost entirely confined to epigraphy, with very few of the buildings being known from actual remains. This is crucial because it means that there might be other phases of building work which we know nothing about, simply because they were not recorded on inscriptions and this could equally well apply in the civilian zone where inscriptions are always far rarer. The period also saw a massive peak in coin issues by provincial mints across the Empire, in the names of Septimius Severus and Caracalla. So, there seems to have been a more widespread agenda in commemorating this dynasty in a variety of media, thereby distorting the record.

104 *Housesteads,* Vercovicium, *the east gate as it may have appeared in the second century*

105 *Hadrian's Wall, turret 26b (Brunton). The 10ft-wide foundation of the Wall, and the turret's 10ft-thick wing wall lie in the centre, while to the right is the 8ft-wide wall built over and up to these earlier features*

The majority of this new work was recorded by auxiliary units, an interesting departure from earlier military building which was almost entirely executed by the legions, at least as far as it is recorded (**106**). Many of the new inscriptions state that the work was reconstructive, an interesting comment not only on the durability of older buildings but also that long periods of dereliction had been tolerated. It may have been part and parcel of a renewal of military structures beginning under Severus and seems to have included a wholesale reconstruction of much of Hadrian's Wall and its associated systems.

Whether the auxiliary units had staff who could design and supervise the work, or whether anonymous legionaries were seconded to do this, is not clear. An inscription of *c.*197-202 from Bowes records that a burnt bathhouse was rebuilt for *cohors I Thracum*. It adds that the work was supervised by Valerius Fronto, prefect of *ala Vettonum* (*RIB* 730). The *ala Vettonum* was probably based nearby at Binchester so they must have had the competence to take charge of the project, which the Thracians did not. At the very least it means we might have underestimated the contribution some auxiliaries could have been making to military building for decades.

This contrasts with the civilian zone which, in the early third century, was characterized by largely 'complete' towns to the extent that they seem to have had their principal public facilities, and were increasingly populated by stone townhouses. There is not a single datable imperial dedication from any town from the mid-second century onwards which can be linked to a specific building. The last one we hear of is the gift

106 *High Rochester,* Bremenium. *Inscription of 216 under Caracalla recording unspecified building work by* cohors I Vardullorum. *The governor's name has been deleted.* RIB *1279*

of a theatre stage at Brough-on-Humber between 140-61, donated by a local aedile (*RIB* 707).

While this must reflect the erratic distribution of inscriptions in the civilian zone, it must also reflect the military predilection for recording their work this way. This makes understanding the erection of stone civic defences from the late second century on, and the only significant civic works thereafter, particularly difficult. There is not one single inscription or literary reference which might provide clues for whether this was a province-wide or local initiative or whether there was any connection with the army. The colonies and, exceptionally for a civitas capital, Exeter made use of earlier military defences for some time. At Exeter the old legionary fortress defences remained to mark the town limits until the late second century when new ones were built to enclose an area some 2.5 times greater.

Considering that of all civic projects the erection of defences and gates is the most closely linked to military architecture this is frustrating especially as they have remained amongst the most durable relics of Roman architecture in the province. Some of the monumental gateways, at Colchester and Verulamium for example, were demonstrably extant some time before the walls and were simply integrated into the new defences. One might speculate that the need to use auxiliaries to build widely in the north was because legionaries had been seconded to towns to supervise urban defences. But that presupposes there was some sort of centralized initiative and fails to explain the lack of inscriptions recording their input. Vitruvius regarded urban defences as a routine part of establishing a town (v.5.1) so there is no automatic need to link them to a specific threat, except where the effect will have been to inhibit normal commercial activity. This is best seen at London where the 'late' riverside wall built in the fourth century served to cut the town off from its life-giving wharves.

107 *The west gate of the Saxon Shore fort at Pevensey,* Anderida. *Date is uncertain but probably very late third century or early fourth. Unlike fort gates of a century or more before, the towers are solid, projecting, bastions*

As a style though the new walls acted generally as stone revetments to earlier earthen ramparts. This sets them apart from the introduction of the Saxon Shore fort system in the south and east during the third century, which represented a new form of military architecture based on freestanding walls (**107, colour plate 20**). The banks of earth within the walls provided access, but this was a parallel feature rather than with earlier walls, where the stone tended to act as revetments to existing banks. In terms of style though, the new shore forts exhibit no sense that the architecture need be anything more than brutally functional. Very few stone-built internal buildings are known from these sites, and there is no evidence at all for any sort of sculptural embellishment to evoke pride or splendour.

The introduction of projecting bastions represents another problem, and seems to link the urban examples into more general military works. Bastions were solid projections from walls which provided static artillery with a wider field of fire. The normal association is the post-367 context when Count Theodosius set about repairing Britain's defences. Nothing in the archaeology has served to confirm that. That they were incorporated *during* construction at some Saxon Shore forts in the later third century is self-evident from the partial bonding at Burgh Castle (*see* **44**). Urban bastions are generally attributed to a later initiative though they clearly drew from and depended on military techniques. Unlike the Saxon Shore fort bastions, though there is more of a sense of urgency in the urban examples, the possibility that military authorities were responsible for converting towns into extensions of the short fort system should not be passed over. We have the London bastion builders to thank for some of London's finest and most important epigraphic and sculptural monuments demolished and utilized as rubble core (*see* **52**). At Caerwent the work was more disciplined, leaving some of the most outstanding examples of Roman urban defences in Britain. Here the projecting semi-octagonal bastions recall the Multangular Tower at York, itself linked to the rather earlier redevelopment of the fortress at the beginning of the fourth century in 305-6 when Constantius I embarked on a northern campaign, followed by his death and the declaration of his son Constantine as emperor the following year (**colour plate 29**). It seems rather hard then to associate the two other than in adopting a broadly similar response to the same architectural trend.

The fourth century in fact is a very complicated picture for military architecture. Style was not entirely forgotten. York's multangular tower (above) was one of a series of hollow polygonal towers designed to create an imposing riverfront façade. At Birdoswald, one of the few places where an inscription demonstrates rebuilding work under the Tetrarchy (*RIB* 1912), the fourth century seems to have seen a gradual decline to semi-dereliction, and the eventual replacement of some fort buildings with timber halls. At Housesteads, deterioration of the walls led to partial demolition of the gates and use of components to repair them. Conversely, South Shields seems to have been modified into a state-of-the-art establishment, complete with Mediterranean-style commandant's house. At the legionary fortresses clearance of some areas seems to have taken place, with the appearance of *II Augusta* at Richborough in the *Notitia Dignitatum* and the disappearance of *XX* from the record presumably being connected.

By the late fourth century a series of towers with walled courtyards and external ditches was built along the Yorkshire coast. Known only from their lower levels, they might have resembled Norman castle keeps and added to a series of military fortifications which now spread right round Britain's shores, including installations at towns in vulnerable locations such as Horncastle (see chapter 4). At Lancaster a mid-fourth-century fort obliterated some of the earlier fort structures, such as the baths, cut through by a ditch. At Caer Gybi in Anglesey a three-sided compound leading down to the sea must be a fortified landing point for naval vessels patrolling the coasts.

Private military building

As well as epigraphic evidence for military buildings by specific units and at specific dates, there is a significant body of evidence for private military building initiatives. The case of the Brough-on-Humber aedile, Marcus Ulpius Januarius, cited above, is extremely rare in an urban context. Very few civilian buildings are commemorated this way on surviving slabs though sporadic finds of what seem to be quite obscure structures like an arch to the god Viridius at Ancaster, and Mars Rigonemetos at Nettleham (*JRS* 1962, 192), suggest that problems with survival in more developed parts of England might be part of the problem. Even so, examples reflect a general bias to recording buildings associated with religion if at all, whether temples or the arched entrances to the precincts.

Soldiers seem to have been fond of acting as individual patrons of building or rebuilding projects, but as with the civilian zone, temples and shrines were favoured. At Benwell an inscription records that the prefect Terentius Agrippa restored a temple to the

Section of Arthur's Oven.

108 *The curious temple which survived to the mid-eighteenth century known as Arthur's O'on, at Carron, just north of the Antonine Wall. Probably a temple dedicated to Victory, the structure was probably built by soldiers garrisoned on, or building, the new Wall*

Mother Goddesses of the Parade Ground and the local Genius (*RIB* 1334). Further east at Wallsend a centurion of *VI Victrix* built a temple to an unknown god (*RIB* 1305). Not surprisingly, the same was true at the legionary fortresses. At York, a temple of Serapis was built before *c.*212 by Claudius Hieronymianus, legate of *VI* (**colour plate 28**), and at Caerleon Titus Flavius Postumius Varus, probably the mid-third-century legate of *II Augusta*, restored a temple to Diana (*RIB* 658, 316).

Perhaps it is significant that even in the civilian zone soldiers were disproportionately responsible for recording their benefactions this way. At Winchester a *beneficiarius consularis* restored what must have been a shrine to the Mother Goddesses, the London mithraeum is unequivocally associated with a veteran of *II Augusta*, and at Dover a *strator consularis* restored a shrine to the Italian Mother Goddesses (*see* **75**, *RIB* 88, and *B* 1977, 426-7). Dover was, however, a fort, and London was of course closely associated with the army through its own garrison.

Such individualism also found other outlets in the military zone at a relatively early date. 'Arthur's O'n' was a circular 'beehive' temple at Carron, two miles north of Falkirk. It survived intact until 1743 but antiquarian drawings and a replica preserve its form (**108**). It was around 9m in height and width, being built of dressed stone in beehive form and had an arched entrance and a window above. It may have had an *oculus* (an open space) at the top. It is not certain that the building was a temple but it is difficult to imagine an alternative function and there is the circumstantial evidence of a relief from Rose Hill, Gilsland, Cumbria. Early accounts mention carved victories and eagles on the walls within, so it may have been a temple to Victory which would have been appropriate for the location, though a garbled report by Sir Robert Sibbald of an inscription still visible in 1707 may be restorable as a dedication to Jupiter Optimus Maximus (*RIB* 2345★). There was almost certainly a statue within because a pedestal existed and a fragment of bronze statue was also found. Being so close to the fort at Falkirk on the Antonine Wall, and the quality of its masonry, makes it virtually certain that the army was responsible for its construction. The temple would probably have fallen out of use by the late second century, along with the abandonment of the Antonine Wall, but such was its structural integrity only deliberate demolition brought its life to an end.

The curious little temple of Antenociticus at Benwell was identified outside the east wall of the fort at Benwell in 1862. Three altars record its dedication to Antenociticus/Anociticus (*RIB* 1327-9). One can be dated to 177-80. The structure's quaint eccentricity suggests a very homemade type of shrine. Unlike Arthur's O'on the building was not particularly ambitious in scale or design but must have been constructed by soldiers as a private initiative (**109**).

The end of military building

Sadly there is nothing to tell us how military architecture was organized in the fourth century. Only the garbled inscription from Ravenscar records the curious command

109 *The mid- to late second-century apsidal temple at Benwell,* Condercum, *dedicated to a local god called Antenociticus but with dedications made by soldiers*

structure involved. Here Justinianus, *praepositus*, and Vindicianus, *masbier* (for *magister*?), had dealt with the fourth-century signal tower work (*RIB* 721). But there is no date, no emperor, and no unit named (*see* **51**). Expressing no, or being unaware of, allegiance to any authority beyond their own these men symbolize the dissipation of Roman military authority into semi-autonomous units where even having the idea to produce an inscription at all, however miserably executed, was a striking event.

With evidence for civilian public building works, apart from defences, being largely confined to the late first and second centuries, military architecture turns out to have been the most sustained programme of building in Roman Britain. After the fifth century architecture, as we know it, entirely disappeared only resurfacing in the seventh and eighth centuries when Saxon church building in stone began. Even then, the principal defining factor seems to have been the availability of Roman building materials — the forts at Reculver and Bradwell, for example, were home to seventh-century churches. It is hard to avoid concluding that, whatever its manifestation, military building remained the foundation of architecture in Britain during the Roman period. It influenced and helped define buildings elsewhere in Britain but it never entered the permanent consciousness of the inhabitants. Once the institution of the army had been withdrawn, architecture temporarily ceased to exist.

8

MILITARY COMMUNITIES

The traditional image of the Roman military community in Britain as a separate social caste has proved astonishingly durable, in spite of the proliferation of modern studies seeing the army as an integral component of a more complex set of social relationships. A recent major historical television series still described the end of Roman Britain as the time 'when the Roman army went back'. Back to where? Certainly not 'to Rome'. This anachronistic sense of separateness had its origins in scholars whose own personal experience had been drawn from military service in the armies of the late nineteenth and twentieth centuries. They were particularly fond of excavating forts, restoring plans, and attempting to shoehorn the erratic nature of the evidence into a regimented scheme. For them, the scattered and tantalising evidence of archaeology and texts like those of Tacitus cried out to be reconstructed into perceptions of a world of order, reliability and standardization, helped along by writers like Josephus. As this was how the British Empire had been won and held, then surely this was how the Roman army had won its territories?

This led to all sorts of assumptions. For example, an inscription naming a unit at a fort meant that was the fort's garrison. An inscription naming *another* unit too was rarely seen as evidence that both units might have been there simultaneously, or in rapid succession, and perhaps even changing places over weeks or months in a single season. Likewise, the ethnic names of military units tended to be taken literally, with little or no acknowledgement of the body of evidence for increasing local recruitment, or even Dio's comment that ethnic titles were sometimes artificially adopted to provide al-fresco units of men hired for their skill with a fabricated identity. Oddly, despite the evidence available today, the idea that foreign recruits continued to arrive like boatloads of immigrants at Staten Island continues to circulate.

Part of the problem is equating the Roman army with modern armies. But this is wholly inappropriate. Where we have administrators, police, customs officers, civil defence, and a battery of other trades, the Roman world depended on the army as its core source of supervisory and professional skills. At Herculaneum, buried by mud and lava from Vesuvius in 79, remains of the fleeing population have been found in recent years scattered, suffocated and burned, on the beach below the wealthy sea-view villas that clustered along the Roman resort's front. One of the bodies is that of the so-called 'Soldier', found face down and still equipped with *gladius* sword and military belts, as well as carpentry equipment (Gore 1984, 572-3). It takes little experience of traditional British archaeology to know that had he been found in Britain his identification as a legionary would have been instantaneous and that, by extension, his presence must mean a nearby fort, which would thereafter subsist as a 'fact'. Herculaneum of course was not a fort, though the fleet was based not far away at Misenum. The Herculaneum 'soldier' was indeed probably a soldier, but going about his business in a wealthy civilian settlement

110 *Chester, Deva. Tombstone of the* XX Valeria Victrix *centurion Marcus Aurelius Nepos who died at the age of 50, dedicated by his anonymous wife. The style is astonishingly crude, even by Romano-British standards.* RIB 491

either in a private capacity or because he had an official post in the city connected with a public building project, security or policing. We will never know, but he is a reminder that the Roman world was not divided into clearly demarcated civilian and military zones.

It is frustratingly true that understanding who made up the Roman army in Britain, or indeed in any province, relies on exceptionally limited evidence. In this book we have already come across an amazing diversity from a relatively very small number of sources. The nominal size of the garrison at York alone must have always been around 5000 legionaries and an unknown number of auxiliaries across a period of at least 300 years. But just seven York soldiers identify themselves as such on tombstones, and a further two in the epitaphs for their wives. The pattern is repeated almost everywhere else, even at Chester where a chance find of dozens of tombstones reused in the city wall still constitutes a minute sample of the original population (**110**). Nevertheless, careful use of this sort of material, together with the recovery of limited numbers of documents and taken together with evidence from elsewhere in the Empire has made it possible for a picture to be built up which exposes the Roman army to have been hugely more complicated than was once thought.

Origins and mobility

The army was overwhelmingly a mobile organization and this went way beyond the movements of units. Individuals were transferred or promoted almost everywhere, quite apart from having perhaps travelled across the Empire to join up. Men of any rank could be moved about. This had consequences not just for personal experience but also in diluting the ethnic units of the army. An important question is whether this mobility endured, or whether there was a steady transition to static, insular, units.

For the man of senatorial status, a legionary command after successfully serving as a military tribune and a praetor was simply one possible step on a career, which would eventually lead to a consulship and then lucrative provincial governorships. Caius Caristianus Fronto commanded *VIIII Hispana* under Vespasian, then being promoted to become governor of Bithynia and Pontus in Asia Minor, rather closer to his hometown of Antioch-in-Pisidia from where the inscription comes that records his career (*ILS* 9485). Lucius Minicius Natalis was legate of *VI Victrix* under Hadrian. He had a home at Tivoli near Rome, near to Hadrian's villa, and like his emperor also came from Spain. He progressed through a variety of commands including his time in Britain before rising to the governorship of Lower Moesia, and finally the crowning glory of his career, the governorship of Africa (*ILS* 1061). For both men, the times as commander of *VIIII Hispana* and *VI Victrix* respectively were just passing phases of senatorial careers. There is no longer any convenient analogy to this in our own time. It is as if a member of the British Cabinet, or the US senate, might routinely expect to spend a spell in a military command in order to groom him or her for a position in administrative and legislative authority.

For those senators who had particular military skills, Britain was a place in which to prepare for other exacting commands, but still needed ample prior military experience. There was a cultural element to this. Onasander, a Greek military writer of the first century AD, was convinced that Roman success was not attributable to luck but 'deeds of generalship' (*The General, Prooemium* 5). He went on to celebrate the credentials that went to make up a good general. A popular work of the day, it gave military leaders something to live up to. Appropriately, he dedicated his work to Quintus Veranius, identifiable as the short-lived governor of Britain in 57. Like Veranius, many other governors of Britain are known to have been experienced military commanders. Aulus Didius Gallus, governor between 52-7, had earlier served as commander of cavalry in Moesia (*ILS* 970). Sextus Julius Severus, governor between *c.*130-3, had been 'warmed up' in Lower Moesia and after Britain was transferred to Judaea (*ILS* 1056) to deal with the aftermath of the Jewish Revolt of 132. Agricola, governor between *c.*77/8-83/4, was unusual in holding a number of posts in Britain. This made strategic sense because, given Britain's particular problems of resistance, military leadership was bound to benefit from extensive experience in Britain itself. But that overlooks the broader priority in senatorial careers which was to provide Rome's ruling class, itself increasingly drawn from provinces across the Roman world, with varieties of experience 'in the field'.

Equestrians had the chance to serve as military tribunes before holding a variety of posts, which could include commands of auxiliary units and the fleet. As the career organization for the Roman senatorial and equestrian élite, the army also meant that cultivated men, or those who considered themselves to be of good families, spent time in Britain as officers and commanders. The poet Juvenal (*fl. c.*78-135) was the commander of an auxiliary cohort in Britain. This is not an absolute certainty, but the poet refers briefly to Britain in his *Satires* (ii.161) while a dedication to Ceres from Aquinum in Italy (*ILS* 2926) records one Decimus Junius Juvenalis whose career included the tribuneship of *cohors I Dalmatarum*, a unit known to have been in Britain at some point during the second century (**colour plate 6**). This is probably the same man.

However remote the forts of the northern frontier were, the close-knit social ties of the élite reduced distances. Lucius Neratius Marcellus was governor between *c.*102-6, and appears in a letter from Vindolanda illustrating the patronage which was central to all Roman professional life. The writer, Flavius Cerealis, then the equestrian prefect of *cohors IX Batavorum* at Vindolanda asks his friend Grattius Crispinus to intercede on his behalf with the governor (*TV* ii.225). We do not know what he wanted, or whether he was successful, but Flavius Cerealis believed that having a 'delightful military service' (*iucundam militiam*) depended on it. What matters here is that regardless of the distant setting, this officer had access to influential friends in high places. Networking was alive and well in the moors of northern Britain.

Cerealis' name is intrinsically interesting in its own right. *Cohors IX Batavorum*, which he commanded, is a reminder that the troops stationed here were (nominally at least) north European in ethnic origin and thus will have been relatively familiar with conditions and climate in the northern provinces. But they were integrated into the Roman world and thus the visual and practical impact that Rome had in this environment was primarily second generation. Cerealis himself bore the praenomen Flavius, a name almost certainly originating in citizenship earned during the reign of a Flavian emperor (and one of course was still ruling until 96). That puts his family's rise back to no earlier than 69/70 which of itself reminds us that even the ruling officer class in late first-century Vindolanda had existed within élite Roman tradition for no more than two generations. We cannot know where Cerealis or his wife, Sulpicia Lepidina, came from but it was likely to be somewhere between Italy, Gaul or Germany.

At Carrawburgh one Aulus Cluentius Habitus, prefect of *cohors I Batavorum*, made a vow to Mithras and was explicit that he came from *Larinum* (Larino) in Italy, giving its new Severan titles as a colony (*RIB* 1545). This places the altar to the reign of Severus or afterwards but the information in the text would have made it clear to educated men at the time that he belonged to a family defended by Cicero more than 250 years before. This was far from an obscure brag. The speech, delivered in 66 BC, was Cicero's longest. It was published and widely admired in antiquity, as were many of his writings. Pliny the Younger regarded it as *optima*, 'the best' (*Letters* i.20.4), showing that knowledge of the speech was current 150 years after it was delivered. Evidently, it still carried enough kudos another century later to make it worth publicising to fellow adherents of Mithras.

Another Italian officer was Marcus Maenius Agrippa though, unlike Juvenal, he made Britain his career, serving as the commander of several auxiliary units as well as the fleet, before rising to become the province's procurator. His career can be dated to the reigns of Hadrian and Antoninus Pius by an inscription from his hometown, *Camerinum* (Camerino) in Italy, which refers to his being sent on a British expedition by Hadrian (*ILS* 2735).

Lucius Aufidius Pantera is recorded on an undated altar found at Lympne, naming him as prefect of the *classis Britannica* (*RIB* 66) (**111**). However, he is also known to have served as the prefect of a cavalry ala in Upper Pannonia in the year 133, a position to which he was probably promoted after his time with the fleet, showing that military command was more significant than specific experience with a single type of warfare (*CIL* xvi.76). Quintus Baienus Blassianus was one of his successors in the British fleet and rose to the prestigious prefecture of Egypt, the second highest post to which an equestrian could aspire (*AE* 1974.123).

By the time we reach the third and fourth centuries it becomes a great deal more difficult to assess the calibre and pedigrees of the men who served in high military office in Britain. Although military inscriptions exhibit a peak in the early third century, for the most part we know little or nothing else about the incumbents. The governors of Britannia Inferior are spectral figures, usually known to us only from one or two inscriptions. Their sheer anonymity was perhaps deliberate. After all, it had been the part played by Clodius Albinus in the civil war of 193-7, which had led to Britain being split in the first place.

An exception is Tiberius Claudius Paulinus, serving as governor of Britannia Inferior by 220, recorded on an inscription from High Rochester, and conveniently also testified as legate of *II Augusta* on a statue base found at Caerwent, close to the legionary base at Caerleon (*RIB* 1280, and 311 respectively) (**112**). The latter has incidentally the value of indicating close administrative and social ties between the civilian civitas capital and its military neighbour though the evidence is unparalleled in Britain. The career progression was logical as the governorship of Inferior was essentially the command of *VI Victrix* at York,

111 *Lympne,* Lemanis. *Altar dedicated to Neptune by Lucius Aufidius Pantera, prefect of the* classis Britannica. *Found in the remains of the later Saxon Shore fort. Hadrianic. RIB 66*

though Paulinus had served as governor of Gallia Lugdunensis in between (*CIL* xiii.3162). But we know extremely little about other governors of this period apart from their names, such as Modius Julius, only explicitly recorded on a gate inscription from Birdoswald, and tentatively dated to around 219 (*RIB* 1914). The names of just two governors of Britannia Superior are known, and nothing else about them.

The position with legionary legates, never particularly promising, is little better. One of the few is Titus Flavius Postumius Varus who tells us that he was a senator, and a legate, on a dedication found at Caerleon which he set up to record his restoration of a temple of Diana (*RIB* 316). The inscription is undated but in 271 a man called Postumius Varus, probably the same, was prefect of Rome (*ILS* 2940). By the fourth century it is impossible to make any sort of meaningful assessment. Nectaridus, for example, named as *comes maritime tractus*, 'count of the maritime area' (Ammianus xxvii.8.1), appears only for us to be told that he was killed during the barbarian conspiracy of 367. Even his post is unparalleled and may actually be a synonym for 'count of the Saxon Shore'.

112 *Caerwent,* Venta Silurum. *Statue base dedicated to Tiberius Claudius Paulinus, legate of* II Augusta, *proconsul of Gallia Narbonensis, and legate of Gallia Lugdunensis, by the Silurian civitas government of* Venta Silurum. *Just prior to 220.* RIB *311*

Up until the early third century though Britain experienced a military leadership made of men drawn from the more general élite of the Roman Empire. Each in his way illustrates a different aspect of the cosmopolitan nature of the way the Roman world operated. Experiencing the army in some shape or form was a common experience for upper class men. To what extent they became integrated in any sense into the societies they found themselves allocated to is less clear. An oddity of Britain was its failure to produce anyone of senatorial status. At lower levels soldiers were more likely to find themselves spending longer in uniform, but not necessarily in Britain.

For soldiers of lower ranks, including centurions, we are much more dependent on finds of tombstones or personal dedications, though the effective cessation of epigraphy in Britain by the late third century makes it impossible to identify individuals thereafter. By and large any tombstone or dedication providing us with information about individual members of the army belongs to the period *c.*50-300. Even so, reticence, economy or indifference means that many tombstones tell us little of value. The tombstones from late first-century Lincoln provide some useful examples which do. Here was buried Gaius Saufeius of *VIIII Hispana,* who came from Heraclea in Macedonia (*RIB* 255). One of his approximate contemporaries and compatriots, Lucius Sempronius Flavinus, declared himself a native of Clunia in Hispania Tarraconensis (*RIB* 256). Titus Valerius Pudens of *II Adiutrix* came from Upper Pannonia (*see* **17**). Yet the men of *II Adiutrix* had clearly all served alongside one another at approximately the same time. Other legions were similarly varied. A veteran of *VI Victrix,* whose Lincoln tombstone must date to at least more than half a century later, was from

113 *Lincoln,* Lindum. *Tombstone of Gaius Julius Calenus from Lyons, veteran of* VI Victrix, *erected by his daughter Julia Sempronia. After 122.* RIB *252*

Lyons in Gaul (**113**), while at Ribchester another centurion of the legion tells us he came from Melitene on the Euphrates (*RIB* 583). Finally, Julius Vitalis, armourer of *XX* at Bath and whom we have already met, was a 'Belgic tribesman', which can only mean Gallia Belgica or southern Britain (*see* **57**).

Numerous examples could be trotted out here without really adding to the essential point which is that the average legionary could come from almost anywhere in the Empire. Such individuals do not tell us a great deal more about their careers. Lucius Licinius Salaga, of *II Adiutrix*, and born in Lyons, served in the army for 20 or more years before dying at Lincoln. It is impossible to be certain that *II Adiutrix* was where he spent his whole military career, especially as the legion had been raised in part from troops taken from the fleet (*RIB* 253). As ordinary rankers it is unlikely that they had been moved widely, but we know for example that after the Boudican Revolt in 60/1 reinforcements were brought in from the continent. The tantalisingly obtuse inscription from the Tyne dated to *c.*155-9 mentions possible reinforcements for the British legions from the two German provinces, vice versa, or the return of detachments sent to the Germanies (*see* **34**). Evidence of African-style pottery found in early third-century contexts in York has been taken as evidence for reinforcements allocated to *VI Victrix* in the aftermath of the civil war of 193-7 (Swan 1992).

In fact, the evidence from the rest of the Empire is for a steadily increasing level of recruitment from the province in which the legion was stationed. The phenomenon began in the first century and increased steadily to the third century when local people constitute the largest numbers of known recruits to legionaries in other provinces (Dobson and Mann 1973, 193). By this date, the legal restriction on only citizens entering legions was academic, thanks to Caracalla's edict of universal citizenship. This does not preclude the possibility of some African recruits at York but the point might be rather overemphasised. Unfortunately, as ever in Britain, the problem is identifying the Britons in legions, but invisibility in the archaeological record does not constitute non-existence.

It was the centurion who was more likely to find himself moved about and, as we shall see, allocated to duties involving him in far more than conventional soldiering. A fragmentary tombstone from Colchester mentions an unnamed centurion who had served in at least three different legions, including *III Augusta* in Numidia and *XX Valeria Victrix* in Britain, while having himself been born in Nicaea in Bithynia (*RIB* 203). Petronius Fortunatus, who served as legionary centurion for several decades, had a spell with *VI Victrix* presumably at York or elsewhere in the northern zone. Before that, his various postings had included *III Gallica* in Syria and *XXX Ulpia Victrix* on the Rhine. He went on to *III Cyrenaica* in Arabia (*ILS* 2658). His experience of Britain was perhaps confined to around five years.

At Piercebridge, a centurion called Gracilis was buried by his wife Aurelia (. . .)illa (*RIB* 1026). The epitaph tells us that he came from Upper Germany, and belonged to *XXII Primigenia*. It is not possible to say where Aurelia came from but there is other evidence from Piercebridge which points to a detachment of *XXII Primigenia* on-site in the early third century in one of several expeditions to Britain which are testified epigraphically. Julius Valentinus, from the same province, made a dedication to Jupiter Dolichenus in the year 217 (*RIB* 1022), while a statue base to the same god refers to the 'army of Germany' (*JRS* 57, 205). Collating this information leads to the conclusion that *XXII Primigenia*, or a vexillation, was operating in northern Britain during the reign of Caracalla in the aftermath of the Severan campaign into Caledonia. This was not the only time that the legion served in Britain (see chapters 2 & 3).

It was quite normal for soldiers, particularly centurions, to find themselves detached as individuals. In this way Julius Candidus, a centurion with *I Italica*, based in Lower Moesia and incidentally where Petronius Fortunatus (above) had begun his career as a centurion, found himself in command of *cohors I Baetasiorum* at Old Kilpatrick on the Antonine Wall in the mid-second century (*B* 1970, 310).

Auxiliaries were recruited originally from all over the Empire. The exotic range of names sported by the units testify to the nominal cultural diversity they represented and included Gauls, Germans, Spaniards, Syrians and Dalmatians, but as we will see below, some of this ethnicity was possibly manufactured by the army. Where we have a specific example of an individual we can sometimes see how an auxiliary soldier managed to combine his own personal origins into a more generalised 'Roman' anonymity. At Colchester a tombstone (*RIB* 201) records Longinus Sdapeze, *duplicarius* of *ala I Thracum* who died after 15 years' service (**11, colour plate 5**). The stone is typically generic in its presentation of the triumphant cavalryman trampling his barbarian foe and associated with symbols of the afterlife in the form of a sphinx and lions, images otherwise only known to the tribes of East Anglia from tribal coins. Longinus himself was from Sardica in Thrace and was 40 years old when he died, but we should not be misled by the fact that the stone is the only one of its type from Colchester.

A glaring space in the area for the inscription tells us all we need to know. This was a standard slab, turned out in a masons' shop for purchase and insertion of an appropriate inscription. An individual for us, by virtue of his rarity, Longinus (or his heirs on his behalf) was in fact submerging himself into provincial Romanized military anonymity. His Thracian world was absorbed into the Roman military and even his personal name was partly Roman in nature though we are also told he was '(son of) Matygus', an emphatically non-Roman name. His use of the victorious horseman was an effective, if unoriginal, way of asserting his successful participation in Roman culture and his personal status within it, now of benefit to his heirs rather than to Longinus himself.

Longinus was commemorated outside the fort or the new colony of Roman Colchester as a Roman. The effect of realism will have been greatly enhanced with lurid colours, and this will have applied to all other tombstones. The usual claim is that it must have been erected around c.43-9, or shortly after. This is too precise. He may have been stationed there in a detachment at any point over the next few decades but it does not affect the point that his tombstone was probably relatively early in date. The unit subsequently found itself in Cirencester (see below) and was out of Britain by the mid-second century.

Such units retained their ethnic identities and names, even if they enlisted new troops from where they were stationed. Sextus Valerius Genialis was another Thracian trooper. Commemorated on a tombstone found at Cirencester (see 2), Genialis' message is even more complex. The epitaph tells us that he was a trooper in ala (I?) Thracum, and his three-part name he was a Roman citizen. But it adds that he was a 'Frisian tribesman', presumably recruited locally when the unit was stationed in his homeland. So, Genialis came from northern Europe, served in a Thracian cavalry unit and styled himself Roman.

Genialis is also a reminder of that some of the ethnicity of these units was acquired rather than inherited. Dio specifically states that 'selected foreign horsemen . . . were given the title Batavians, being named after the island in the Rhine called Batavia because the Batavians are superb horsemen' (lv.24.7). He seems to be saying that ethnic titles could be manufactured by the Roman army to create an artificial sense of pride based on popular reputations of excellence. There is no ready modern equivalent, but it was as if a national army had a unit of crack soldiers created and called 'Gurkhas', after the celebrated units of the British army, but with no ethnic connection apart from the name. The passage is another reminder of how simplistic perceptions of the Roman army were in early modern times, with ethnic titles being taken completely literally. It is difficult to avoid the conclusion that most auxiliary units bore no more relation to their nations 'of origin' than many modern European football teams.

In any case, genuine or fabricated ethnicity was very rapidly diluted by recruitment from provinces in which units were stationed. An altar from Adamklissi in Dacia (ILS 9107, CIL iii.14214) records members of a single unnamed auxiliary unit drawn from Gaul (12), Spain (3), Britain (2), Africa, Noricum and Raetia (1 each). In some senses the appropriated ethnicity of the cohort or ala provided such disparate groups with unity, almost resembling modern football teams which bear ethnic titles of no relevance whatsoever to many of their members.

Dilution of ethnic units was underway in the first century but the general stability of frontiers and dispositions of units from the early second century on may have helped encourage soldiers to form relationships in the vicinity of their forts. This, however, may be an illusion created in part by the limited evidence for short-term relocations of units — of which there is enough though to show that it was routine for units to be split up and redeployed in short order.

Conventional religious dedications were also a means in which Roman soldiers from disparate communities expressed their *Romanitas* while commemorating their personal origins. At Birrens *cohors II Tungrorum equitata* included Raetians making a dedication to Mars and Imperial Victory, and soldiers from two other districts making their own dedications to Ricagambeda and Viradechthis respectively (*RIB* 2100, 2107-8). The wording, the deities, and the ethnic origins might differ but the end-result was the same — members of the unit making religious dedications in a common manner.

Enjoying careers spent in different provinces of the Empire was not restricted to the military but it was probably the main way men enjoyed this experience. The limited evidence available suggests that soldiers or at any rate their associates, did not necessarily move around alone. At Chesters Lurio 'the German', who — to be pedantic — does not actually specify that he was a soldier, buried his sister Ursa, his wife Julia, and his son Canio (*RIB* 1483). Equally reticent about his own status is Dionysius Fortunatus on a tombstone in honour of his mother Aurelia Lupula, from Risingham (*RIB* 1250). While either of these men may or may not have been paid-up members of the Roman army, passing through or permanent residents, they remind us that the Roman fort was a straggling gaggle of humanity which included extended families and the general emotional flotsam of all communities. In the same way, the ships of Nelson's navy went to sea replete with female comforts for the tars, and carpetbaggers followed the Union Army into the defeated Confederate States after 1865.

Skills

As an organization with so many professional demands, the Roman army also depended on specialist skills, discussed in more detail in chapter 5. The auxiliary regiments are the most obvious manifestation of this, but it also extended to skilled individuals, for example in medicine, drawn from elsewhere in the Empire and also integrated into the greater military community, bringing into Britain a range of professions. At Chester there are two examples of Greek doctors, recorded in Greek inscriptions. Hermogenes, *hiatros*, dedicated an altar to Soteres, and Antiochos dedicated another to Asklepios, Hygiaea and Panakeia, while at Binchester one Marcus Aurelius [. . .]ocomas also dedicated an altar to Aesculapius and Salus (*RIB* 461, *JRS* 1969, 235, *RIB* 1028). The names, and their chosen deities, make it likely they came from the Eastern Empire. The medical profession was traditionally monopolised by Greeks, though there was an equal distrust amongst educated Romans of Greek doctors on the grounds of their having suspect motives, a view uncompromisingly stated by Pliny the Elder *c*.75. This helps explain the appearance at Housesteads of Anicius Ingenuus, *medicus ordinarius* with *cohors I Tungrorum*. He was only 25 when he died and shows that ordinary auxiliary units could count trained in-house health-carers amongst rankers (*RIB* 1618).

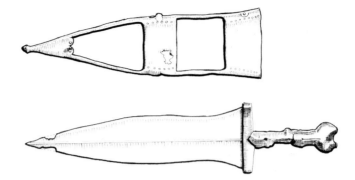

114 *Military dagger (*pugio*) found at Copthall Court, London. Length 410mm*

The picture is rather thin but professional Greek and Roman medicine is generally associated in Britain with military establishments. This would certainly make sense with the suggested association between the army and healing spas in the north-west provinces. Oculists' stamps, used for impressing names and information into ointment cakes to treat eye conditions, are much better known in Britain and more widely distributed. However, even this has been taken as evidence that itinerant practitioners and third-party distributors were more necessary in a province which enjoyed less general access to the professions (Frere and Tomlin 1992).

Soldiers in the community

The distribution of memorials bearing inscriptions, and even artefacts (**114**), shows that soldiers were present almost everywhere in Roman Britain, making the classic distinction between military and civilian zones misleading. This is with the proviso that the military taste for inscriptions guarantees their conspicuousness in the record — but that is really the point. More visible embodiments of Romanization now, they were also more visible then. Thus the small town at Dorchester-on-Thames (Oxon) has produced a single inscription, an altar to Jupiter and the Spirits of the Emperors dedicated by one Marcus Varius Severus, a *beneficiarius consularis*, a soldier detached to the governor's staff (*RIB* 235). The post is well known from the military zone, but another is testified at Winchester, *Venta Belgarum*, itself also the only legible stone inscription from the town (*RIB* 88). At London we even find one Veldeius, *equisio consularis*, 'groom on the governor's staff', recorded on a letter at Vindolanda (*TV* ii.310).

The more soldiers an official could have detached to his staff, the greater his prestige. Perhaps this was why in *c*.111-13, during his governorship of Bithynia and Pontus, Pliny the Younger was informed by Gavius Bassus, 'prefect of the Pontic shore', that the ten *beneficiarii*, two cavalrymen and a centurion assigned him from the provincial garrison by imperial order were insufficient for his needs. Trajan, then emperor, advised Pliny that this was not in the public interest, but it remains unclear what Bassus needed, or thought he needed, the men for (*Letters* x.21-22). This was not the only time Pliny was faced with demands for more seconded troops to accompany an official (see Maximus, in chapter 5).

The evidence from cemeteries is unreliable because burials themselves rarely provide specific information about the owner's former life and they virtually never survive in association with tombstones. Cremations, which dominate the first- and second-century

115 *London. South-east corner of the fort as exposed after bomb-damage clearance in the 1940s. The discovery explained the shape of the town's defensive line, and showed that the fort had been a major feature of the provincial capital. See* **116**

record, usually lack evidence for sex. Inhumations, characteristic of the third and fourth centuries, are more useful. In the south-Fosse Way burial group at Cirencester, male burials outnumbered females by more than 2:1. In the smaller group to the north, the ratio was at best 5:1. The explanation offered is that Cirencester may have attracted a disproportionately high number of retired soldiers and officials who were less likely to be married (Wells 1982). Being unidentified as individuals, this is obviously unverifiable, and unmarried soldiers are not noted for their capacity to live without women, unless it was not the fashion for Romano-British women 'to kiss before they are married'. But the tombstone evidence from earlier periods shows a similar bias. Lincoln has 65 percent adult males, against 10 percent women and 10 percent juvenile females. Most of those males were soldiers, based on the epitaphs. Neither case of course explains where the women were, unless they were more usually buried in less conspicuous ways, matching their higher degree of social and legal invisibility. But it remains possible the prevailing view was that soldiers were better accommodated on their own than with wives. All we can say is that women are simply more difficult to find either on tombstones or in their physical remains.

The picture certainly reflects that argued for Egypt where soldiers were thoroughly integrated into civilian communities. In Cirencester's case the possibility arises that even urban life in general in Britain was dominated by men, and thus perhaps by soldiers and ex-soldiers. London will probably have been the place where soldiers were the most conspicuous in a civilian context (**24**, **40**, **82**). Here, the presence of the fort which almost certainly housed the governor's personal garrison will have been responsible for that, though little of the evidence from London actually says that any given individual was so employed (**115 & 116**). Gaius Pomponius Valentis was probably a *beneficiarius tribuni*, recorded on a tombstone found in High Holborn (*JRS* 1962, 190-1). The stone is incomplete, so we do not know if he died on duty in London while working for a tribune,

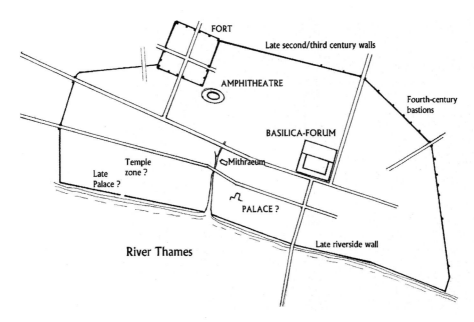

116 *London. The plan shows how the fort was integrated into the early third-century defences, along with what must be its associated amphitheatre (see* **115***). Finds of military equipment and inscriptions recording soldiers are common in the city*

himself working to the governor. Ulpius Silvanus, veteran of *II Augusta*, was responsible for commissioning a relief sculpture depicting the Mithraic Tauroctony, found in the London mithraeum. That the stone itself seems to have been carved in Orange in Gaul raises the possibility that the mithraeum was a place Silvanus visited, perhaps regularly, while in transit to a home elsewhere in Britain (**75**). Of course it is impossible to say, though London was such a major point of transit that it was inevitable that its fluid population would have included many serving members of the Roman armed forces, regardless of garrison residents. Marcus Ulpius Maximus, *primus pilus* of an unnamed legion, appears on a lead sealing found in the wharf deposits at Billingsgate (*B* 1990, 369). Perhaps no more than a simple stray item detached from goods passing on to a military base, he might also have worked in London, detached to the governor's staff to police the port of entry to the province.

The recent discovery of a hoard of 43 gold *aurei* in Plantation Place, London, with a terminal date under Marcus Aurelius, was exceptional, not only for being all gold and recovered during an excavation, but also for being found in a Roman building. It illustrates the unique role London played in the province. In many respects the evidence London has produced matches that found at major military sites rather than other towns. While its special role as a provincial capital must have played a part in its vast ceramic, numismatic, epigraphic and general artefact record, it may be that its substantial military population had as much or even more to do with it. It is impossible to attribute the hoard to anyone in particular but a military officer is one of the most likely candidates, alongside traders and provincial government officials.

Governors of course were not confined to London or the northern frontier zone, and this may explain Olus Cordius Candidus, *strator consularis* (horse and stable overseer to the governor), recorded on an altar found at Dover (*B* 1977, 426-7). Dover was a significant port from early in the Roman period, guarded by a fort of conventional second-century design, and later by a fort of the Saxon Shore. Candidus could have been passing through with a governor, or was perhaps permanently stationed there to look after transport for the governor. Interestingly the only other example of this position in London has been found on a tombstone at Irchester (Northants), though in this case Anicius Saturninus may simply have been buried at his home (*RIB* 233).

In 128 Hadrian inspected *III Augusta* and its associated auxiliaries at Lambaesis in North Africa. Happily his address survives on an inscription, and amongst his comments was the acknowledgement that 'you [centurions] are kept apart due to your many jobs all over the place', a highly revealing comment (*ILS* 2487). Bath is an apparently civilian site with one of the highest representations of military personnel, though as we saw in chapter 6 this may have been for generally different reasons than London, with the exception of the 'centurion in charge of the region', Gaius Severius Emeritus, who recorded his repair work to a holy place caused by vandalism (*RIB* 152) (**117**). His unit is unnamed so he must have been detached to serve in a policing capacity in the spa area, unlike the other tombstones and altars which probably belong to soldiers visiting the location for private reasons unless they too had been allocated to police duties. It is frustrating that the epitaphs tell us nothing about the reason for their deaths, and whether they had died while on pilgrimages or on official duties. Perhaps this was what had called Vivius Marcianus of *II Augusta* to London where he died. His wife took care of the funeral (*see* **24**). His rank is not specified though he carries the badges of office, a staff and scroll. Marcus Favonius Facilis, centurion of *XX*, is always regarded as belonging to the legion's time at Colchester (**9**, **colour plate 1**). But, Tacitus' account of the plundering of the Iceni by centurion after the death of Prasutagus in 59/60 makes it entirely possible that Facilis was detached from *XX* for police duties in the region and could conceivably have participated in the rampant exploitation of East Anglia in the preamble to the Boudican Revolt. It is impossible to say, but this is no more or less likely than the conventional explanation for his tombstone's find-spot.

Publius Aelius Bassus, a veteran centurion of *XX*, was buried in a tomb in or near Watercrook in Cumbria (*RIB* 754). A long way from his nominal base at Chester, his burial seems to have been administered by Aelius Surinus, a centurion with *VI*. The text provides no explanation for their association, or the location. That detachments of both legions were active in the north-west is known from a variety of inscriptions (for examples *RIB* 2034, and *B* 1989, 331-3), but it is quite possible that the men had been allocated to policing duties in the area, with Bassus opting to retire there. Either way, it is a reminder that soldiers were as liable to end their lives as veterans in remote places as they were in the great colonies of Colchester, Lincoln and York. Evidence from Egypt supports the impression that soldiers were widely used for this sort of work (Alston 1999).

In chapter 7 the role of the military architect is discussed, and although the evidence is limited military architects could clearly be instructed to assist urban communities with building. This merging of the two orders may have become more pronounced in the

117 *Altar from Bath*, Aquae Sulis. *The text records the restoration of the 'sacred place' (*locum religiosum) to the virtue and spirit of the emperor (*virtuti et n(umini)) by Gaius Severius Emeritus, centurion of the region (*c(enturio) reg(ionarius)), who must have been detached from a legion to serve in this capacity. The text is intriguingly slapdash in layout, indefensible even on the grounds of style. Line 4, for example, ends early, and the last word has had to be crammed in.* RIB 152

fourth century once towns came to resemble fortified centres, and as production of military equipment was concentrated in the town-based state manufactories. In this sense the analogy of a modern army is really quite suspect. The Roman soldier was utilised in a much more extensive range of roles than modern troops are, except in national emergencies, and thus enjoyed a day-to-day familiarity with communities that today's armed services do not. Roman troops were liable to find themselves allocated to policing traffic, while locals petitioned district-centurions. We would call this martial law, but it was quite normal in the Roman Empire. The wide dispersal of troops on various different duties is testified for *cohors I Tungrorum* on a tablet from Vindolanda and also for *cohors XX Palmyrenorum* from Dura-Europos in Syria (*TV* i.154; Alston, 157). What we can see in either case is how units were in a permanent state of fragmentation amongst different duties, and consequently dispersed across the province.

Families and marriage

If soldiers were an integral part of Romano-British society in all contexts, it is not surprising that they formed relationships with women and had families. It probably seems that female personal possessions would be useful evidence for the presence of women in military communities, but in fact this is not really the case. For a start, most artefacts like coins and pottery are not attributable in that sense except where a pot is marked with a female name graffito, such as Sacra who appears at Castleford (Cool 1998, 357). Fragments of personal adornment, such as hairpins, earrings and bracelets, suggest their presence but strictly speaking these could derive from a casual presence rather than mothers and wives. Nonetheless, their existence, even in modest amounts, shows that women must have been part of the community, but perhaps normally being excluded from the fort proper. At Castleford the quantity of this sort of artefact was observed to increase greatly in the second-century *vicus*.

The Vindolanda letters recording the correspondence between officers' wives is ample proof that they at least lived legitimately within the military community in the late first century, intriguingly mirrored by the finds of children's and women's leather shoes. Claudia Severa, wife of Aelius Brocchus, commanding officer at *Briga* (unknown) in northern Britain engages in social arrangements with her friend Sulpicia Lepidina, and refers to her own small son. Of course, as officers' wives they belonged to an entirely different social stratum from the 'poor bloody infantry', and the letters are exceptional (*TV* ii.292-3).

Tombstones and other inscriptions provide us with virtually the only other evidence for the nature of families and marriage in Roman Britain. Cemetery excavations may produce statistics about sex ratios, age at death, disease, and so on but they tell us nothing about how society was divided up. One of the peculiarities of tombstones in Britain is not only that soldiers are always disproportionately represented, even at civilian sites, but also women and children are disproportionately well represented amongst the balance. This makes it possible, or even likely, that many of these women and children were military dependants, though only some are specifically described as such.

The soldier was a comparatively privileged member of Roman society and those of rank could afford slaves, and could afford to free them. This generated further links into the civilian communities around forts and deeper into Britain. Marcus Aufidius Maximus, a centurion with *VI Victrix*, is commemorated on two dedications made for him at Bath by his freedman Aufidius Eutuches (*RIB* 143-4). Eutuches, we might imagine, had been despatched to the spa to make the dedication on his patron's behalf or perhaps had travelled in his entourage along with other dependants, these dedications being his way of expressing his thanks.

At South Shields the loyalty was expressed the other way. Here, Victor, freedman of Numerian, a trooper in *ala I Asturum*, was remembered by his former master in a particularly extravagant tombstone (**118**). It has been suggested that their relationship was sexual — we have no way of knowing — but either way Numerian seems to have been responsible for bringing a young man (Victor was 20) who was a Moorish tribesman into northern Britain as part of his personal estate. Not all slaves were freed, but some of those who continued in that role found ways to establish their own group identity within the military community. Thus a slave, whose name is lost, but belonged to someone called Hardalio, was buried by his fellow members of the *collegium conservorum*, 'guild of slaves', at Haltonchesters on the Wall (*RIB* 1436).

If soldiers were able to bring their slaves, or at least acquire them, they were certainly able to acquire family dependants. Considering that military tombstones dominate the record, it is a pity that so little is known about the origins of women who turn up in military areas. A very good example is Aurelia (…)illa, mentioned on the tombstone of her husband, Gracilis (see above). That he was a serving centurion with *XXII Primigenia* suggests that she must have accompanied him on the expedition under Caracalla (211-17).

118 *South Shields,* Arbeia. *Tombstone of Victor the Moor, freedman of Numerianus, trooper in* ala I Asturum, *who was 'most devotedly escorted [to the tomb]' after dying at the age of 20. The reclining deceased is a well-known Roman funerary banquet motif, but the style, for example the blocks on which the bed is placed, is Eastern and of late second- or early third-century date.* Ala I Asturum *is testified at Benwell in 205-8 and 238 but these need not preclude a presence at South Shields in the same period or before.* RIB 1064 / P 248

This is an interesting, apparent, corroboration of the reference in Dio to the presence of 'not a small number of children and females' in the baggage train of Varus' army in the year 9 just before he and three legions were wiped out (Dio lvi.20.2). This rather alters the popular impression of the Roman army on campaign. But Varus was remarkable for his complacency — noted by historians of the time. There are very few such general references to women in Roman military baggage and it is quite possible that Gracilis had been in Britain for long enough to acquire a wife. We have, after all, no idea how long *XXII Primigenia* was in Britain apart from the fact that it was long enough for several inscriptions to be made and survive from the episode; this could easily have been several years.

There is also the question of women's legal status, particularly with respect to marriage to ordinary soldiers (as opposed to officers). Aurelia calls Gracilis her 'husband', but in the early Empire soldiers were barred from legal marriage. In 44, one of Claudius' measures was to allow soldiers to enjoy the privileges enjoyed by married men, to compensate them for not being able to have legal wives (Dio lx.24.3). The statement is rather oblique as the kind of privileges involved meant, for example, control of the wife's property, she being legally transferred as a chattel from her father to her husband. If there was no wife, then some of the privileges were rather academic. So, perhaps the provision was one which superficially sustained the ban on legal marriages while at the same time tacitly recognizing the inevitability of liaisons and allowing the soldiers concerned to benefit from their wives' property. When Septimius Severus made it officially legal for a soldier to live with his wife he was probably only acknowledging reality rather than significantly altering any practices (Herodian iii.8.5), though it is quite likely that the legal position had encouraged soldiers to commemorate their wives in a way that avoided mentioning their relationship. The circumstantial evidence at Piercebridge suggests that Aurelia buried her husband after Severus had changed the law and there would therefore have been no obstruction to her naming him as her husband.

All this speculation is rather complicated by a single letter from Pliny the Younger to Trajan. Sent during his time as governor of Bithynia and Pontus, it is tied to the years 111-13. Short and to the point, the letter transmits a petition by one Publius Accius Aquila.

> Having been asked, lord, to send you a letter by Publius Accius Aquila, a centurion with the sixth cohort of cavalry, through which he begs your indulgence concerning the status of his daughter, I considered it difficult to say no, seeing that I know how much you are accustomed to offer patience and humanity with requests from soldiers.

> Pliny the Younger, *Letters* x.106 (trans. author)

Trajan's reply (x.107), clarifies the position by explicitly granting the soldier's daughter *civitatem Romanam*, 'Roman citizenship', and sent confirmation in writing. Accius Aquila was demonstrably a Roman citizen, though whether he was a legionary, detached to command auxiliary cavalry or a citizen recruited directly into an auxiliary centurionate in his own right is not clear. But it does not really matter. The fact that his daughter was of unsettled status demonstrates that Aquila and the mother were not joined in a marriage or liaison of equal rank. The daughter was therefore either illegitimate or perhaps had been born to a wife of intermediate status, such as a Latin citizen, or a provincial, *peregrina*. Any question about this being of sufficient taboo to affect the information on tombstones seems therefore to be irrelevant speculation. Clearly, Accius Aquila had no reservation about publicising the existence of his family to the governor and also the emperor. If there were any potential recriminations they were clearly gathering dust from lack of use. Indeed, it is plain that Trajan normally acceded to such requests. Here then, in one letter, we have evidence that soldiers had families of lesser status than themselves, while in service, and that the 'system' allowed for routine requests to have the offspring elevated to equal status. There is no reason whatsoever why the same should not have been true for the citizen soldiery in Britain.

At York, Gaius Aeresius Saenus commemorated his wife Flavia Augustina and her two infant children (*RIB* 685) (*see* **55**). Saenus was, however, a veteran of *VI Victrix* and his wife had died at the age of 39. She seems old, by the standards of the day, to have been the mother of two children aged one year and three days, and one year, nine months and five days respectively. Perhaps Saenus had erected a retrospective monument to three members of his family who may have died at different dates, some time earlier than when he had the stone made. He might, for instance, have waited until he left the army before his wife could be acknowledged. Even if Pliny's letter suggests there was no problem with admitting to the presence of a family, protocol might have required that the wife at least be marginalized into invisibility in the record we have. This explains why some women were buried without any reference to their position. Nigrina was buried at Greatchesters by Aurelius Casitto of *VI Victrix*, without making any mention of a personal connection or offspring (*RIB* 1746). Nigrina died at the age of 40, old enough to have been a wife and mother of some standing. One might entertain idle speculation that she was a prostitute of whom Casitto, frequently passing this way, was especially fond but in the Boot Hill cemeteries of the Roman frontier, Nigrina is yet another female whose presence is unexplained.

There are many less helpful tombstones, particularly when the deceased is a woman in a military zone and there is no mention of a potential husband. Titullinia Pussitta, a Raetian, was buried at Netherby (*RIB* 984). Her epitaph leaves us none the wiser about how she got there, and whether or not she was married. The resident unit was *cohors I Aelia Hispanorum* which if nothing else suggests it was a mixed marriage if there was one at all, though as we have seen the unit might have been manned by many more types than Spaniards. Perhaps the detail was omitted to pay lip service to the law then nominally in force, or simply to save on the text. At Carlisle Aurelia, the 'very dear' wife of one Ulpius Apolinaris (sic) was buried with a portrait tombstone (*RIB* 959). Although explicitly a wife, we can only suggest that her husband was probably a soldier, given the location, and the same must apply to another stone from nearby (**54, 119**).

Titullinia's homeland does show that women in the military zone could be as cosmopolitan in origin as the men. At Carvoran, Aurelia Aia, the 'very pure wife' of Aurelius Marcus, was buried (*RIB* 1828). She came from Dalmatia and the unit testified at the fort in the *Notitia* was *cohors II Dalmatarum*, which had been in Britain since 105 at the latest. Her husband does not state his rank or unit but it is probable that he had either brought her with him or possibly even been sent her. Flavia Baetica's name makes Spain a possible place of origin for her, but perhaps several generations before. She appears on the tombstone of her son Afutanius, whom she had had by Bassus, a centurion with *cohors II Tungrorum* at Birrens (*RIB* 2115). The Tungrians themselves came from Belgium but, strictly speaking, in this case it is impossible to be sure where either of them came from. The son Afutanius, however, was probably born in Britain and this shows how difficult it is to draw conclusions from names.

But then Apion, the fleet recruit at Misenum mentioned in chapter 5, also told his Egyptian family that his official name for military purposes was 'Antonius Maximus' (*SP* 112) which makes some of the turgid analysis of the ethnic origin of Roman soldiers on the basis of their names potentially futile. No historian or archaeologist examining an inscription of Antonius Maximus would ever guess he was once called Apion and came from Egypt without the papyrus to hand. Antonius is also a human symbol of the artefact evidence we have for cultural influence. Not only was he likely to bring his own possessions with him, but he would also have sought like-replacements as well as perhaps forming part of an ethnic Egyptian cabal. This would have demanded, and perhaps produced, Egyptian goods, as well as those each one of them picked up along the way to

119 *Carlisle,* Luguvalium. *Tombstone of Aurelia Aureliana, an all-purpose, anodyne and uninformative Roman name, who died at 41, and dedicated by her husband Ulpius Apolinaris (sic). RIB 959*

their new base. For Antonius we can read every ethnic recruit to a military unit in Britain, until local recruiting gradually supplanted them.

It is the letters from Vindolanda which have so memorably brought to modern attention the presence not only of officers' wives engaging in spirited efforts to maintain normal social contact in the blustery hills of northern Britain, on forts which we also know to have stunk from tanneries, and been awash with mud and rain (*TV* ii.291). The same letter makes a mention of a child. The text of the letter is vibrant with a sense of immediacy and an enthusiasm for life but it brushes over the reality of a world in which infant mortality was still high. Sadly, it is the memorials of the children, which at once evoke the tragedy of child deaths, while also illustrating that the military fort was also where children played, just as in towns. Birdoswald has produced few tombstones, but amongst their number are those commemorating Aurelius Concordius, son of the commanding officer, who died aged one year and five days (*RIB* 1919), and another which seems to record the deaths of two brothers, Decibalus who survived only a few days, and Blaesus who lived to the age of 10 (*RIB* 1920). That a third brother was apparently responsible for the stone might mean they were orphans, an interestingly unexpected (but inevitable) dimension to military lives on the northern frontier.

The best-known woman from all Roman Britain, apart from Boudica, is Regina, wife and freedwoman of one Barates the Palmyrene, buried at South Shields (*RIB* 1065) (*see* **84**). Barates tells us nothing about his role in life. He has been linked to the standard bearer of the same name, recorded on a tombstone from Corbridge though in fact the name there is spelled differently and is incomplete, appearing as [Ba]rathes (*RIB* 1171). But given South Shields' location he must have been connected with the army, even if no more than as a trader or artisan. Regina, exceptionally, is named as a member of the

Catuvellauni. As Barates' former slave, and then his wife, she will have had little choice in where she went but it is interesting to see that here we have a woman relocated across Britain. It certainly means that the military zone did not only involve the exclusive injection of males and shows that members of the wider population of the island were drawn into greater mobility.

The only other instance of a British wife is Verecunda Rufilia, wife of Excingus, who died at the age of 35 (*RIB* 621). A Dobunnian woman, she was buried at Templeborough (Yorks). Unfortunately, Excingus does not identify his own post though a unit testified at the fort from two other tombstones is *cohors IIII Gallorum* (see below). Whether or not Excingus was a soldier, or whether he was an authentic Gaul, does not affect the fact that Verecunda died some way from home.

The *canabae* and *vici*

This is an enormous subject, confounded by a lack of large-scale excavation, and impossible to explore in much detail here. Almost every fort developed a straggling community beyond its gates, given time. But it is too simplistic to see these as specifically 'civilian', compared to the military fort compound. The probability is that the extra-mural settlements were really blurred extensions of the fort proper, containing both elements of the military establishment as well as military families, veterans, traders, travellers, and local civilians. Those growing up around the legionary fortresses were known as *canabae* (from the Greek word *kanabos*, for a hut or shack, so literally the 'hutments'), and those outside auxiliary forts as *vici*. The physical evidence is plain to see at Housesteads and Vindolanda to this day (**colour plate 30**), but aerial photography has tracked large areas of apparently unregulated settlement outside the gates of numerous other forts. Epigraphy and excavation have revealed traces at other sites.

The crucial question is, who lived in them? On the face of it, the logical conclusion would be that this was evidence for local civilians clustering around the forts to trade and mingle but that relies to some extent on overlooking the army as a more complex cultural organisation. It also scarcely fits with the description of the 'Brittunculi' at Vindolanda, and nor is it easy to reconcile with the army's interests and needs. The Vallum feature of the Hadrian's Wall system may have been initially devised in part to restrict the growth of *vici*, or at any rate to exclude undesirables from the Wall zone and restrict access only to approved and trusted traders. The land around a fort, or fortress, was under military control but it was possible for the settlements to be allowed a certain amount of autonomy. This is testified at fortresses on the Continent, and at some forts in Britain, which makes it likely that the latter's legionary fortresses were also organised this way (Mason 1987). The degree of legal status, and quality of physical infrastructure, varied according to the level and location of the military establishment but it means that the *canabae* and *vici* represent a legal and social conflation of Roman military and urban life even if their development was piecemeal and individual.

It is more likely that the *canabae* and *vici* started life as places where fort trades might be established. They would also have been settlements for traders and prostitutes who followed the military baggage train and veterans who continued to ply trades learned when in the ranks, even if individual Britons were drawn in through sexual or commercial relationships. This special role is perhaps reflected in how weights, used on scales for measuring commodities, were found in much larger numbers in the *vicus* at Castleford, rather than within the forts. It is fairly evident from tombstones that the population around a fort was not restricted to serving soldiers. Thus at Templeborough, Cintusmus, a soldier with *cohors IIII Gallorum* was buried, as was Crotus, veteran of the same unit and buried by his wife, Flavia Peregrina, herself literally Flavia 'the Provincial' (*RIB* 619-20).

It is also possible that small units of troops, passing through, were accommodated here on an ad-hoc basis. It would be wrong to see the settlements as somehow extraneous or incidental to the fort proper. In many senses they were as routine a part of the fort as the headquarters and granaries. Equally, the abandonment of a fort or the long-term absence of the garrison, must have had an extremely significant effect on the economic viability of the *vicus*, unless there were other economic or social circumstances involved. Chester's *canabae* was extensive by the late first century and thus during the time that the fortress was being established and consolidated. In spite of the hiatus in the fortress's development during the second century this does not seem to have affected the transition to stone houses in the *canabae*. Regina (*see* **84**), mentioned above, might have been British but she came to South Shields with a Syrian husband. Her tombstone is likely to have been manufactured by a compatriot of his — either, or both of who, might have been soldiers, or civilians who followed the army. Lurio, 'the German', also mentioned above, seems to have lived with an extended family near Caerleon. Not identified as a soldier, he looks suspiciously like a civilian who came to Britain following a military market.

Some of the settlements seem to have been formalised on conventional lines. The *curia Textoverdi*, recorded on an altar dedicated to Sattada from near Vindolanda, commemorates a name and a goddess otherwise unknown (*RIB* 1695). Perhaps a community of foreign nationals, the name may also preserve the occupation of weaving from *textor*, 'a weaver'. But more common was a name taken from the fort. This links the *vicus* community more closely to the military than it does to a local population gathered around the fort. Thus we have the *vicani Vindolandesses* on a thoroughly Roman dedication to Vulcan and the Spirits of the Emperors from Vindolanda (*RIB* 1700). Just the sort of dedication, which might have been made by the resident unit anyway, this is either a gesture of community solidarity and mutual interest, or perhaps an indication that old habits die hard, and was made by veterans residing close to their old barracks. Even more explicitly, an altar from Carriden was dedicated to Jupiter by 'the *vicus* dwellers at the fort of *Velunia*' (*JRS* 1957, 229-30). Evidence from Chester includes traces of a variety of deities ranging from Minerva and Aesculapius to the Nymphs and Mother Goddesses (Mason, *op. cit.* 147, 151-2). The inscription from Housesteads which has been reconstructed as *d(ecreto) vica(norum)*, 'decree of the *vicus* dwellers' is as easily (or more easily) restored as a fragment of a name on a tombstone or an altar, so may be discarded as suspect (*RIB* 1616).

Where extra-mural settlements yield attributable evidence at all it is generally for an extension of Roman military culture and life, rather than for a Romanized British community. It is impossible to imagine that local people did not come into the communities, but unfortunately we tend only to know about British people if they came from further afield, such as Verecunda Rufilia (above). Similarly, the quaint little temple to Antenociticus at Benwell might have commemorated a local deity but it was Roman soldiers who built and visited this shrine (**109**). Given this symbiotic dependence on the fort and the soldiers based or passing through there, it is not surprising that the *vici* and *canabae* were generally unable to survive the running down of the fortresses and forts. This is quite unlike the urban settlements further south. Even if the Roman towns ceased to function as such, location and habit tended to encourage an urban revival in the medieval period, even if centuries had elapsed. But the *vici* of the northern frontier were apparently unable to subsist as villages or towns, the moment the forts themselves moved into decline.

Evidence for third- and fourth-century activity at Chester's *canabae* has proved relatively elusive — and in any case, the legion disappears from the record by the late third century. At Vindolanda the coin-list for the fort runs well into the fourth century, by which time the *vicus* coin list had long tailed off. At Housesteads, the coin list goes no further than the 320s in the vicus, but lasts another 50 years in the fort. Such evidence is always difficult to interpret but at the very least coin-loss, and thus usage, in the fort *vicus* had dissipated long before the fort. Perhaps the *vicus* activities had been removed to within the fort. Either way, what had once been comparable had become different. Like so much else that was Roman about Roman Britain, the civilian settlements of the military zone depended on a thriving army for their existence.

Recruitment of British units

Some regions, and thus families, will have been permanently affected by the recruitment of men into auxiliary units to serve elsewhere in the Empire. The exceptional size of Britain's garrison must have created problems for the Roman army, and the convenience of recruiting locally cannot have been avoided, with possible consequences for the availability of troops to be sent elsewhere. As early as the year 80, a British unit appears on a diploma, which must mean that some of the men had served since 55 (see Dobson and Mann 1973, 198, n. 37). By Trajan's reign some 14 units serving abroad are known to have been raised in Britain, and the numbers of soldiers involved will have amounted to 9-10,000 men, though the Adamklissi monument shows that 'British' recruits need not have been restricted to nominally British units, and that those units in time will have been drawn from all the places to which they were allocated. An example is Lucco 'the Dobunnian', recorded as a member of *cohors I Britannica* in Pannonia in 105, while by the 140s a *numeri Brittonum* formed part of Upper Germany's garrison (CIL xvi.49 and xiii.8495). The *cohors Cornoviorum* recorded as being *the* garrison at Newcastle in the *Notitia Dignitatum* is an exceptional instance of what seems to be a British unit, raised in the canton governed from Wroxeter, and stationed in the province. However, in the fourth century things were very different when it came to military organisation. An ad-hoc levying of units from the cantons is quite in context with an age that seems to have seen working parties from the civitas capitals repairing Hadrian's Wall.

Raising the cohorts of 'Britons' to be sent 'abroad' only represents the equivalent of a couple of medium-sized towns, though in practice it meant the removal of healthy young men, probably drawn from higher echelons of their communities, at a critical time in their lives. Depending on the length of time men continued to be sourced from the tribes of origin and send abroad, the effects will have been more than transitory. The 'compensation', such as it was, came in the form of auxiliary units introduced into Britain, whose members must have consorted with women in the vicinities of their forts. It is unfortunate that the British units are only named as such, the tribes having effectively been 'disappeared'.

Those whose careers were successfully completed were able to return to Britain, with savings and donatives, and perhaps foreign wives, though whether they did so or not is a moot point. Their re-integration into indigenous society will have meant injections of capital, as well as providing another dimension to Roman cultural synthesis. Having said that, we do not have any specific evidence for an individual. This is interesting because we might expect some of these veteran careers to be recorded on surviving tombstones in Britain. None are which means that either none have, by chance, survived, or that ex-soldiers of British origin generally subscribed to the same lack of interest in tombstones as their civilian counterparts, or ultimately that in fact 'returnees' were highly unusual. Even Julius Vitalis, Belgic armourer with *XX*, was of ambiguous origin (*see* **57**).

By the fourth century, in any case, recruitment had become hereditary and compulsory. We know this to have been the law but there is no verification in the form of tombstones or dedications in Britain other than the indirect evidence in their absence. There is a slim possibility that this had first occurred under Severus Alexander (222-35) for frontier troops. However, that relies on trusting a reference in his biography known generally to be suspect for other detail. It says, 'territory captured from the enemy was handed over to the commanders and troops of the *limitanei* on condition that they could only keep it if their sons became soldiers' (*SHA* lviii.4).

Whatever the truth, British soldiers seem to have reflected their own background culture by fading back into the 'Celtic' fringe from which they were recruited, whether they served in Britain or elsewhere. If further proof were needed of this disparity between the 'foreign' invading troops and the indigenous soldiers, it is that even Britons who ended up completing their careers and lives elsewhere in the Empire seem little more likely to have engaged in the visible classical epigraphic culture. One of the few very rare examples is Aemilius, *cives Dumnonius*, 'citizen of the Dumnonii', whose tombstone at Cologne recorded the fact and his service with the *classis Germanica* (AE 1956.249). His modest lack of restraint serves only to illustrate the silence amongst his fellow British recruits. Marcus Ulpius Quintus, *frumentarius* in Rome on detachment from *VI Victrix*, tells us he was of the Nervian voting tribe from Gloucester (ILS 2365). Like Antonius Maximus, his true family origin is entirely obfuscated by a name telling us he belonged probably to the second century (thanks to Trajan's *praenomen* and *nomen*). Perhaps, like Publius Accius Aquila's daughter, he was a legionary's son by a local Gloucester woman, and who benefited from Trajan's accommodating policy of elevating the children of his soldiers.

9
CONCLUSION

This book has attempted to summarise the role of the Roman army in Britain, both in a narrative and in more detailed discussions of themes. Throughout, the basic thesis has been that Britain found in the Roman army its principal, but conditional, means of access to the Roman and greater classical world. The army is now, and always has been, the most conspicuous feature of the Roman archaeological record in Britain, and this extends from tombstones to buildings. It also dominates the historical record. As a result, while we know a reasonable amount about the early governorships and the progression of conquest, we know scarcely anything equivalent about urban development or the countryside. The question is whether that military domination is an accurate reflection of how things were in antiquity.

We use the word 'foreign' to describe almost anything imported from, or recognised about, another country. In the Roman Empire this was not so straightforward because a province could be at once itself, and also part of the Empire. But 'foreign' is a handy term to describe how the Britons may have perceived the incoming Roman provincial culture, even if many of them were prepared to accept and even adopt it. This 'foreign' culture, whether in the form of tombstones, major buildings, or samian pottery, is quite simply more visible than the indigenous culture. Literacy and architecture exemplify this. It owed its ingress to Britain more to the army than any other aspect of antiquity, but it almost seems that visibility and foreignness go hand-in-hand (**120**). In the end, it may be that the Roman army was just the most efficient and dense medium through which this visible foreign culture entered, and saturated the surviving record, although the paradox is that its visibility in the record is not matched by durability once the systems bringing it in had elapsed. This tends to suggest that the induction of Roman culture was a consequence of military action and colonisation rather than the result of a deliberate policy of integration.

We should not have a problem with accepting that a small proportion of the population could be so dominant in the terms that subsist as the most visible. There are plenty of historical examples. The evidence of the Saxon invasions is that a very small number of people were able to make a dramatic impact on language in eastern Britain, manifested in the names of rivers, and the *-castra*-based endings of so many Roman settlements with which they labelled them. The Spanish conquest of the Americas was conducted by a very few soldiers compared to the general population, and who had a devastating effect on indigenous cultures so out of proportion to their numbers that were it not an unalterable historical fact we might have trouble crediting it. In the Southern States of North America the white plantation owners dominate in every respect the *visible* remains of their settlements. Yet, those very plantations often retain the documentary evidence that the owners may have numbered a hundredth or fewer of the people living there. The slaves are relatively invisible in the archaeological and linguistic record of their period.

120 *Lincoln,* Lindum. *Tombstone of Sacer, son of Bruscus, and his family. Although apparently a rare case of a civilian tombstone in a town where most are military, Sacer is identified as a* civis Senoni, *'citizen of the Senones', a region in Umbria. It is therefore probable that he was an immigrant, attracted to the military trade, or a veteran, perhaps recorded on the missing part of the slab, which survives only through being built into the church of St Mary-le-Wigford.* RIB 262

During the time that the Roman army maintained its energetic cultural injection, it was not exclusively segregated from society into its forts and fortresses. Soldiers, whether serving or as veterans, mingled throughout Romano-British society at all times and in all places. Not only were soldiers the force through which civilians accessed imperial authority by feeling its effects, or soliciting its benefits, but it was also through soldiers that civilians experienced the aesthetic, literary and more general cultural impact of Roman civilization or its brutality in the arena. This might take the form of looking at the tombstone of Longinus outside Colchester, or it might involve a petition to Gaius Severius Emeritus, centurion of the region at Bath (**117**). The soldiers of course had their own cultural and linguistic traditions as well as the Roman world's instinctive capacity to accommodate. This explains the widespread adaptation of local names and labels for places, and their enthusiastic respect for local, 'Celtic', deities like Coventina.

This relationship is found elsewhere in the Empire, but what makes Britain special is that soldiers always remained more conspicuous in the record though similar patterns exist in some other frontier provinces. But however locally important Coventina was, she is only known to us because of the Romans who venerated her (*see* **70**). Preserved by the Roman world, she also disappeared with it. With certain exceptions, the military momentum remained essential to sustaining the one-way cultural effect of Romanization. One of those exceptions was the fourth-century villa culture, characterised by its clumsy aping of élite

Roman rural life and its ramshackle versions of classical culture trapped in a provincial idiom. Of course, we have no idea who even owned the villas but whoever they were they represented a minute proportion of the general population who, for the most part, are invisible and anonymous. When this military mechanism of access to Roman civilization was withdrawn, the dynamic seems to have dwindled with it, in spite of efforts by the upper tier of society to ally themselves with a more remote and exotic culture.

Epigraphic evidence has served as one of the bedrocks of this book. Inscriptions provide fixed points in the ever-changing universe of archaeological evidence. As a record it is naturally unsatisfactory. The distribution is variable. Many stones are illegible or only semi-legible. Some, despite being complete, are cryptic and incoherent — at least to our eyes. But there are easily detectable patterns, one of which is the preponderance of those erected in the name of, or by, a soldier or a veteran. This is largely regardless of the classification into which we would place a site. Lincoln was a colony for most of its time as a Roman settlement. Yet nearly half the tombstones from the site come from a period of at most 25 years in the first century when it was a legionary fortress, while potential military dependants or immigrants from other provinces constitute most of the remainder.

How can this be, unless the indigenous civilian population rarely bothered with inscriptions, or scarcely ever? The absence of Britons in other provinces is a fundamental part of the evidence. No Briton ever achieved a position of imperial eminence, and even the swaggering *Romanitas* of Carausius was swept aside as the aberration of an international criminal. Aemilius, the *classis Germanica* Dumnonian, is a modest exception. Even Britain's meagre epigraphic haul manages to include men and women from almost everywhere in the Empire, yet the testified presence of Britons in, say, Africa, Greece or Italy is almost non-existent. Perhaps being a Briton was not something one recorded, or Britons did not travel far, or it was simply not something a Briton ever usually thought, or was inclined, to do. And if they rarely troubled themselves with tombstones in Britain or anywhere else, we have to ask if that meant they had limited interest in literacy or investing their time and money in becoming 'Roman' at all (**120**).

In general, the provincial and civitas capitals are more difficult to interpret because most have produced little or nothing at all in the way of epigraphy, and those that have, do so in far smaller quantities than London, the colonies and major towns like Cirencester. Cirencester, known to have had a briefly occupied first-century fort on the same site, has a high proportion (one-third) of military tombstones. This is surely remarkable, considering its later high status as a regional provincial capital. London, with its long-term garrison fort, has produced a similar proportion. Indeed there is enough evidence from London to argue that it was to all intents and purposes a military town, more like Corbridge but all the richer and more sophisticated for being closer to the continent. Some other urban settlements, like Verulamium, where the existence of a fort at all has remained only a hypothesis based on a few finds of military equipment, have produced virtually no epigraphy at all.

A lack of epigraphy may provide the basis for a case that some of these settlements did not have forts on the same or a nearby site, and that the community may have exhibited markedly less of what we call a Roman lifestyle. The distribution of urban bathing establishments, as public or private facilities, may even reflect this. London is the perfect example of a town where an apparently civilian settlement exhibits the epigraphic and architectural evidence for a military-biased community. At sites where tombstones are present at all, it is usually the case that somewhere between one-third and two-thirds are those of soldiers or veterans. Although the overall total is always in favour of men (including civilians), there is a slight bias amongst the non-military component to women and children. The latter are all potential military dependants, even if the fact is not stated, leaving us with the possibility that 70-90 percent of all tombstones at some 'urban' sites are actually from the military period, or a veteran military community within the urban population. Even the remainder, the 'civilian' males, may be made up of men who were ex-army or in some way connected with the military.

The implications for how we interpret the towns are quite significant. This is not the place to engage in a detailed discussion of how, or why, Romano-British towns appear to have suffered a long-term decay. But some points do need to be considered. In historical, epigraphic and archaeological terms, what we see is the steady disappearance or decline of material that we interpret as evidence for towns as commercial civilian settlements during the fourth century. New public building, for example, ceases. Some public buildings seem eventually to be abandoned, or are demolished. Population density, in the form of private buildings, appears to diminish though this is almost impossible to measure in any valid way. Of course, this is natural to some extent because any major building programme will be followed by a long period of maintenance, rather than a continuity of major construction work. Our reliance on Victorian housing and public buildings, including even sewers, is a case in point. But there is no doubt that by the fourth century, the character of the towns as manifested in the archaeological record had radically altered. Paradoxically, urban defences appear to be enhanced, even if this was at the expense of commercial facilities, as at London where the wharves were cut off by the late riverside wall.

The virtual absence of the towns from any of our historical or literary sources, including the *Notitia*, makes it extremely difficult to know what was going on. But the significant epigraphic evidence for a large military, or veteran, population at certain Romano-British towns in the first and second centuries, is followed by some evidence for a bias to males in urban inhumation cemeteries of the third and fourth. Unfortunately, there are no later inscriptions to help us assess whether this means places like Cirencester in the third and fourth centuries still had large military or veteran populations. The interesting possibility arises that, if this was the case, some of the reinforcements to urban fortifications may have been connected with making the towns into extensions of the fort system, while perhaps a removal of some of the urban military component in the opportunistic usurper wars of the third and fourth centuries may have bled the towns of the very people on which they depended.

At Caerwent, for example, a number of significant changes occurred in the mid-fourth century. The north and south walls of the defences were augmented with bastions, and the gates in both walls blocked up (**121**). This suggests that all traffic into and out of the settlement was now forced to pass through the main east-west street. Meanwhile, the basilica was largely demolished (a phenomenon observed elsewhere) which must mean that civic organisation was now managed from somewhere else or given up altogether, perhaps in favour of some sort of para-military town government. At any rate it is hard to see how the town could not now have been some sort of quasi-fort rather than a civilian settlement. This would help explain the consummate indifference to existing monuments, such as tombstones

122 *Caerwent,* Venta Silurum, *the south defences, looking east. The walls were reinforced here with six bastions on the south and five on the north in the mid-fourth century and the gates in these walls were blocked up. Given that the nearby fortress of* II Augusta *at Caerleon seems to have been abandoned by this time, it may be that some of the forces became part of the urban community here which had long had connections with the legion and whose population was probably made up in part of veterans or serving soldiers (see, for example,* RIB *310 and 312).*

and memorials, utilised as fill for new bastions or wall core (**52**). It would also help explain the bias towards males in some late inhumation cemeteries. Of course, the absence of any units allocated to towns from the *Notitia* makes this no more than a theory, but it reflects the need to avoid assuming that military and civilian were necessarily separate spheres.

Whatever the position within the towns, the soldiers were still part of a great imperial institution which tied them and their facilities into the broader Roman Empire. The *Notitia*'s lists were what defined Britain in the eyes of the Empire — an island of garrisons and military commands. And this meant that they needed to be paid. Britain took a relentless psychological battering in the fourth century. By the end, most major buildings were positively antique, relics of a different time and energy when imperial urbanization of the provincial proletariat was at its zenith. Now the towns were fortified strongholds, merging into a series of militarised compounds ranging from the derelict walls of Housesteads and Birdoswald (**122, colour plate 22**) to the port-strangling riverside wall at London (**116**) and the walled enclosure at Horncastle. By the end of the fourth century, even the villas — those rural mysteries — were falling into decay. Amidst all this the Empire could still proudly count the swaggering names of military units still allocated to Britain, recorded in the *Notitia*. It is impossible to say where reality ended and the dreams began. The units lost by Magnentius, or those accompanying Constantine III, are totally unknown. All we do know is that the money to pay whoever was left stopped.

The money is really at the heart of the matter. Roman Britain began with the salaries of invading Roman troops and the loans made to the tribal leaders and ended when it stopped. The money was the conduit along which the foreign culture of Roman goods, ideas, tastes,

122 *Housesteads,* Vercovicium. *The north gate, photographed (anon.) about 1924, and preserving a symbolic image of the derelict northern forts, including here the blocked north gate and moss-covered ruin, now largely cleaned up by modern custodians. The large, worked, blocks show that the gate towers had been partially dismantled to provide the blocking masonry. At most gates along the Wall, gate blockings have been removed*

images and rulers flowed. Accepting the cash was part of accepting the system, so long as it was there to accept. Roman Britain ended when the money stopped arriving to pay those troops. Even the decline of the *vici* is symbolic of the fact. It is impossible to say how many 'soldiers' were left by this stage. Whoever they were, and wherever they were, the forts and towns were abandoned and the system ceased to exist. This is a fact and it does not need sustained or even detailed excavation to demonstrate it. And, as the military system decayed into oblivion it seems that the Romanitas of Britain went with it, despite the efforts of some communities to cling onto it. The survival of some of the great Roman military buildings long after the army had left bears witness to the record it left (**colour plate 32**).

Like most unbidden guests, the army was more welcome when it had left. Bede, the eighth-century chronicler of British history, was one of many post-Roman authorities who recorded a tradition of bleating for help for generations after the Roman system collapsed in Britain. Perhaps that was how it had always been. In the vast miasma of artefacts we interpret as the evidence for Roman Britain, the truth may be that the army was always the spine and foundation for it all, but more by accident than design. Where we can attribute artefacts or monuments to men or women of a particular type, the soldiers dominate — regardless of time or place. The Roman army was the source and stimulus of the classical world in Britain, but it was only ever transient.

Rome, tho' her eagle thro' the world had flown,
Could never make this Island all her own.

Edmund Waller (1606-87), *Panegyric to My Lord Protector*

APPENDIX 1:
ARMY ORGANISATION

Although various features of the Roman army and its organization in Britain appear throughout the book, the following summary should prove useful for reference while reading and while consulting other works.

Provincial command

The governor of Britain was an imperial legate, *legatus*. He is always described as being of propraetorian status, that is he had served as a praetor, though in practice the governors of Britain were a level higher, having been consuls. This was a fiction to preserve the status of the emperor, himself of proconsular status.

It was usual, but not essential, for a provincial governor to have at least served a term as a military tribune, if not a legionary commander. Septimius Severus (193-211) missed out both but still rose to prestigious provincial governorships before taking command of an army and becoming emperor. Agricola, on the other hand, served as a tribune and as a legionary legate in Britain before becoming governor.

Legions

The Roman legions fluctuated in number throughout the period. In 23 there were 25 listed by Tacitus, making a total army of about 240-250,000 men if one accepts the statement that auxiliaries amounted to the same approximate total (*A* iv.5). By the end of Antoninus Pius' reign in 161 this had risen to 28 legions and a total of 310-320,000 (*CIL* vi.3492). A further list is provided by Dio for the early third century, where he lists 19 legions surviving from Augustus' time and a further 14 raised since then (lv.23.2ff). Those disappearing along the way, like *VIIII Hispana*, are simply omitted.

Between 43-69 Britain had at least four, and very probably more at certain points. Only for the year 60 do we have the certain information that *II Augusta*, *VIIII Hispana*, *XIIII Gemina* and *XX* were in Britain. The invasion force, of which we only know *II Augusta* to have been part, probably also included part or all of *VIII Augusta*.

Although *XIIII* was replaced with *II Adiutrix* in the 70s, it had left once more by 89, reducing the legionary garrison to three. In or around 122 *VI Victrix* arrived to replace *VIIII*, unless the latter was already gone. The three legions, *II Augusta*, *VI* and *XX*, remained in Britain thereafter. *XX* is last heard of on the coinage of Carausius in 286-93, while the other two survived in name at least to be mentioned in the *ND*, though it is improbable that either in numbers or appearance they resembled their earlier manifestations.

The individual names of the legions have occasioned some debate. It is worth explaining first that the Latin for a legion, *legio*, is a female word and thus all the titles take female forms.

II Augusta owed its titles simply to origins under Augustus. *II Adiutrix* indicated its creation as an 'assistant' legion in the mid- to late 60s. The additional titles *Pia Fidelis*, 'loyal and trusty', presumably belong to its decision to accept Vespasian in the civil war of 69. *VI Victrix* was also Augustan in origin and like *II Augusta* fought in the Spanish campaigns of 27-13BC. *VIIII Hispana* earned its title in Spain. *XIIII Gemina* had presumably been combined out of two. Its additional titles, *Martia Victrix*, are generally supposed to belong to awards handed out after the suppression of Boudica in 60-1. *Victrix* means a conqueress. As any associated title has to be female too we have *Martia*, a word adapted from Mars. Interestingly, *Marte* and *Victrix* appear in Virgil's *Aeneid* in book vii, lines 540-44. However, the basic meaning is not in doubt, 'the Fourteenth legion, made of two, warlike and victorious'. *XX Valeria Victrix* presents a more complex problem. It too may have earned its titles in 60-1. One suggestion is that it records a personal name though this would be rather unusual and there is no obvious contemporary candidate. *Valeria* is an extremely common female name so the answer may lie hidden in that somewhere, though the word may be adapted from *valere*, 'to be strong'. Perhaps the alliteration alone was attractive and matched the symmetry of the double X in the legion's numeral, while reflecting the *XIIII*'s name. In fact, the award at this date of either name is supposition rather than testified, and it has been suggested that *XX*'s awards were not made until after the Battle of Mons Graupius in 83 or 84 (Tomlin 1992).

In his review of the legions in the early third century, Dio implies that *Valeria* somehow refers to their adoption by Augustus when he became emperor, even though 'not everyone called them Valerians and no longer use that name' (lv.23.6-7). In this respect the allusion may belong way back in Rome's quasi-mythical historical past, when Publius Valerius Publicola drove Tarquinius Superbus from Rome in 509 BC (Horace, *Satires*, i.6.12), and thus be synonymous with loyalty to the state. Tarquinius' expulsion ended the monarchy and opened the Republic and it was Augustus' claim to have restored the Republic. Attractive though this is, Dio may simply have picked up a piece of later folk myth attached to the names which had no basis in truth. In any case there is no evidence for the legion ever being named just *Valeria*, and both titles are missing from earlier inscriptions (**9**) so unfortunately we must content ourselves with recognizing various possibilities.

In the first and second century each legion consisted of about 5500 men, made up about 5000 citizen legionaries, and a block of 120 cavalry, as well as officers and others. The legionaries were divided into centuries of 80 men. Six centuries of 480 troops made nine of the ten cohorts. The first cohort had five double centuries, numbering 800 men.

The century was commanded by a centurion, with an *optio* his number two. The centurions were classed by status according to the level of the century and cohort in which they served. The centurion of the first century of the first cohort was the *primus pilus*. Each cohort had a clerk, *tesserarius*, a standard bearer, *aquilifer*, and a trumpet-blower, *bucinator*. The legion as a whole had a standard bearer, *signifer*, a camp prefect, *praefectus castrorum*, and six military tribunes, one of whom was of senatorial status and on a career path which would lead to a legionary command and perhaps a provincial governorship. The legion was commanded by a *legatus*. He was literally an imperial delegate and a man of senatorial status who would eventually hold a consulship, followed by provincial governorships. For a few, the path led right to the top. In 43, *II Augusta* was commanded by Titus Flavius Vespasianus, eventually to become the Emperor Vespasian (69-79).

Service length varied. During the time in question it was supposed to be 20 years. By the second century the average was 23-6 years (le Bohec 2000, 64). Marriage was technically prohibited until the time of Septimius Severus but circumstantial evidence suggests that marriage was not unusual.

Auxiliaries

There were besides [the legions], fleets, cavalry and light infantry, drawn from the provinces, in commanding positions in our possessions, amounting to very little less in total. But it would be misleading to provide a detailed account because they moved about as required. Their numbers were sometimes increased, and sometimes reduced.

Tacitus, A iv.5.6

Dio adds the fact that he was unable to provide exact figures for the auxiliaries in Augustus' reign, and tells us nothing about their numbers in his own time (lv.24.5).

The statement by Tacitus gives us a broad picture of the auxiliary troops of the Roman Empire. They were roughly equivalent to the legionaries in total, which at the time he wrote means 125,000 men. Given that the Duke of Wellington's force in 1815 started out at 100,000, two-thirds of whom were non-British, the number does not seem very great. The most revealing comment though is that their numbers were subject to constant variation.

Additional information comes from Tacitus' account of the civil war. In the year 69, Vitellius entered Rome: 'The front of the line was marked by the eagles of four legions, while the standards of four other legions could be seen on either side. They were followed by the colours of 12 cavalry wings. Then came the infantry and the cavalry, followed by 34 auxiliary infantry cohorts, distinguished by their national names or their equipment . . .' (*H* ii.89).

Auxiliaries were used as the main frontier garrisons, but were also placed first in the front line on the battlefield. Usually, they were posted away from their nominal homelands. This included Britain, and a number of units are known, stationed elsewhere in the Empire. They were less well paid than legionaries and had to serve 25 years to earn an honourable discharge and citizenship. This event was sometimes recorded on small bronze tablets, commemorating the discharge of auxiliaries in a given province on a given date. The diplomas, *diplomata*, form an invaluable record of snapshots of the auxiliary garrison across the militarised provinces, and they confirm Tacitus' image of a force in perpetual flux.

Units were divided up according to their nominal strengths. This was often very nominal indeed. In the auxiliary infantry regiments a *cohors peditata quingenaria* was 'a 500-strong infantry cohort'. In fact, it was made up of six 'centuries' of 80 troops, not including officers. The larger infantry unit was called a *cohors peditata milliaria*, but instead of being 1000-strong it was made up of ten centuries of 80 men, producing a 'milliary cohort' of 800. At Birdoswald, from at least 205-8, the garrison was *cohors I Aelia Dacorum milliaria*, or the 'First cohort of Aelian Dacians, 1000-strong'.

In the auxiliary cavalry regiments an *ala quingenaria* was a cavalry wing of nominal 500 strength but this time made up of 16 *turmae* of 32 men each, making 512 not including officers. A 'large wing' was called an *ala milliaria* and had 24 *turmae*, making 768 men. Britain, like all provinces, had only one such unit, *ala Petriana*, stationed at Stanwix, the largest fort on the Wall.

Other auxiliary units were made from a combination of infantry and cavalry. This was achieved by adding four *turmae*, or 128 men, to a small infantry cohort, making 608 men in what was now called a *cohors equitata quingenaria* ('500-strong mounted cohort'). Eight *turmae* added to a large cohort created a unit of 800 foot and 256 cavalry or 1056 men, called a *cohors equitata milliaria* ('1000-strong mounted cohort'). A number of inscriptions from Risingham name the *cohors I Vangionum milliaria equitata*, or 'First part-mounted cohort of Vangones, 1000-strong'. Promotion from the ranks was usually denoted by pay. *Duplicarius*, for example, meant double-pay and usually referred to the second-in-command of a *turma* (*see* **11**).

Although the physical evidence from forts shows that they were built to reflect these nominal and actual strengths, we now know from *diplomata*, the strength roster found at Vindolanda, and other information, that day-to-day manpower varied immensely. Soldiers could be sick or otherwise unfit for duty, sent away in large detachments to serve elsewhere, or seconded to the governor's staff. Some time around 78-84, a trooper in the auxiliary cavalry unit of *ala Gallorum Sebosiana* was serving as a *sing(ularis consularis)* to the governor, Gnaeus Julius Agricola (*Brit* xxix, 1998, 74, no. 44). In a few instances we only know of a unit as a vexillation, or detachment, for example the *vexillation Sueborum Longovicianorum Gordianae*, 'the Vexillation of Suevians of *Longovicium* [Lanchester], styled the Gordians' (*RIB* 1074 for 238-44).

The most useful way of understanding a unit and its fort, is to see the latter as the nominal base where units records were maintained and to which soldiers would return. But the soldiers in residence at any one time were likely to vary depending on duties and detachments, while troops from other units were quite likely to pass through in detachments or as individuals. Thus we have *cohors Bracarum in Britannia* some time in the mid-second century, yet the unit is otherwise unknown in Britain and is otherwise testified in North Africa (*ILS* 9002). It is worth bearing in mind a comment made by Mike Bishop, 'It has long been traditional to attempt to associate a particular type of unit with a base of a given size, but recent scholarship — and most significantly the excavation of Elginhaugh — has tended to highlight the futility of this pursuit' (Bishop in Abramson *et alia*, 311).

Most auxiliary unit names sport an ethnic component. The usual assumption is that at the very least this recorded the original province where the unit was raised, and from where new recruits were raised to begin with. Even if local recruitment supplanted those from the province of origin, the title was retained. But it was also possible for ethnicity to be supplanted quite early on. Sextus Valerius Genialis was a late first-century Frisian cavalryman with a Thracian *ala* (**2**). The case of the Egyptian fleet recruit called Apion, awarded the Roman name of Antonius Maximus on arrival in Italy (see Chapter 8), shows that individual ethnicity was also suppressed. Apion himself indicates no regret. Dio also tells us that under Augustus a unit of cavalry, made up of picked men, were named

Batavians simply to appropriate the kudos of a region with a reputation for producing first-class horsemen (lv. 24.7).

Some of the units were awarded special privileges, as a reward for achievements and which were commemorated in their names. This was usually Roman citizenship, for example, the *cohors I fida Vardullorum milliaria equitata civium Romanorum,* 'the First part-mounted loyal cohort of Vardulli, 1000-strong', at High Rochester (RIB 1279, for the year 216). It was also common in the third century for such units, as well as legions (*see* **40**), and this one was no exception, to adopt the name of the incumbent emperor as an honorific, and tactful, label. Here the unit was given the name *Antoniniana* for the official name of Caracalla. In other cases, the unit name might record special skills, thus *cohors I Hamiorum sagittaria,* 'the First cohort of Hamian archers' (RIB 1778). All such titles were often abbreviated and sometimes omitted altogether.

As well as the mainstream auxiliaries, there were also several lesser forms of auxiliary unit. These were more casually organised, less well paid, and did not earn citizenship on retirement. They proliferate in later records, particularly the *ND*, even though many of the older, more conventional, units are listed side by side. These include the *numerus*, which means no more than 'number', applied it seems to almost any kind of unit apart from cavalry (see Southern 1987). One of the most exotic, and seemingly inappropriate, is the *numerus Barcariorum Tigrisiensium Arbeia,* 'unit of Tigris boatmen', based at South Shields (*ND* xl.22). There is a possibility that this was a manufactured title, especially if this was the unit, which just described itself as a *numerus barcariorum* at Lancaster (*RIB* 601; and see Chapter 8). Other specialist units classified as *numeri* are the *exploratores,* 'scouts', such as those based at High Rochester alongside *cohors I Vardullorum* between 238-44 (*RIB* 1262).

Cavalry units of similar status to the *numeri* were known as the *cuneus*, which means 'wedge'. In Britain these first appear in the third century, for example the *cuneus Frisionum Aballavensium Philippianorum,* 'cavalry unit of Frisians at *Aballava* [Burgh-by-Sands], styled the Philippians' (*RIB* 883, for the year 241, but found at Papcastle). Almost entirely known only from the *ND* are the *equites,* units of cavalry assigned to a variety of locations such as Saxon Shore forts and several unknown places. They variously fell under the command of the Duke of the Britons, the Count of the Saxon Shore, and the Count of the British provinces. Those listed under the latter are not assigned to any locations, suggesting they were mobile.

APPENDIX 2:
GLOSSARY OF TERMS

The following list may be useful, in addition to the definitions of units described in Appendix 1.

Aquilifer	bearer of the legionary eagle standard
Beneficiarius	a soldier on detachment, usually qualified by the office to which he was attached. For example, *beneficiarius consularis* means a soldier detached to the governor's staff, *legati* to a legionary commander's staff, *tribuni* to a legionary tribune, *praefecti* to a prefect's staff and so on. Invariably abbreviated on inscriptions to BF.
Bucinator	trumpeter
Centurio praeposito	centurion in command, abbreviated to CENT PP, or C PP
Cornicularius	staff clerk
Curator	soldier of a *turma* in charge of supplies
Custos armorum	custodian of armour and equipment
Eques singularis Augusti	trooper of the imperial bodyguard, *eques singularis consularis* of the governor's bodyguard and so on
Fabricensis/fabriciensis legionis	armourer of the legion
Frumentarius	literally a corn-dealer, but the word had come to mean a military spy
Imaginifer	bearer of the imperial portrait standard
Medicus	surgeon
Mensor	surveyor
Pedites singularis Augusti	soldier of the governor's bodyguard
Praefectus castrorum	camp prefect
Praepositus curam agens horreorum	officer in charge of the granaries
Signifer	standard-bearer of the century
Speculator	legionary serving as a secretary on the governor's staff
Strator consularis	soldier in charge of the governor's horses and stables
Tesserarius	keeper of the century's password
Tribunus militum	military tribune
Vexillarius	flag-bearer

APPENDIX 3:
AUXILIA IN BRITAIN

(order as *RIB* 2401, Table I, with additions)

This is a summary list of auxiliary units testified in Britain. Very few are specifically dated to the first century, while second-century records are largely confined to diplomas. As a result the nominal base for each unit up until the beginning of the third century is not usually known. More is known for the first half of the third century but thereafter virtually the only source is the Notitia Dignitatum (ND), the contents of which can only be broadly attributed to the fourth century. Regardless of how frequently units are testified in a single place, the fact remains that they could have been widely dispersed, or dispatched elsewhere, in between (see for example Alston 1995, Appendix I). Where units are testified from the tombstone of an individual it is important to remember that the individual might have been the only member of his unit present at the location. The dedications to Antenociticus at Benwell, and Coventina at Carrawburgh are good examples. Likewise lead sealings (RIB 2411) only apply to goods shipped by the unit, perhaps from elsewhere. References are selected here, preferring always inscriptions which are dated, unless these are not available.

Alae (cavalry units)

*ala Augusta Gallorum Petriana milliaria civium
   Romanorum*
Diplomas: 98, 122, 124, 127, 135
Inscriptions: Carlisle, Corbridge, Stanwix
   (*RIB* 957, 1172, 2411.84)
ND: Stanwix

ala Agrippiana Miniata
Diploma: 122

ala I Hispanorum Asturum
Diplomas: 98, 122, 124, 127, 145-6, 158
Inscriptions: Benwell 205-8, 238 (*RIB*
   1337, 1334), South Shields (*RIB* 1064)
ND: Benwell

ala II Asturum
Diplomas: 122, 127
Inscriptions: Chesters 176-84, 221, 221-2
   (*RIB* 1463-4, 1465, 1466)
ND: Chesters

ala Augusta ob virtutem appellate
Diplomas: nil, but perhaps identical with
   another known by a different name
Inscriptions: Chesters 122-38 (*B* 1979,
   346), Carlisle 180-92 (*RIB* 946), Old
   Carlisle 185, 188, 191, 197, 213, 242,
   (*RIB* 903, 893, 894, 895, 905, 897)

ala Gallorum Indiana
Inscriptions: Cirencester before 135 (*RIB*
   108)

ala Gallorum Picentiana
Diplomas: 122, 124
Inscriptions: Malton (*B* 1971, 291)

ala Augusta Gallorum Proculeiana
Diplomas: 114-130, 135, 145-6, 158

ala Gallorum Sebosiana
Diplomas: 103, 122, 127, 158, 178

Inscriptions: Carlisle 78-84 (*B* 1998, 74), Lancaster 262-6 (*RIB* 605)

ala Gallorum et Thracum Classiana civium Romanorum
Diplomas: 105, 122, 178

ala I Herculea
ND: '*Olenacum*' (Ilkley or Elslack)

ala I Pannoniorum Sabiniana
Diplomas: 122, 127, 145-6, 178
Inscriptions: Haltonchesters (*RIB* 1433)
ND: Haltonchesters

ala I Pannoniorum Tampiana
Diplomas: 103, 122

ala Sarmatarum
Inscriptions: Ribchester (*RIB* 594-5)

ala I Thracum
Diplomas: 103, 124
Inscriptions: Cirencester, Colchester, Caerleon (*RIB* 109, 201, 2415.39)

ala I Tungrorum
Diplomas: 98, 105, 122, 135, 158
Inscriptions: Mumrills (*RIB* 2140)

ala Hispanorum Vettonum civium Romanorum
Diplomas: 103, 122, 158, 178
Inscriptions: Bath, Bowes, Binchester, Y Gaer (*RIB* 159, 730, 1028, 1035, 403, 405)

ala Augusta Vocontiorum civium Romanorum
Diplomas: 122, 127, 178
Inscriptions: Newstead (*RIB* 2121)

Cohortes (cohorts, infantry or mixed infantry and cavalry)

cohors I Aelia Dacorum milliaria
Diploma: 127, 145-6, 158
Inscriptions: Birdoswald 205-8, 235-8, 237, 238-44, 259-68, 270-3, 276-82 (*RIB* 1909, 1896, 1875, 1893, 1882, 1883, 1886, *JRS* 1961, 194
ND: see PNRB p.221, note 44

cohors I Augusta Nervia/Nervana Germanorum milliaria equitata
Diplomas: 122, 127, 158, 178
Inscriptions: Bewcastle, Burgh-by-Sands, Birrens (*RIB* 966, 2041, 2093, 2097)

cohors I Tungrorum milliaria
Diplomas: 103, 122, 127, 135, 146
Inscriptions: Vindolanda 90-100 (*TV* ii.154), Castlecary 139-61 (*RIB* 2155), Housesteads undated (*RIB* 1578, 1580, 1584-6, 1591)
ND: Housesteads

cohors II Tungrorum milliaria equitata civium Latinorum
Inscriptions: Cramond (*RIB* 2135, revised), Birrens 157-8 (*RIB* 2110), Castlesteads 241 (*RIB* 1983)

cohors I Vangionum milliaria equitata
Diplomas: 103, 122, 124, 135, 158, 178
Inscriptions: Vindolanda (*TV* ii.181), Risingham 205-8, 211-17, 213 (*RIB* 1234, 1237, 1235), Benwell (*RIB* 1328), Chesters (*RIB* 1482)

cohors I fida Vardullorum milliaria equitata civium Romanorum
Diplomas: 98, 122, 124, 135, 145-6, 158, 159, 178
Inscriptions: Castlecary 138-61 (*RIB* 2149), Lanchester 175-8 (*RIB* 1083), High Rochester 218-22, 220, 225-35, 238-41 (*RIB* 1272, 1280, 1281, 1262), Cappuck (*RIB* 2118)

cohors I Afrorum equitata civium Romanorum
Diploma:122

cohors I Alpinorum
Diploma: 103

cohors I Aquitanorum
Diplomas: 122, 124, 127
Inscriptions: Brough-on-Noe 158 (*RIB* 283), Bakewell (*RIB* 278), Carrawburgh 130-3? (*RIB* 1550), Brancaster third century on (*RIB* 2466)

cohors I Asturum equitata
ND: Chesters — probably an error, see
cohors II Asturum below

cohors II Asturum equitata
Diplomas: 105, 122, 124, 127
Inscriptions: Great Chesters 225 (*RIB*
1738), Llanio (*RIB* 407-8)

cohors I Baetasiorum civium Romanorum
Diplomas: 103, 122, 124
Inscriptions: Bar Hill 139-61 (*RIB* 2170),
Old Kilpatrick 139-61 (*B* 1970, 310),
Maryport (*RIB* 830, 837-8, 842-3),
Reculver third century on (*RIB* 2468)
ND: Reculver

cohors I Batavorum equitata
Diplomas: 122, 124, 135, 178
Inscriptions: Carrawburgh 213-22, 237
(*RIB* 1544, 1553)
ND: Carrawburgh

cohors III Batavorum
Inscriptions: Vindolanda *c*.92-103 (*TV*
ii.26)

cohors IX Batavorum
Inscriptions: Vindolanda *c*.92-103 (*TV*
ii.159)

cohors I Bracaraugustanorum equitata?
Inscriptions: York (*RIB* 649)

cohors Bracarum
Inscription: *ILS 9002 in Britannia, c.*160

cohors III Bracaraugustanorum equitata
Diplomas: 103, 122, 124, 127, 145-6, 158
Inscriptions: Manchester (*RIB* 2469.i-iii),
Melandra Castle (*RIB* 2469.iv)

cohors IIII Breucorum
Diplomas: 122
Inscriptions: Bowes 130-3 (or *IIII
Delmatarum*) (*RIB* 739), Ebchester 213-
22 (*RIB* 1101), various northern
locations (*RIB* 2470)

[cohors?] Brittonum (type of unit unknown)
Inscriptions: Castlecary (*RIB* 2152)

cohors I Celtiberorum
Diplomas: 105, 122, 127, 145-6, 158
cohors I Aelia Classica
Diplomas: 145-5, 158
Inscriptions: H Wall turret 25a (*B* 1986,
386)
ND: 'Tunnocelo'

cohors I Cornoviorum
ND
*cohors I Ulpia Traiana Cugernorum civium
Romanorum*
Diplomas: 103, 122, 124
Inscriptions: Cramond (*RIB* 2313),
Newcastle 213 (*B* 1980, 405),
Carrawburgh (*RIB* 1524)

cohors I Dalmatarum/Delmatarum
Diplomas: 122, 124, 135, 158
Inscriptions: Maryport (*RIB* 832),
Chesters (*JRS* 1957, 229)

cohors II Dalmatarum/Delmatarum
Diplomas: 105, 122, 127, 135
Inscriptions: Carvoran (*RIB* 1795)
ND: Carvoran

cohors IIII Delmatarum
Diplomas: 103, 122
Inscriptions: Hardknott (*JRS* 1965, 222)

cohors I Frisiavonum/Frixagorum?
Diplomas: 105, 122, 124, 158, 178
Inscriptions: Melandra Castle (*RIB* 279),
Manchester (*RIB* 577-9), Rudchester?
— see note to *RIB* 1395

cohors II Gallorum equitata
Diplomas: 122, 127, 145-6, 158, 178
Inscriptions: Old Penrith (*RIB* 917, with
B 1995, 390, (g)), Old Penrtih 225-38,
244-9 (*RIB* 929, 915)

cohors IIII Gallorum equitata
Diplomas: 127, 145-6, 158, 178
Inscriptions: Castlehill 138-61 (*RIB*
2195), Vindolanda 212-13, 213-35, 223,
276-82 (*RIB* 1705, 1686, 1706, 1710),
Templeborough (*RIB* 619-20, 2472.1-
2), Risingham (*RIB* 1227, 1249),

Castlesteads (*RIB* 1979-80)
ND: Vindolanda

cohors V Gallorum equitata
Diplomas: 122, 127, 158
Inscriptions: Cramond 138-61 (*RIB* 2134), South Shields 213, 222 (*B* 1985, 325-6, *RIB* 1060)

cohors I Hamiorum sagittaria
Diplomas: 122, 124, 127, 135, 158
Inscriptions: Carvoran 136-8, 163-6 (*RIB* 1778, 1809), Bar Hill 139-61 (*RIB* 2167, 2172)

cohors I Hispanorum equitata/cohors I Aelia Hispanorum milliaria equitata (same unit, doubled)
Diplomas: 98, 103, 105, 122, 124, 127, 145-6, 178
Inscriptions: Maryport *c.*123-38 (*ILS* 2735 with *RIB* 823), Netherby 213-22, 222 (*RIB* 976-9)
ND: Bowness or Stanwix (see PNRB p.221, note 49)

cohors II Hispanorum
Diploma: 178

cohors I Lingonum equitata
Diplomas: 105, 122
Inscriptions: High Rochester 139-43 (*RIB* 1276), Lanchester 238-44 (*RIB* 1091-2)

cohors II Lingonum equitata
Diplomas: 98. 122, 124, 127, 158, 178
Inscriptions: Ilkley (*RIB* 635, 2475), Moresby (*RIB* 798, 800), Brough-under-Stainmore (*RIB* 2411.106, 108)
ND: Drumburgh

cohors III Lingonum equitata
Diplomas: 103, 122, 178

cohors IIII Lingonum equitata
Diplomas: 103, 145-6, 158
Inscriptions: Wallsend (*RIB* 1299-1302, 2411.109, 2476.1-2)
ND: Wallsend

cohors I Menapiorum
Diplomas: 122, 124
cohors I Morinorum et Cersiacorum
Diplomas: 103, 122, 178
ND: Ravenglass

cohors I Nerviorum
Diploma: 105
Inscription: Caer Gai (*RIB* 418)

cohors II Nerviorum civium Romanorum
Diplomas: 98, 122, 124, 127
Inscriptions: Whitley Castle 213, 214-17 (*RIB* 1202-3), Wallsend (*RIB* 1303), Carrawburgh (*RIB* 1538), Vindolanda (*RIB* 1683), High Rochester (*B* 1983, 337), Brough-under-Stainmore (*RIB* 2411.111-40)

cohors III Nerviorum
Diplomas: 124, 127, 135
Inscriptions: Vindolanda (*RIB* 1691), Maryport (*JRS* 1967, 204-5), Newstead (*RIB* 2411.142)
ND: Maryport

cohors IIII Nerviorum
Diplomas: 114-30, 135

cohors VI Nerviorum
Diplomas: 122, 124, 127, 135, 145-6
Inscriptions: Rough Castle 139-61 (*RIB* 2144-5), Bainbridge 205, 206 (*JRS* 1969, 246, RIB 722), Great Chesters (*RIB* 1731)
ND: Bainbridge

cohors I Pannoniorum equitata?
Inscriptions: Cawfields (*RIB* 1667). More likely *II Pannoniorum*

cohors II Pannoniorum
Diplomas: 105, 124
Inscriptions: Beckfoot (*RIB* 880), Cawfields (*RIB* 1667), Vindolanda (*RIB* 2411.143)

cohors V Pannoniorum?
Inscriptions: Brough-under-Stainmore (*RIB* 2411.144)

cohors V Raetorum equitata
Diploma: 122
Inscription: Carrawburgh (*RIB* 1529)

cohors VI Raetorum
Trajanic: in Britain under the prefect C.
  Rufius Moderatus. diploma. CIL
  iii.5202
Inscriptions: Great Chesters 166-9 (*RIB*
  1737), Brough-under-Stainmore (*RIB*
  2411.147-51)

cohors I Sunicorum/Sunucorum
Diplomas: 122, 124, 127
Inscriptions: Carnarfon 198-209 (*RIB*
  430)

cohors I Thracum equitata civium Romanorum
Diplomas: 122, 127, 158, 178
Inscriptions: Bowes 197-202, 205-8 (*RIB*
  730, 740), Birdoswald 205-8 (*RIB* 1909)

cohors II Thracum equitata
Diplomas: 103, 122, 178
Inscriptions: Mumrills 139-61 (*RIB*
  2142), Moresby (*RIB* 797, 804)
ND: Moresby

cohors VI Thracum
Inscriptions: Gloucester, 1st century (*RIB*
  121), Brough-under-Stainmore (*RIB*
  2411.152-60)

cohors VII Thracum
Diplomas: 122, 127, 135, 158, 178
Inscriptions: Brough-under-Stainmore
  (*RIB* 2411.161-92, 194-240)

cohors ?? Thracum
Inscription: Wroxeter (*RIB* 291)

cohors Usiporum
Text: in Britain in 83 (Tacitus, *Agr* 28.1,
  and Dio lxvi.20)

*cohors II Vasconum equitata civium
  Romanorum*
Diplomas: 105, 122

Vexillationes (vexillations of units otherwise not testified)

vexillatio M[a]r[sacorum?]
Inscriptions: Old Penrith 222-35 (*RIB*
  919)

vexillatio G(aesatorum) R(aetorum)
Inscriptions: Cappuck (*RIB* 2117), Great
  Chesters (*RIB* 1724), Risingham (*RIB*
  1216-17)

vexillatio Germa[no]r(um) V[o]r[e]d(ensium)
Inscription: Old Penrith (*RIB* 920)

vexil(latio) Raetor(um) et Noricor(um)
Inscription: Manchester (*RIB* 576)

*vexillatio Sueborum Lon(govicianorum)
  Gor(dianae)*
Inscription: Lanchester, 238-44 (*RIB*
  1074)

Cunei

*c[u]neus Frisionum Aballavensium
  Philipp(ianorum)*
Inscription: Papcastle, 241 (*RIB* 883)

*cuneus Frisiorum Ver(covicianorum)
  Se(ve)r(iani) Alexandriani*
Inscriptions: Housesteads, 222-35 (*RIB*
  1594)

c(uneus) Fris(iorum) Vinovie(nsium)
Inscription: Binchester (*RIB* 1036)

cuneus Sarmatarum, Bremetenraco
ND: Ribchester

Equites

equites Catafractariorum
ND: 'Morbio' (unknown). Under
  command of *dux Britanniarum*. ND
  xl.21
equites Crispianorum
ND: Doncaster? or Jarrow?

equites Delmatarum
ND: 'Praesidio'
equites Dalmatarum Branodunensium
ND: Brancaster

equites stablesianorum Garrionnensium
ND: Burgh Castle

eq(uites) [St]ratonicianorum
Inscription: Brougham (*RIB* 780)

Milites

milites Tungrecanorum
ND: Dover

Numeri (and other unspecified units)

numerus Abulcorum, Anderidos
ND: Pevensey

numerus Alamannorum
Text: in Britain in 372 (Ammianus
    xxix.4.7)

numerus Barc(ariorum)
Inscription: Lancaster (*RIB* 601)

numerus Barcariorum Tigrisiensium, Arbeia
    (perhaps identical with the previous)
ND: South Shields

numerus Batavorum
Text: in Britain in 367 (Ammianus
    xxvii.8.7)

numerus Concangensium
Inscription: Binchester (*RIB* 2480.1-2)

numerus Defensorum, Braboniaco
ND: Kirkby Thore

numerus Directorum, Verteris
ND: Brough

*numerus Explorator(um) Brem(eniensium)
    Gor(diani)*
Inscription: High Rochester 238-44 (*RIB*
    1262)

(numerus?) Expl[oratores Habitancenses?]
Inscription: Risingham 213 (*RIB* 1235)

numerus Exploratorum, Lavatrae
ND: Bowes

numerus Exploratorum, Portum Adurni
ND: Portchester

numerus Fortensium, Othonae
ND: Bradwell-on-Sea

numerus Herulorum
Text: in Britain in 367 (Ammianus
    xxvii.8.7)
numerus Hnaudifridi
Inscription: Housesteads (*RIB* 1576)

numerus Joviorum
Text: in Britain in 367 (Ammianus
    xxvii.8.7)

numerus Longovicanorum, Longovicio
ND: Lanchester

numerus Magne<c>e(n)s(ium)
Inscription: Carvoran (*RIB* 1825)

*n(umerus) Maur[o]rum Aur(elianorum)
    Valeriani Gallieniq(ue), Aballaba*
Inscription: Burgh-by-Sands 253-8 (*RIB*
    2042)
ND: Burgh-by-Sands

numeri Moesiacorum
Text: in Britain in 360 (Ammianus xx.1.2)

numerus Nerviorum Dictensium, Dicti
ND: Wearmouth?

numerus Pacensium, Magis
ND: Burrow Walls?

numerus Raetorum Gae[sa]torum
Inscription: Risingham 213 (*RIB* 1235)

*n(umerus) eq(uitum) Sar[m(atarum)]
    Bremmetenn(acensium)*
Inscription: Ribchester 238-44 (*RIB* 583),
    Bainesse, near Catterick (*RIB* 2479)

numerus Solensium, Maglone
ND: Old Carlisle?

numerus Supervenientium Peturiensium, Derventione
ND: Malton

numerus S(yrorum) s(agittariorum)?
Inscription: Kirkby Thore (*RIB* 764)

numerus Turnacensium, Lemannis
ND: Lympne

numerus Victorum
Text: in Britain in 367 (Ammianus xxvii.8.7)

numerus vigilum, Concangios
ND: Chester-le-Street

Areani or *Arcani*
Text: in Britain 368-9 (Ammianus xxviii.3.8)

Venatores
venatores Banniesses
Inscription: Birdoswald (*RIB* 1905)

Unspecified

Aeruli
Text: in Britain in 360 (Ammianus xx.1.2)
Batavii
Text: in Britain in 360 (Ammianus xx.1.2)

Others

These units are listed in the *Notitia* under the command of the *comes provinciarum Britanniarum*.
equites catafractarii juniores
equites scutarii juniores
equites Honoriani seniores
equites Stablesiani
equites Syri
equites Taifali
Victores juniores Britannici
Primani juniores
Secundani juniores

Diploma References

98: CIL xvi.43
103 (Jan 19): CIL xvi.48 (RIB 2401.1)
114-30 (but not 122, 124, or 127): CIL xvi.88 (RIB 2401.7)
'Trajanic': CIL iii.5202
122 (Jul 17): CIL xvi.69
127 (Aug 20): Nollé (forthcoming)
135 (Apr 14): CIL xvi.82 (RIB 2401.8)
145-146 (Dec 10-Dec 9): CIL xvi.93 (RIB 2401.10)
146 (Jan-Mar): diploma. RMD 97 (RIB 2401.9)
158 (Feb 27): Brit. xxviii (1992), 463-4, no. 28, and Brit. xxvi (1995), 389-90 (f)
159 (estimated): CIL xvi.130 (RIB 2401.12)
178 (Mar 23): RMD 184, and Brit. xxvi (1995), 390, (g)

REFERENCES AND FURTHER READING

References

A	Tacitus, *Annals*
AE	*L'année Epigraphique*
Agr	Tacitus, *Agricola*
B	*Britannia* (published by the Society for the Promotion of Roman Studies, London)
CA	Coulston and Phillips 1988
CF	Cunliffe and Fulford 1982
CIL	*Corpus Inscriptionum Latinarum* (Berlin 1863-)
CSIR	*Corpus Signorum Imperii Romani*
H	Tacitus, *Histories*
ILS	*Inscriptionum latinae selectae*, published by H. Dessau 1892-1916
JRS	Journal of Roman Studies
LAC 8	London Association of Classical Teachers, *LACTOR* no. 8, 'Inscriptions of the Roman Empire AD14-117'. Volume 4 in this series, 'Inscriptions of Roman Britain', is also a very convenient source of texts and inscriptions for those without access to *RIB*. Copies may be obtained from 5 Normington Close, Leigham Court Road, London SW16 2QS
KA	Keppie and Arnold 1984
P	Phillips 1977
PNRB	*Place Names of Roman Britain* (Rivet and Smith 1979)
RIB/RIB95	Collingwood and Wright, second edition 1995
SHA	*Scriptores Historiae Augustae*
SP	*Select Papyri, Vol. 1,* Loeb Classical Library no. 266
TV	*Tab Vindol* (see Bowman 1994, and Bowman and Thomas 1996)

Further reading

The number of books and articles concerning the Roman army in Britain and across the Empire is so vast that the following form only the tiniest proportion. However, those listed have proved the most useful in assembling this book. The various classical references found throughout the text are most easily found in the Penguin Classics series, or the Loeb Classical Library (Harvard).

Abramson, P., Berg, D.S., and Fossick, M.R., *Roman Castleford Excavations 1974-85. Volume II: the Structural and Environmental Evidence*, West Yorkshire Archaeology Service

Allason-Jones, L., 1999, 'Women and the Roman army in Britain', in Goldsworthy, A., and Haynes, I., 1999 (Eds)

Allason-Jones, L., and Bishop, M.C., 1988, *Excavations at Roman Corbridge: the Hoard*, English Heritage Archaeological Report no. 7, London

Allason-Jones, L., and McKay, B., *Coventina's Well*, Trustees of the Clayton Collection, Chesters Museum

Allen, J.R.L., and Fulford, M.G., 1996, 'The distribution of South-East Dorset Black Burnished Category 1 pottery in South-West Britain', *Britannia* xxvii, 223-82

Allen, J.R.L., and Fulford, M.G., 1999, 'Fort Building and Military Supply: Later Second and Third Centuries', *Britannia* xxx, 163-84

Alston, R., 1995, *Soldier and Society in Roman Egypt*, Routledge, London

Alston, R., 1999, 'Ties that bind: soldiers and societies' in Goldsworthy, A., and Haynes, I., 1999 (Eds)

Beevor, A., 1998, *Stalingrad*, Penguin, London

Bezeczky, T., 1996, 'Amphorae Inscriptions – Legionary Supply?', *Britannia* xxvii, 329-36

Bidwell, P.T., 1980, *Roman Exeter: Fortress and Town*, Exeter City Council, Exeter

Biggins, J. Alan, and Taylor, D.J.A., 1999, 'A Survey of the Roman Fort and Settlement at Birdoswald', *Britannia* xxx, 91-110

Birley, A., 1979, *The People of Roman Britain*, Batsford, London

Birley, E., 1969, 'Septimius Severus and the Roman army', *Epigraphische Studien* viii.63-82

Biró, M., 'The inscriptions of Roman Britain', *Acta Archaeologica Academiae Scientarum Hungaricae* xxvii, 13-58

Bishop, M.C. (ed), 1985, *The Production and Distribution of Roman Military Equipment; Proceedings of the Second Roman Military Equipment Seminar*, British Archaeological Reports International Series no. 275, Oxford

Bishop, M.C., and Coulston, J.N.C., 1993, *Roman Military Equipment*, Batsford, London

Black, E.W., 1998, 'How Many Rivers to Cross', *Britannia* xxix, 306-7

Bowman, A.K., 1994, *Life and Letters on the Roman Frontier. Vindolanda and its People*, British Museum Press, London

Bowman, A.K., and Thomas, J.D., 1996, 'New writing tablets from Vindolanda', *Britannia* xxvii, 299-328

Braund, D., 1984, 'Observations on Cartimandua', *Britannia* xv, 1-6

Breeze, D., and Dobson B., 1987, *Hadrian's Wall*, Penguin, London

Briggs, A., 1959, *The Age of Improvement*, Longman, London

Burnham, B.C., and Wacher, J., *The 'Small Towns' of Roman Britain*, Batsford, London

Bushe-Fox, J.P., 1949, *Fourth Report on the Excavation of the Roman Fort at Richborough, Kent*, Research Report of the Society of Antiquaries of London no. 16, London

Clay, P., and Mellor, J.E., 1985, *Excavations in Bath Lane, Leicester*, Archaeological Report No. 10, Leicester Museums Publication No. 65, Leicester

Collingwood, R.G., and Wright, R.P., 1995, *The Roman Inscriptions of Britain I. Inscriptions on Stone*, second edition with addenda and corrigenda by R.S.O. Tomlin, Alan Sutton, Stroud

Connolly, P., 1981, *Greece and Rome at War*, Macdonald, London

Cool, H.E.M., and Philo, C., 1998, *Roman Castleford Excavations 1974-85. Volume 1: The Small Finds*, West Yorkshire Archaeological Service

Cool, H.E.M., Jackson, C.M., and Monaghan, J., 1999, 'Glass-making and the Sixth Legion at York', *Britannia* xxx, 147-61

Coulston, J.C., and Phillips, E.J., 1988, *Corpus Signorum Imperii Romani. Great Britain Volume I, Fascicule 6: Hadrian's Wall West of the North Tyne, and Carlisle,* British Academy, Oxford University Press, Oxford

Crow, J., 1995, *Housesteads*, English Heritage, London

Crummy, P., 1990, 'Metrological Analysis', *Current Archaeology* no. 122, 91-3

Cunliffe, B., 1968, *Fifth Report on the Excavations of the Roman Fort at Richborough*, Research Report of the Society of Antiquaries of London no. 23, London

Cunliffe, B., 1975, *Excavations at Portchester Castle I: Roman*, Research Report of the Society of Antiquaries of London no. 32, London

Cunliffe, B., 1988, *The Temple of Sulis Minerva at Bath. Volume 2. The Finds from the Sacred Spring*, Oxford University Committee for Archaeology Monograph no. 16, Oxford

Cunliffe B.W., and Fulford, M.G., 1982, *Corpus Signorum Imperii Romani. Great Britain Volume I, Fascicule 2: Bath and the Rest of Wessex*, British Academy, Oxford University Press, Oxford

Dannell, G.B., and Wild, J.P., 1987, *Longthorpe II. The Military Works-Depot: an Episode in Landscape History*, Britannia Monograph series no. 8, Society for the Promotion of Roman Studies, London

Dark, P., 1999, 'Pollen Evidence for the Environment of Roman Britain', *Britannia* xxx, 247-72

de la Bédoyère, G., 1998 (i), *Hadrian's* Wall, Tempus, Stroud

de la Bédoyère, G., 1998 (ii), 'Carausius and the Marks RSR and I.N.P.C.D.A.', *Numismatic Chronicle* 158, 79-88

de la Bédoyère, G., 1999, *Companion to Roman Britain*, Tempus, Stroud

de la Bédoyère, G., 2002, *Gods with Thunderbolts*, Tempus, Stroud

Dearne, M.J., and Branigan, K., 1995, 'The use of coal in Roman Britain', *Antiquaries Journal* lxxv, 71-105

Dobson, B., and Mann, J.C., 1973, 'The Roman Army in Britain and Britons in the Roman Army', *Britannia* iv, 191-205

Eckardt, H., 'The Colchester child's grave', *Britannia* xxx, 57-90

Erim, K.T., 1982, 'A new relief showing Claudius and Britannia from Aphrodisias', *Britannia* xiii, 277-82

Evans, E., 1994, 'Military Architects and Building Design', *Britannia* xxv, 143-64

Faulkner, N., 2000, *The Decline and Fall of Roman Britain*, Tempus, Stroud

Field, F.N., and Hurst, H., 1984, 'Roman Horncastle', *Lincs Hist. and Archaeology*, vol. 18

Frere, S.S., and Tomlin, R.S.O., 1992, 'Oculists' Stamps', in *The Roman Inscriptions of Britain. Volume II, Instrumentum Domesticum Fascicule 4*, Alan Sutton, Stroud

Fulford, M.G., 1996, *The Second Augustan Legion in the West of Britain*, The Ninth Annual Caerleon Lecture, National Museums and Galleries of Wales

Goldsworthy, A., 2000, *Roman Warfare*, Cassell, London

Goldsworthy, A., and Haynes, I., 1999 (Eds), *The Roman Army as a Community*, Journal of Roman Archaeology supplementary series no. 34, Portsmouth, Rhode Island

Gore, R., 1984, 'The Dead Do Tell Tales At Vesuvius', *National Geographic*, vol. 165, no. 5 (May), Washington DC

Greene, K., 1978, *The Pre-Flavian Fine Wares. Report on the Excavations at Usk 1965-1976*, University of Wales, Cardiff

Halkon, P., 1998, 'A Roman Relief Depicting Victory from Bolton, East Yorkshire', *Britannia* xxix, 322-5

Hanson, W.S., 1978, 'The organisation of Roman military timber-supply', *Britannia* ix, 293-305

Hassall, M.W.C., 1976, *Aspects* – not located mentioned in Rivet and Smith on p. 221

Hattatt, R., 1987, *Brooches of Antiquity. A third selection*, Oxbow Books, Oxford

Haynes, I., 'Military service and cultural identity in the *auxilia*', in Goldsworthy, A., and Haynes, I., 1999 (Eds)

Henig, M., 1978, *A Corpus of Roman Engraved Gemstones from British Sites*, British Archaeological Reports (British Series) no. 8, Oxford (2nd edition)

Henig, M., 1995, *Art in Roman Britain*, Batsford, London

Henig, M., 1999, 'Artistic patronage and the Roman military community in Britain', in Goldsworthy, A., and Haynes, I., 1999 (Eds)

Henig, M., Cleary, R., and Purser, P., 2000, 'A Roman Relief of Mercury and Minerva from Aldsworth, Gloucestershire', *Britannia* xxxi, 362-3

Hind, J.G.F., 1989, 'The invasion of Britain in AD 43 – an alternative strategy for Aulus Plautius', *Britannia* xx, 1-21

Holder, P.A., 1980, *Studies in the Auxilia of the Roman Army from Augustus to Trajan*, Cambridge

Hope, V.M., 1997, 'Words and pictures: the interpretation of Romano-British tombstones', *Britannia* xxvii, 245-58

James, S., 1988, 'The fabricae: state arms factories of the Later Roman Empire' in Coulston, J.C.N., (Ed), *Military Equipment and the Identity of Roman Soldiers*, Proceedings of the Fourth Roman Military Equipment Conference, Oxford, *BAR* S394

Johns, C., 1996, *The Jewellery of Roman Britain. Celtic and Classical Traditions*, UCL Press, London

Johnson, A., 1983, *Roman Forts*, A & C Black, London

Jones, M., 2002, *Roman Lincoln*, Tempus, Stroud

Kendal, R., 1996, 'Transport Logistics associated with the Building of Hadrian's Wall', *Britannia* xxvii, 129-52

Keppie, L.J.F., and Arnold, B.J., 1984, *Corpus Signorum Imperii Romani. Great Britain Volume I, Fascicule 4: Scotland*, British Academy, Oxford University Press, Oxford

King, A., 1999, 'Animals and the Roman army: the evidence of animal bones', in Goldsworthy, A., and Haynes, I., 1999 (Eds)

Le Bohec, Y., 2000, *The Imperial Roman Army*, Routledge, London (reprinting a 1994 Batsford title, translated from the French 1989)

Mack, R.P., 1975, *The Coinage of Ancient Britain*, Spink, London

Mason, D.J.P., 'Chester: the Canabae Legionis', *Britannia* xviii, 143-68

Mason, D.J.P., 2000, 'Chester, the Elliptical Building', *Current Archaeology*, no. 167

McCarthy, M., 2002, *Roman Carlisle*, Tempus, Stroud

McWhirr, A., Viner, L., and Wells, C., 1982, *Romano-British Cemeteries*, Cirencester Excavation Committee, Cirencester

Millett, M., 1990, *The Romanization of Britain*, Cambridge University Press, Cambridge

Murphy, D., Staton, R., Walsh-Atkins, P., and Whiskerd, N., 1998, *Britain 1815-1915*, HarperCollins, London

Pearson, A., 2002, *The Roman Shore Forts*, Tempus, Stroud

Phillips, E.J., 1977, *Corpus Signorum Imperii Romani. Great Britain Volume I, Fascicule I: Corbridge, Hadrian's Wall East of the North Tyne*, British Academy, Oxford University Press, Oxford

Philpott, R.A., 1999, 'A Romano-British Brooch Type from North-Western and Northern England', *Britannia* xxx, 274-86

Pitts, L.F., and St Joseph, J.K., 1985, *Inchtuthil. The Roman Legionary Fortress*, Britannia Monograph no. 6, London

Pollard, R.J., 1988, *The Roman Pottery of Kent*, Kent Archaeological Society, Maidstone

Rankov, N.B., 1987, 'M. Oclatinius Adventus in Britain', *Britannia* xviii, 243-9

Reade, J., 1999, 'An Eagle from the East', *Britannia* xxx, 286-8

Reece, R., 1997, *The Future of Roman Military Archaeology*, The Tenth Annual Caerleon Lecture, National Museums and Galleries of Wales

Rivet, A.L.F., and Smith, C., *The Place-Names of Roman Britain*, Batsford, London

Rogers, I., 1996, 'The Conquest of Brigantia and the Development of the Roman Road System in the North-West', *Britannia* xxvii, 365-8

Rook, A., 1978, 'The development and operation of Roman hypocausted baths', *Journal of Archaeological Science* 5, 281

Sauer, E., 1999 (i), 'The Augustan Army spa at Bourbonne-les-Bains', in Goldsworthy, A., and Haynes, I., 1999 (Eds)

Sauer, E., 1999 (ii), 'The Military Origins of the Roman Town of Alchester, Oxfordshire', *Britannia* xxxi, 289-96

Shirley, E.A.M., 1996, 'The Building of the Legionary Fortress at Inchuthil', *Britannia* xxvii, 111-18

Smith, A.H.V., 1997, 'Provenance of Coals', *Britannia* xxvii, 297-324

Southern, P., 1989, 'The Numeri of the Roman Imperial Army', *Britannia* xx, 81-140

Southern P., and Dixon, K.R., 2000, *The Late Roman Army*, Routledge, London (reprinting a 1994 Batsford title)

Speidel, M.P., 1987, 'The Chattan War, the Brigantian Revolt and the Loss of the Antonine Wall', *Britannia* xviii, 233-6

Speidel, M.P., 1998, 'The Risingham *Praetensio*', *Britannia* xxvii, 356-9

Stephens, G.R., 1987, 'A Severan Vexillation at Ribchester', *Britannia* xviii, 239-42

Strickland, T.J., 1999, 'What kind of community existed at Chester during the hiatus of the 2nd century?' in Goldsworthy, A., and Haynes, I., 1999 (Eds)

Swan, V.G., 1992, 'Legio VI and its men: African legionaries in Britain', *Journal of Roman Pottery Studies* 5, 1-33

Swan, V.G., and Philpott, R.A., 2000, 'Legio XX VV and Tile Production at Tarbock, Merseyside', *Britannia* xxxi, 55-67

Tinniswood, A., *Belton House, Lincolnshire*, National Trust, London

Todd, M., *The Roman Town at Ancaster. The Excavations of 1955-1971*, Universities of Nottingham and Exeter

Tomlin, R.S.O., 1992, 'The Twentieth Legion at Wroxeter and Carlisle', *Britannia* xxiii, 141-58

Tomlin, R.S.O., 1998, 'Roman Manuscripts from Carlisle', *Britannia* xxix, 31-84

Wacher, J., 1995, *The Towns of Roman Britain*, Batsford, London

Walker, D.R., 1988, 'The Roman Coins', in Cunliffe 1988

Waller, Edmund, 1745, *The Works of Edmund Waller Esq.,* Fenton, London, 116

Walthew, C.V., 1981, 'Possible standard units of measurement in Roman military planning', *Britannia* xii, 15-36

Webster, G., and Dudley, D.R., 1965, *The Roman Conquest of Britain*, London

Wells, C., 1982, 'The Human Burials' in McWhirr *et alia*

White, R., and Barker, P., 1998, *Wroxeter. Life and Death of a Roman City*, Tempus, Stroud

Willis, S., 1996, 'The Romanization of Pottery Assemblages during the First Century AD', *Britannia* xxvii, 179-222

Wilmott, T., 1997, *Excavations of a Roman fort [Birdoswald] on Hadrian's Wall and its successor settlements: 1987-92*, London

Zienkiewicz, D., 1986, *The Legionary Fortress Baths at Caerleon*, Cardiff

Zienkiewicz, D., 1993, 'Caerleon: The Legionary Museum Site 1983-5', *Britannia* xxiv, 27-140

INDEX